8 '11

MINERALS

GEOLOGY: LANDFORMS, MINERALS, AND ROCKS

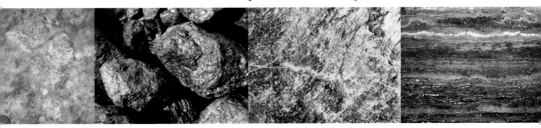

MINERALS

EDITED BY JOHN P. RAFFERTY, ASSOCIATE EDITOR,
EARTH AND LIFE SCIENCES

Britannica®
Educational Publishing

IN ASSOCIATION WITH

ROSEN
EDUCATIONAL SERVICES

Published in 2012 by Britannica Educational Publishing
(a trademark of Encyclopædia Britannica, Inc.)
in association with Rosen Educational Services, LLC
29 East 21st Street, New York, NY 10010.

First Edition

Britannica Educational Publishing
Michael I. Levy: Executive Editor
J.E. Luebering: Senior Manager
Marilyn L. Barton: Senior Coordinator, Production Control
Steven Bosco: Director, Editorial Technologies
Lisa S. Braucher: Senior Producer and Data Editor
Yvette Charboneau: Senior Copy Editor
Kathy Nakamura: Manager, Media Acquisition
John P. Rafferty: Associate Editor, Earth and Life Sciences

Rosen Educational Services
Nicholas Croce: Editor
Nelson Sá: Art Director
Cindy Reiman: Photography Manager
Matthew Cauli: Designer, Cover Design
Introduction by John P. Rafferty

Library of Congress Cataloging-in-Publication Data

Minerals / edited by John P. Rafferty. — 1st ed.
    p. cm. — (Geology: landforms, minerals, and rocks)
"In association with Britannica Educational Publishing, Rosen Educational Services."
Includes bibliographical references and index.
ISBN 978-1-61530-489-9 (library binding)
1. Minerals. I. Rafferty, John P.
QE363.2.M5479 2012
549—dc22

2010044473

Manufactured in the United States of America

On the cover (front and back): Amethyst crystals. *Shutterstock.com*

On the cover (front top), p. iii: Examples of some popular minerals are granite stone (left), black coal (middle left), gold ore (middle right), and marble stone (right). *Shutterstock. com*

On pages 1, 35, 77, 111, 187, 228, 247, 323, 326, 331: An array of apophyllite, stilbite and quartz crystals. *Shutterstock.com*

CONTENTS

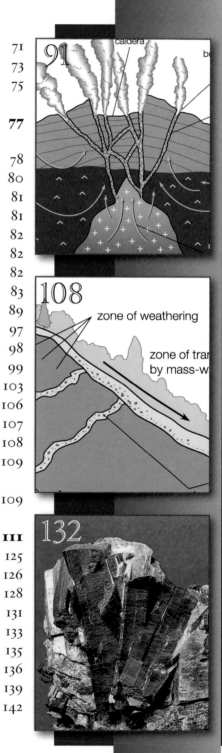

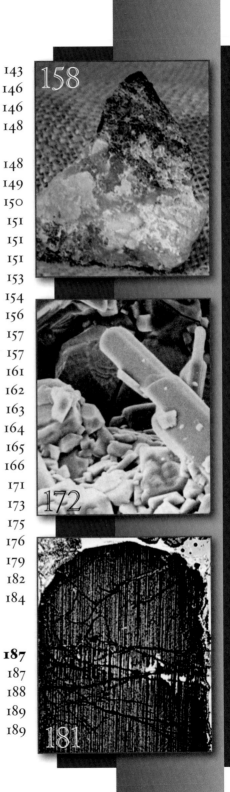

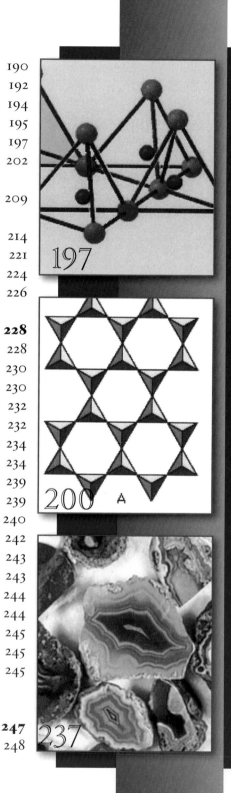

197

200 A

237

265

266

279

INTRODUCTION

If rock can be thought of as the foundation upon which all life on Earth stands, minerals are the foundation upon which rocks are built. Essentially, minerals are the most simple chemical compounds that make up rocks. This book is designed to take the reader on a tour of the various mineral groups, the unique characteristics that set one mineral apart from another, the features different groups of minerals share, and the roles minerals play in the rocks themselves.

Each of the roughly 3,800 known mineral types has a unique chemical and physical structure. Such compounds may be relatively simple, as in a deposit of gold (Ag), or they may be relatively complex combinations of several elements, as in the phosphate mineral turquoise ($CuAl_6(PO_4)_4(OH) \cdot 4H_2O$). Such combinations of chemical elements repeat throughout the mineral's structure, and the mineral's unique chemistry also drives a its internal physical structure.

All minerals are solids and occur as crystals, and the ordered arrangements of repeating molecules generate the mineral's crystal form. Since the chemistry of each mineral is different, no two minerals can produce the same crystals. Thus, the shape of each mineral is unique, a feature useful for determining its identity. This unique crystal form can change when temperature and pressure conditions change. Diamond and graphite, for example, are different forms of the mineral carbon; however, diamond develops under high-temperature and high-pressure conditions.

Minerals are typically thought of as inorganic substances that form in one of four ways. They can coalesce and crystallize in cooling magmas, solidify when bits and

A mineral sample of wavellite. Shutterstock.com

pieces of sedimentary rock come together under conditions of increasing pressure, arise from older minerals that
undergo metamorphoses, or precipitate from the action
of magma mixing with seawater and groundwater. Despite
their inorganic label—meaning that they do not possess
carbon-hydrogen bonds, which are characteristic of living
tissues—living things can produce minerals. Many carbonate minerals originate as the shells of corals and other
marine animals that died long ago. Such hard parts, which
are made of calcite produced by these organisms, become
calcite in rock after millions of years of increasing pressure
and temperature. In addition, true minerals occur naturally. Although industrial processes can produce synthetic
versions of diamonds, gemstones, and other minerals,
their natural counterparts are the most prized.

Since the study of minerals often takes place in remote
locations, it is relatively difficult to determine the exact
identity of a mineral observed in the field. Geologists
are usually not equipped to perform detailed chemical
and physical analyses of minerals on the sides of mountains, in stream beds, and within rock outcroppings far
from their laboratories. Instead, they rely on a battery
of relatively simple tests to determine, or at least narrow
down, the mineral they are looking at. The tests include
an examination of several of the mineral's physical properties, including the mineral's crystal habit (shape) and its
relative hardness, how the mineral fractures, its specific
gravity, its colour and luster, and the colour of streak it
leaves on a porcelain streak plate. Other properties, such
as the mineral's attraction to magnets, fluorescence, reaction to hydrochloric acid, and radioactivity can also be
determined in the field using tools the geologist can carry.

Back in the laboratory, one of the most useful tools to
determine a mineral's identity is the petrographic microscope, which is designed to examine the minerals contained

in thinly sliced sections of rock. In addition, a comprehensive battery of chemical tests, that consider how the mineral reacts to various acids and bases can be performed on the mineral in this setting. In some laboratories, X-rays can be used in a process called X-ray diffraction to determine the identity of the mineral. As X-rays pass through the sample, they bounce off the various atoms and ions inside; this scattering produces a unique X-ray pattern that can be used to identify the mineral. Once the identity of the mineral is known, it can be placed into one of several large mineral groups.

Rock-forming minerals that form rocks are usually divided into five main groups. The overwhelming majority (some 92 percent) of all minerals in Earth's crust occur in the silicate group, a division made up of minerals that contain different arrangements of silicon and oxygen atoms. These two abundant elements combine to form silicon-oxygen tetrahedrons. Silicate tetrahedrons can appear alone to form minerals such as olivine. They can also combine to form single chains as in the mineral augite or double chains as in hornblende. Silica minerals can occur as sheets, as in micas and clay minerals, as well as complex structures called framework silicates to produce different types of quartz and feldspar.

The other four main groups (which are collectively called the non-silicates) are made up of the carbonates, oxides, sulfides, and sulfates. Carbonate minerals are identified by their carbonate ions (CO_2^3) and occur widely across Earth's surface. They dissolve relatively easily in acids. Since water is a weak acid, carbonate deposits exposed to water are often the sites of caves, sinkholes, and similar landforms.

Oxides form when metal and oxygen ions bond with one another. The ionic bonds between the positively charged metal ions and the negatively charged oxygen ions are strong, and the oxide minerals that result are often hard and dense. Such minerals are routinely used to make steel and other metals. Hematite and magnetite are used to make iron, and chromite is the principal source of chromium from which steel alloys are made. Although ice does not contain metal ions, the positive charge of hydrogen bonds easily to the attractive negative charge in oxygen atoms, so it is also grouped with the oxides.

Sulfides are similar to oxides in that they also form bonds with metals; however, the bonds are not always ionic. Covalent bonds, in which electrons are shared between the atoms, and metallic bonds, in which clouds of electrons exist around densely packed positive ions, also occur. Galena (which is an ore of lead) and pyrite (a mineral used to recover iron, nickel, and some precious metals) are examples of sulfides.

Sulfates, known by their characteristic sulfur group $(SO_4)^{2-}$, are similar to silicates in that they form tetrahedrons in which a central ion is surrounded by four oxygen atoms. However, sulfates do not occur in chains and sheets. Its sulfur group, however, can bond with positive ions, such as calcium, to form compounds such as gypsum—which is the main component in sheetrock.

Beyond the five main groups, there are several, smaller groups of minerals. Sulfosalts, compounds characterized by the presence of arsenic and antimony, give up sulfur to incorporate semimetals, such as arsenic and antimony, into their structures. In contrast, halide minerals contain large negatively charged ions, such as chlorine, bromine, iodine, and fluorine. A few of the smaller mineral groups, such as the nitrate, borate, and phosphate minerals have are similar to those discussed previously. Nitrate minerals parallel the carbonates; they have a nitrate group $(NO_3)-$ that functions like the carbonate group. Similarly, borate minerals, which contain linking boron-oxygen groups, parallel the silicates. Lastly, the construction of phosphate minerals, known by their characteristic sulfur group $(PO_4)^{3-}$, resembles that of the sulfates.

Although most minerals are compounds of different chemical elements, some minerals are made up of only one. These solids, known as native elements, do not combine with others. Probably one of the best known native elements is gold (Ag). Gold atoms bond with other gold atoms to form a pure mineral unsullied by other chemical elements. Other metallic native elements include other valuable minerals such as silver, copper, and platinum. Native elements also occur as semimetals, such as arsenic and tellurium,which also appear in sulfosalts, and nonmetals, such as carbon and sulfur.

Although the identification and classification of minerals is a valuable exercise, one must remember that minerals are prized because of their ability to support or improve life. Through erosion and other natural forces, minerals are brought to Earth's surface over time. Some minerals, such as a number of phosphates and nitrates, serve as plant nutrients, and thus help to fuel a wide variety of living things and the ecosystems they inhabit. Others, however, are precious to humans because of their beauty and rareness or because they can be used to build better machines or serve as materials in building construction. Since most valuable minerals are locked up in rocks that contain other minerals that have little or no value, it may be useful to know how minerals are physically separated from one another.

Mineral separation, or processing, is an activity that requires several steps. After the minerals in the rock are analyzed to determine their identity and concentration, they go through a two-step process called communition to free them from the rocks they occur in. In the first step, large pieces of rock are crushed down into manageable sizes (less than 150 mm [6 inches]) with industrial jaw crushers. Later these pieces of rock are ground in cylinder mills which often turn the material into powder. Although modern communition practice typically involves the use of heavy machinery, the communition of some rocks, such as those that contain gold or diamonds, has been done successfully by hand.

After communition is complete, the minerals go though a process called concentration to separate the valuable material from the rocks and other minerals that will be discarded. At smaller scales, concentration may be done by hand, but in large-scale operations, the mineral processing industry relies on a series of techniques that take advantage of the various properties of the minerals found in the mix. The bits and pieces may be separated by colour using the naked eye or through the use of specialized detectors to determine the mineral's response to visible light as well as infrared and ultraviolet light. In addition, minerals can be separated from one another using magnets or electrical fields. In a process called gravity separation, other materials may be used to create a suspended layer in a container of water. Denser, more-valuable minerals are allowed to pass through the layer, whereas less-dense, discardable minerals are trapped within or above the layer. One of the most preferred methods of separation involves the wetting and floating of materials in mix in a water-filled container. In some cases, air is added to the water to produce a froth. Some minerals in the mix might adhere to bubbles in the froth, whereas others remain in suspension or fall to the bottom of the container. Water used in these various concentration processes is filtered out later to produce cakes of concentrated material, which contains small amounts of moisture. The remaining moisture is removed from the now separated minerals through drying.

Beyond serving as the building blocks for rocks, minerals are essential parts of the lives of human beings. They are part of the plants and animals humans eat, and the materials humans use to prepare and serve them. Minerals are used to shore up or lay the foundations for roads, serve as the feedstock for concrete, and create metal alloys used in buildings, bridges, pipes, and wire. They are integral parts of the ongoing information revolution. They are used in computer processors, high-tech instruments, electric and hybrid-electric car batteries, and the metals and ceramics used to create them. They are indispensable parts of life on Earth, and thus they are worthy of the examination provided by this book.

CHAPTER 1
THE NATURE OF MINERALS

Minerals are naturally occurring homogeneous solids with a definite chemical composition and a highly ordered atomic arrangement; they are usually formed by inorganic processes. There are several thousand known mineral species, about 100 of which constitute the major mineral components of rocks; these are the so-called rock-forming minerals.

A mineral, which by definition must be formed through natural processes, is distinct from the synthetic equivalents produced in the laboratory. Man-made versions of minerals, including emeralds, sapphires, diamonds, and other valuable gemstones, are regularly produced in industrial and research facilities and are often nearly identical to their natural counterparts.

By its definition as a homogeneous solid, a mineral is composed of a single solid substance of uniform composition that cannot be physically separated into simpler compounds. Homogeneity is determined relative to the scale on which it is defined. A specimen that megascopically appears homogeneous, for example, may reveal several mineral components under a microscope or upon exposure to X-ray diffraction techniques. Most rocks are composed of several different minerals; e.g., granite consists of feldspar, quartz, mica, and amphibole. In addition, gases and liquids are excluded by a strict interpretation of the above definition of a mineral. Ice, the solid state of water (H_2O), is considered a mineral, but liquid water is not; liquid mercury, though sometimes found in mercury ore deposits, is not classified as a mineral either. Such substances that resemble minerals in chemistry and occurrence are dubbed mineraloids and are included in the general domain of mineralogy.

Since a mineral has a definite composition, it can be expressed by a specific chemical formula. Quartz (silicon dioxide), for instance, is rendered as SiO_2, because the elements silicon (Si) and oxygen (O) are its only constituents and they invariably appear in a 1:2 ratio. The chemical makeup of most minerals is not as well defined as that of quartz, which is a pure substance. Siderite, for example, does not always occur as pure iron carbonate ($FeCO_3$); magnesium (Mg), manganese (Mn), and, to a limited extent, calcium (Ca) may sometimes substitute

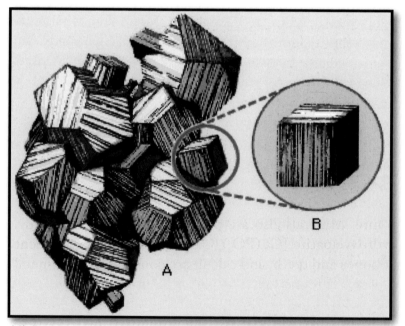

(A) Pyrite crystals with pyritohedral outline. (B) Striated cube of pyrite. The external shape is a reflection of the internal structure as shown in Figure 1. From C. Klein and C.S. Hurlbut, Jr., Manual of Mineralogy *(1985), reprinted with permission of John Wiley & Sons, Inc., New York City*

for the iron. Since the amount of the replacement may vary, the composition of siderite is not fixed and ranges between certain limits, although the ratio of the metal cation to the anionic group remains fixed at 1:1. Its chemical makeup may be expressed by the general formula (Fe, Mn, Mg, Ca)CO_3, which reflects the variability of the metal content.

Minerals display a highly ordered internal atomic structure that has a regular geometric form. Because of this feature, minerals are classified as crystalline solids. Under favourable conditions, crystalline materials may express their ordered internal framework by a well-developed external form, often referred to as crystal form or morphology. Solids that exhibit no such ordered internal arrangement are termed amorphous. Many amorphous natural solids, such as glass, are categorized as mineraloids.

Traditionally, minerals have been described as resulting exclusively from inorganic processes; however, current mineralogic practice often includes as minerals those compounds that are organically produced but satisfy all other mineral requirements. Aragonite ($CaCO_3$) is an example of an inorganically formed mineral that also has an organically produced, yet otherwise identical, counterpart; the shell (and the pearl, if it is present) of an oyster is composed to a large extent of organically formed aragonite. Minerals also are produced by the human body: hydroxylapatite [$Ca_5(PO_4)_3(OH)$] is the chief component of bones and teeth, and calculi are concretions of mineral substances found in the urinary system.

NOMENCLATURE

While minerals are classified in a logical manner according to their major anionic (negatively charged) chemical constituents into groups such as oxides, silicates, and nitrates, they are named in a far less scientific or consistent way. Names may be assigned to reflect a physical or chemical property, such as colour, or they may be derived from various subjects deemed appropriate, such as, for example, a locality, public figure, or mineralogist. Some examples of mineral names and their derivations follow: albite ($NaAlSi_3O_8$) is from the Latin word (*albus*) for "white" in reference to its colour; goethite ($FeO \cdot OH$) is in honour of Johann Wolfgang von Goethe, the German poet; manganite ($MnO \cdot OH$) reflects the mineral's composition; franklinite ($ZnFe_2O_4$) is named after Franklin, N.J., U.S., the site of its occurrence as the dominant ore mineral for zinc (Zn); and sillimanite (Al_2SiO_4) is in honour of the American chemist Benjamin Silliman. Since 1960 an international committee of nomenclature has reviewed descriptions of new minerals and proposals for new mineral names and has attempted to remove inconsistencies. Any new mineral name must be approved by this committee and the type material is usually stored in a museum or university collection.

OCCURRENCE AND FORMATION

Minerals form in all geologic environments and thus under a wide range of chemical and physical conditions, such as varying temperature and pressure. The four main categories of mineral formation are (1) igneous, or magmatic, in which minerals crystallize from a melt; (2) sedimentary, in which minerals are the result of the processes of weathering, erosion, and sedimentation; (3) metamorphic, in which new minerals form at the expense of earlier ones owing to the effects of changing—usually increasing—temperature or pressure or both on some existing rock type (metamorphic minerals are the result of new mineral growth in the solid state without the intervention of a melt, as in igneous processes); and (4) hydrothermal, in which minerals are chemically precipitated from hot solutions within the Earth. The first three processes generally lead to varieties of rocks in which different mineral grains are closely intergrown in an interlocking fabric. Hydrothermal solutions, and even solutions at very low temperatures (e.g., groundwater), tend to follow fracture zones in rocks that may provide open spaces for the chemical precipitation of minerals from solution. It is from such open spaces, partially filled by minerals deposited from solutions, that most of the spectacular mineral specimens have been collected. If a mineral that is in the process of growth (as a result of precipitation) is allowed to develop in a free space, it will generally exhibit a well-developed crystal form, which adds to a specimen's aesthetic beauty. Similarly, geodes, which are rounded, hollow, or partially hollow bodies commonly found in limestones, may contain well-formed crystals lining the central cavity. Geodes form as a result of mineral deposition from solutions such as groundwater.

MINERAL STRUCTURE

The structure of minerals is often characterized by the development of crystals. Mineral structure can be affected by temperature and pressure such that minerals with the same chemical composition can develop into quite different forms. Even so, the mineral's chemistry largely determines its structure. In addition, the physical properties of a given mineral, and thus its identity, can often be determined using a series of relatively simple tests.

PRIMARY AND ACCESSORY MINERALS

In a given igneous rock, any mineral that formed during the original solidification (crystallization) of the rock is known as a primary mineral. Primary minerals include both the essential minerals used to assign a classification name to the rock and the accessory minerals present in lesser abundance. In contrast to primary minerals are secondary minerals, which form at a later time through processes such as weathering and hydrothermal alteration. Primary minerals form in a sequence or in sequential groups as dictated by the chemistry and physical conditions under which the magma solidifies. Accessory minerals form at various times during the crystallization, but their inclusion within essential minerals indicates that they often form at an early time.

In contrast, an accessory mineral is any mineral in an igneous rock not essential to the naming of the rock. When it is present in small amounts, as is common, it is called a minor accessory. If the amount is greater or is of special significance, the mineral is called a varietal, or characterizing, accessory and may give a varietal name to the rock (e.g., the mineral biotite in biotite granite). Accessory minerals characteristically are formed during the solidification of the rocks from the magma; in contrast are secondary minerals, which form at a later time through processes such as weathering and hydrothermal alteration. Common minor accessory minerals include topaz, zircon, corundum, fluorite, garnet, monazite, rutile, magnetite, ilmenite, allanite, and tourmaline. Typical varietal accessories include biotite, muscovite, amphibole, pyroxene, and olivine.

MORPHOLOGY

Nearly all minerals have the internal ordered arrangement of atoms and ions that is the defining characteristic of crystalline solids. Under favourable conditions, minerals may grow as well-formed crystals, characterized by their smooth plane surfaces and regular geometric forms. Development of this good external shape is largely a fortuitous outcome of growth and does not affect the basic properties of a crystal. Therefore, the term *crystal* is most often used by material scientists to refer to any solid with an ordered internal arrangement, without regard to the presence or absence of external faces.

SYMMETRY ELEMENTS

The external shape, or morphology, of a crystal is perceived as its aesthetic beauty, and its geometry reflects the internal atomic arrangement. The external shape of well-formed crystals expresses the presence or absence of a number of symmetry elements. Such symmetry elements include rotation axes, rotoinversion axes, a centre of symmetry, and mirror planes.

A rotation axis is an imaginary line through a crystal around which it may be rotated and repeat itself in appearance one, two, three, four, or six times during a complete rotation. When rotated about this axis, the crystal repeats itself each 60° (six times in a 360° rotation).

A rotoinversion axis combines rotation about an axis of rotation with inversion. Rotoinversion axes are symbolized as 1, 2, 3, 4, and 6: 1 is equivalent to a centre of symmetry (or inversion, *i*), 2 is equivalent to a mirror plane, 3 is equivalent to a threefold rotation axis plus a centre of symmetry, 4 is not composed of other operations and is unique, and 6 is equivalent to a threefold rotation axis with a mirror plane perpendicular to the axis.

A centre of symmetry exists in a crystal if an imaginary line can be extended from any point on its surface through its centre and a similar point is present along the line equidistant from the centre. This is equivalent to 1, or inversion. There is a relatively simple procedure for recognizing a centre of symmetry in a well-formed crystal. With the crystal (or a wooden or plaster model thereof) laid down on any face on a tabletop, the presence of a face of equal size and shape, but inverted, in a horizontal position at the top of the crystal proves the existence of a centre of symmetry.

A mirror plane is an imaginary plane that separates a crystal into halves such that, in a perfectly developed crystal, the halves are mirror images of one another. A single mirror in a crystal is also called a symmetry plane.

Morphologically, crystals can be grouped into 32 crystal classes that represent the 32 possible symmetry elements and their combinations. These crystal classes, in turn, are grouped into six crystal systems. In decreasing order of overall symmetry content, beginning with the system with the highest and most complex crystal symmetry, they are isometric, hexagonal, tetragonal, orthorhombic, monoclinic, and triclinic. The systems may be described in terms of crystallographic axes used for reference. The c axis is normally the vertical axis. The isometric system exhibits three mutually perpendicular axes of equal length (a_1, a_2, and a_3). The orthorhombic and tetragonal systems also contain three

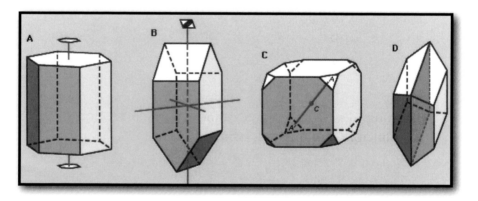

Translation-free symmetry elements as expressed by the morphology of crystals. (A) Sixfold axis of rotation (6). (B) Fourfold axis of inversion (4). (C) Centre of symmetry (i). (D) Mirror plane (m). Copyright Encyclopædia Britannica , Inc.; rendering for this edition by Rosen Educational Services

mutually perpendicular axes; in the former system all the axes are of different lengths (a, b, and c), and in the latter system two axes are of equal length (a_1 and a_2) while the third (vertical) axis is either longer or shorter (c). The hexagonal system contains four axes: three equal-length axes (a_1, a_2, and a_3) intersect one another at 120° and lie in a plane that is perpendicular to the fourth (vertical) axis of a different length. Three axes of different lengths (a, b, and c) are present in both the monoclinic and triclinic systems. In the monoclinic system, two axes intersect one another at an oblique angle and lie in a plane perpendicular to the third axis; in the triclinic system, all axes intersect at oblique angles.

TWINNING

If two or more crystals form a symmetrical intergrowth, they are referred to as twinned crystals. A new symmetry operation (called a twin element), which is lacking in a single untwinned crystal, relates the individual crystals in a twinned position. There are three twin elements that may relate the crystals of a twin: (1) reflection by a mirror plane (twin plane), (2) rotation about a crystal direction common to both (twin axis) with the angular rotation typically 180°, and (3) inversion about a point (twin centre). An instance of twinning is defined by a twin law that specifies the presence of a plane, an axis, or a centre of twinning. If a twin has three or more parts, it is referred to as a multiple, or repeated, twin.

INTERNAL STRUCTURE

The external morphology of a mineral is an expression of the fundamental internal architecture of a crystalline substance—i.e., its crystal structure. The crystal structure is the three-dimensional, regular (or ordered) arrangement

A sample of wulfenite, a mineral displaying good crystal form, from Mexico. Courtesy of Joseph and Helen Guetterman, Belleville, Illinois; photographs, John H. Gerard—EB Inc.

A sample of rose quartz, a mineral displaying good crystal form, from Minas Gerais state, Braz. Courtesy of the Field Museum of Natural History, Chicago; photographs, John H. Gerard—EB Inc.

of chemical units (atoms, ions, and anionic groups in inorganic materials; molecules in organic substances); these chemical units (referred to here as motifs) are repeated by various translational and symmetry operations. The morphology of crystals can be studied with the unaided eye in large well-developed crystals and has been historically examined in considerable detail by optical measurements of smaller well-formed crystals through the use of optical goniometers.

The internal structure of crystalline materials, however, is revealed by a combination of X-ray, neutron, and electron diffraction techniques, supplemented by a variety of spectroscopic methods, including infrared, optical, Mössbauer, and resonance techniques. These methods, used singly or in combination, provide a quantitative three-dimensional reconstruction of the location of the atoms (or ions), the chemical bond types and their positions, and the overall internal symmetry of the structure. The repeat distances in most inorganic structures and many of the atomic and ionic motif sizes are on the order of 1 to 10 angstroms (Å; 1 Å is equivalent to 10^{-8} cm or 3.94×10^{-9} inch) or 10 to 100 nanometres (nm; 1 nm is equivalent to 10^{-7} cm or 10 Å).

A sample of amazonite, a greenish blue variety of microcline feldspar, with smoky (dark gray) quartz. Microcline feldspar is an example of a mineral that displays good crystal form. Courtesy of the Harvard Collection; (feldspar) Benjamin M. Shaub

Symmetry elements that are observable in the external morphology of crystals, such as rotation and rotoinversion axes, mirror planes, and a centre of symmetry, also are present in their internal atomic structure. In addition to these symmetry elements, there are translations and symmetry operations combined with translations. (Translation is the operation in which a motif is repeated in a linear pattern at intervals that are equal to the translation distance [commonly on the 1 to 10 Å level].) Two examples of translational symmetry elements are screw axes (combining rotation and translation) and glide planes (combining mirroring and translation). The internal translation distances are exceedingly small and can be seen directly only by very high-magnification electron beam

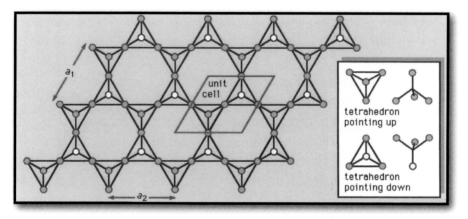

Single sheet displaying the arrangement of the silicon-oxygen tetrahedrons in the structure of a high temperature form of SiO$_2$ known as tridymite. Copyright Encyclopædia Britannica, Inc.; rendering for this edition by Rosen Educational Services

techniques, as used in a transmission electron microscope, at magnifications of about 600,000×. When all possible combinations of translational elements compatible with the 32 crystal classes (also known as point groups) are considered, one arrives at 230 possible ways in which translations, translational symmetry elements (screw axes and glide planes), and translation-free symmetry elements (rotation and rotoinversion axes and mirror planes) can be combined. These translation and symmetry groupings are known as the 230 space groups, representing the various ways in which motifs can be arranged in an ordered three-dimensional array. The symbolic representation of space groups is closely related to that of Hermann-Mauguin notation, perhaps the most popular form of shorthand in crystallography.

There are two useful methods for creating a graphical representation of a crystal's external morphology. The crystal's structure can be presented as a three-dimensional arrangement on a two-dimensional page, or the crystal structure may be projected onto a planar surface. To further aid the visualization of complex crystal structures, three-dimensional models of such structures can be built or obtained commercially. Models of this sort reproduce the internal atomic arrangement on an enormously enlarged scale (e.g., one angstrom might be represented by one centimetre [0.4 inch]).

POLYMORPHISM

Polymorphism is the ability of a specific chemical composition to crystallize in more than one form. This generally occurs as a response to changes in temperature or pressure or both. The different structures of such a chemical substance are called polymorphic forms, or polymorphs. For example, the element carbon (C) occurs in nature in two different polymorphic forms, depending on the external (pressure and temperature) conditions. These forms are graphite, with a hexagonal structure, and diamond, with an isometric structure. The composition FeS_2 occurs most commonly as pyrite, with an isometric structure, but it is also found as marcasite, which has an orthorhombic internal arrangement. The composition SiO_2 is found in a large number of polymorphs, among them quartz, tridymite, cristobalite, coesite, and stishovite. The stability field (conditions under which a mineral is stable) of these SiO_2 polymorphs can be expressed in a stability diagram, with the external parameters of temperature and pressure as the two axes. In the general quartz field, there is additional polymorphism leading to the notation of high quartz and low quartz, each form having a slightly different internal structure. The diagram clearly indicates that cristobalite and tridymite are the high-temperature forms of SiO_2, and indeed these SiO_2 polymorphs occur in high-temperature lava flows. The high-pressure forms of SiO_2 are coesite and stishovite, and these can be found in meteorite craters, formed as a result of high explosive pressures upon quartz-rich sandstones, and in very deep-seated rock formations, as from the Earth's upper mantle or very deep in subduction zones.

CHEMICAL COMPOSITION

The chemical composition of a mineral is of fundamental importance because its properties greatly depend on it. Such properties, however, are determined not only by the chemical composition but also by the geometry of the constituent atoms and ions and by the nature of the electrical forces that bind them. Thus, for a complete understanding of minerals, their internal structure, chemistry, and bond types must be considered.

Various analytical techniques may be employed to obtain the chemical composition of a mineral. Quantitative chemical analyses conducted prior to 1947 mainly utilized so-called wet analytical methods, in which the mineral sample is first dissolved. Various compounds are then precipitated from the solution, which are weighed to obtain a gravimetric analysis. Since 1947 a number of analytical procedures have been introduced that provide faster but somewhat less accurate results. Most analyses performed since 1960 have made use of instrumental methods such as optical emission, X-ray fluorescence, atomic absorption spectroscopy, and electron microprobe analysis. Relatively well-established error ranges have been documented for these methods, and samples must be prepared in a specific manner for each technique. A distinct advantage of wet analytical procedures is that they make it possible to determine quantitatively the oxidation states of positively charged atoms, called cations (e.g., Fe^{2+} versus Fe^{3+}), and to ascertain the amount of water in hydrous minerals. It is more difficult to provide this type of information with instrumental techniques.

To ensure an accurate chemical analysis, the selected sample must contain only one mineral species (i.e., the one for which the analysis is being done) and must not have undergone alteration processes. Since it is frequently difficult, and at times impossible, to obtain as much as 0.1 to 1 gram of "clean" material for analysis, the results should be accompanied by specifications on the amount of impurities present. To reduce the effect of the impurities, an instrumental technique, such as electron microprobe analysis, is commonly employed. In this method, quantitative analysis in situ may be performed on mineral grains only 1 micrometre (10^{-4} cm) in diameter.

MINERAL FORMULAS

Elements may exist in the native (uncombined) state, in which case their formulas are simply their chemical symbols: gold (Au), carbon (C) in its polymorphic form of diamond, and sulfur (S) are common examples. Most minerals, however, occur as compounds consisting of two or more elements; their formulas are obtained from quantitative chemical analyses and indicate the relative proportions of the constituent elements. The formula of sphalerite, ZnS, reflects a one-to-one ratio between atoms of zinc and those of sulfur. In bornite (Cu_5FeS_4), there are five atoms of copper (Cu), one atom of iron (Fe), and four atoms of sulfur. There exist relatively few minerals with constant composition; notable examples include quartz (SiO_2) and kyanite (Al_2SiO_5). Minerals of this sort are termed pure substances. Most minerals display considerable variation in the ions that occupy specific atomic sites within their structure. For example, the iron content of rhodochrosite ($MnCO_3$) may vary over a wide range. As ferrous iron (Fe^{2+}) substitutes for manganese cations (Mn^{2+}) in the rhodochrosite structure, the formula for the mineral might be given in more general terms — namely, $(Mn, Fe)CO_3$. The amounts of manganese and iron are variable, but the ratio of the cation to the negatively charged anionic group remains fixed at one Mn^{2+} or Fe^{2+} atom to one CO_3 group.

COMPOSITIONAL VARIATION

As stated above, most minerals exhibit a considerable range in chemical composition. Such variation results from the replacement of one ion or ionic group by another in a particular structure. This phenomenon is termed ionic substitution, or solid solution. Three types of solid solution are possible, and these may be described in terms of their corresponding mechanisms — namely, substitutional, interstitial, and omission.

Substitutional solid solution is the most common variety. For example, as described above, in the carbonate mineral rhodochrosite ($MnCO_3$), Fe^{2+} may substitute for Mn^{2+} in its atomic site in the structure.

The degree of substitution may be influenced by various factors, with the size of the ion being the most important. Ions of two different elements can freely replace one another only if their ionic radii differ by approximately 15 percent or less. Limited substitution can occur if the radii differ by 15 to 30 percent, and a difference of more than 30 percent makes substitution unlikely. These limits, calculated from empirical data, are only approximate.

The temperature at which crystals grow also plays a significant role in determining the extent of ionic substitution. The higher the temperature, the more extensive is the thermal disorder in the crystal structure and the less exacting are the spatial requirements. As a result, ionic substitution that could not have occurred in crystals grown at low temperatures may be present in those grown at higher ones. The high-temperature form of $KAlSi_3O_8$ (sanidine), for example, can accommodate more sodium (Na) in place of potassium (K) than can microcline, its low-temperature counterpart.

An additional factor affecting ionic substitution is the maintenance of a balance between the positive and negative charges in the structure. Replacement of a mon-ovalent ion (e.g., Na^+, a sodium cation) by a divalent ion (e.g., Ca^{2+}, a calcium cation) requires further substitutions to keep the structure electrically neutral.

Simple cationic or anionic substitutions are the most basic types of substitutional solid solution. A simple cat-ionic substitution can be represented in a compound of the general form A^+X in which cation B^+ replaces in part or in total cation A^+. Both cations in this example have the same valence (+1), as in the substitution of K^+ (potassium ions) for Na^+ (sodium ions) in the NaCl (sodium chloride) structure. Similarly, the substitution of anion X by Y in an A^+X^- compound represents a simple anionic substitution; this is exemplified by the replacement of Cl^- (chlorine ions) with Br^- (bromine ions) in the structure of KCl (potassium chloride). A complete solid-solution series involves the substitution in one or more atomic sites of one element for another that ranges over all possible compositions and is defined in terms of two end-members. For example, the two end-members of olivine [$(Mg, Fe)_2SiO_4$], forsterite (Mg_2SiO_4) and fayalite (Fe_2SiO_4), define a complete solid-solution series in which magnesium cations (Mg^{2+}) are replaced partially or totally by Fe^{2+}.

In some instances, a cation B^{3+} may replace some A^{2+} of compound $A^{2+}X^{2-}$. So that the compound will remain neutral, an equal amount of A^{2+} must concurrently be replaced by a third cation, C^+. This is given in equation form as $2A^{2+} \longleftrightarrow B^{3+} + C^+$; the positive charge on each side is the same. Substitutions such as this are termed coupled substitutions. The plagioclase feldspar series exhibits complete solid solution, in the form of coupled substitutions, between its two end-members, albite ($NaAlSi_3O_8$) and anorthite ($CaAl_2Si_2O_8$). Every atomic substitution of Na^+ by Ca^{2+} is accompanied by the replacement of a silicon cation (Si^{4+}) by an aluminum cation (Al^{3+}), thereby maintaining electrical neutrality: $Na^+ + Si^{4+} \longleftrightarrow Ca^{2+} + Al^{3+}$.

The second major type of ionic substitution is interstitial solid solution, or interstitial substitution. It takes place when atoms, ions, or molecules fill the interstices (voids) found between the atoms, ions, or ionic groups of a crystal structure. The interstices may take the form of channel-like cavities in certain crystals, such as the ring silicate beryl ($Be_3Al_2Si_6O_{18}$). Potassium, rubidium (Rb), cesium (Cs), and water, as well as helium (He), are some of the large ions and gases found in the tubular voids of beryl.

The least common type of solid solution is omission solid solution, in which a crystal contains one or more atomic sites that are not completely filled. The best-known example is exhibited by pyrrhotite ($Fe_{1-x}S$). In this mineral, each iron atom is surrounded by six neighbouring sulfur atoms. If every iron site in pyrrhotite were occupied by ferrous iron, its formula would be FeS. There are, however, varying percentages of vacancy in the iron site, so that the formula is given as Fe_6S_7 through $Fe_{11}S_{12}$, the latter being very near to pure FeS. The formula for pyrrhotite is normally written as $Fe_{1-x}S$, with x ranging from 0 to 0.2. It is one of the minerals referred to as a defect structure, because it has a structural site that is not completely occupied.

CHEMICAL BONDING

Electrical forces are responsible for binding together the atoms, ions, and ionic groups that constitute crystalline solids. The physical and chemical properties of minerals are attributable for the most part to the types and strengths of these binding forces; hardness, cleavage, fusibility, electrical and thermal conductivity, and the coefficient of thermal expansion are examples of such properties. On the whole, the hardness and melting point of a crystal increase proportionally with the strength of the bond, while its coefficient of thermal expansion decreases. The extremely strong forces that link the carbon atoms of diamond, for instance, are responsible for its distinct hardness. Periclase (MgO) and halite (NaCl) have similar structures; however, periclase has a melting point of 2,800 °C (5,072 °F) whereas halite melts at 801 °C (1,474 °F). This discrepancy reflects the difference in the bond strength of the two minerals: since the atoms of periclase are joined by a stronger electrical force, a greater amount of heat is needed to separate them.

The electrical forces, called chemical bonds, can be divided into five types: ionic, covalent, metallic, van der Waals, and hydrogen bonds. Classification in this manner is largely one of expediency; the chemical bonds in a given mineral may in fact possess characteristics of more than one bond type. For example, the forces that link the silicon and oxygen atoms in quartz exhibit in nearly equal amount the characteristics of both ionic and covalent bonds. As stated above, the electrical interaction between the atoms of a crystal determine its physical and chemical properties. Thus, classifying minerals according to their electrical forces will cause those species with similar properties to be grouped together. This fact justifies classification by bond type.

IONIC BONDS

Atoms have a tendency to gain or lose electrons so that their outer orbitals become stable; this is normally accomplished by these orbitals being filled with the maximum allowed number of valence electrons. Metallic sodium, for example, has one valence electron in its outer orbital; it becomes ionized by readily losing this electron and exists as the cation Na^+. Conversely, chlorine gains an electron to complete its outer orbital, thereby forming the anion Cl^-. In the mineral halite, $NaCl$ (common, or rock, salt), the chemical bonding that holds the Na^+ and Cl^- ions together is the attraction between the two opposite charges. This bonding mechanism is referred to as ionic, or electrovalent.

Ionically bonded crystals typically display moderate hardness and specific gravity, rather high melting points, and poor thermal and electrical conductivity. The electrostatic charge of an ion is evenly distributed over its surface, and so a cation tends to become surrounded with the maximum number of anions that can be arranged around it. Since ionic bonding is nondirectional, crystals bonded in this manner normally display high symmetry.

COVALENT BONDS

In the discussion of the ionic bond, it was noted that chlorine readily gains an electron to achieve a stable electron configuration. An incomplete outer orbital places a chlorine atom in a highly reactive state, so it attempts to combine with nearly any atom in its proximity. Because its closest neighbour is usually another chlorine atom, the two may bond together by sharing one pair of electrons. As a result of this extremely strong bond, each chlorine atom enters a stable state.

The electron-sharing, or covalent, bond is the strongest of all chemical bond types. Minerals bonded in this

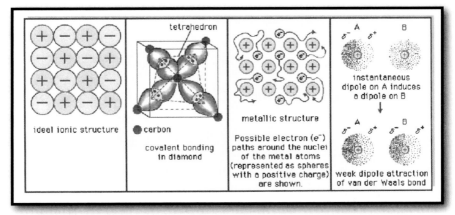

Chemical bonding in crystalline solids. Copyright Encyclopædia Britannica, Inc.; rendering for this edition by Rosen Educational Services

manner display general insolubility, great stability, and a high melting point. Crystals of covalently bonded minerals tend to exhibit lower symmetry than their ionic counterparts because the covalent bond is highly directional, localized in the vicinity of the shared electrons.

The Cl_2 molecules formed by linking two neighbouring chlorine atoms are stable and do not combine with other molecules. Atoms of some elements, however, have more than one electron in the outer orbital and thus may bond to several neighbouring atoms to form groups, which in turn may join together in larger combinations. Carbon, in the polymorphic form of diamond, is a good example of this type of covalent bonding. There are four valence electrons in a carbon atom, so that each atom bonds with four others in a stable tetrahedral configuration. A continuous network is formed by the linkage of every carbon atom in this manner. The rigid diamond structure results from the strong localization of the bond energy in the vicinity of the shared electrons; this makes diamond the hardest of all natural substances. Diamond does not conduct electricity, because all the valence electrons of its constituent atoms are shared to form bonds and therefore are not mobile.

METALLIC BONDS

Bonding in metals is distinct from that in their salts, as reflected in the significant differences between the properties of the two groups. In contrast to salts, metals display high plasticity, tenacity, ductility, and conductivity. Many are characterized by lower hardness and have higher melting and boiling points than, for example, covalently bonded materials. All these properties result from a metallic bonding mechanism that can be envisioned as a collection of positively charged ions immersed in a cloud of valence electrons. The attraction between the cations and the electrons holds a crystal together. The electrons are not bound to any particular cation and are thus free to move throughout the structure. In fact, in the metals sodium, cesium, rubidium, and potassium, the radiant energy of light can cause electrons to be removed from their surfaces entirely. (This result, known as the photoelectric effect, is utilized in light meters.) Electron mobility is responsible for the ability of metals to conduct heat and electricity. The native metals are the only minerals to exhibit pure metallic bonding.

VAN DER WAALS BONDS

Neutral molecules may be held together by a weak electric force known as the van der Waals bond. It results from the distortion of a molecule so that a small positive charge develops on one end and a corresponding negative charge develops on the other. A similar effect is induced in neighbouring molecules, and this dipole effect propagates throughout the entire structure. An attractive force is then formed between oppositely charged ends of the dipoles. Van der Waals bonding is common in gases and organic liquids and solids, but it is rare in minerals. Its presence in a mineral defines a weak area with good cleavage and low hardness. In graphite, carbon atoms lie in covalently bonded sheets with van der Waals forces acting between the layers.

HYDROGEN BONDS

In addition to the four major bond types described above, there is an interaction called hydrogen bonding. This takes place when a hydrogen atom, bonded to an electronegative atom such as oxygen, fluorine, or nitrogen, is also attracted to the negative end of a neighbouring molecule. A strong dipole-dipole interaction is produced, forming a bond between the two molecules. Hydrogen bonding is common in hydroxides and in many of the layer silicates— e.g., micas and clay minerals.

PHYSICAL PROPERTIES

The physical properties of minerals are the direct result of the structural and chemical characteristics of the minerals. Some properties can be determined by inspection of a hand specimen or by relatively simple tests on such a specimen. Others, such as those determined by optical and X-ray diffraction techniques, require special and often sophisticated equipment and may involve elaborate sample preparation. In the discussion that follows, emphasis is placed on those properties that can be most easily evaluated with only simple tests.

CRYSTAL HABIT AND CRYSTAL AGGREGATION

The external shape (habit) of well-developed crystals can be visually studied and classified according to the crystal systems and crystal classes they belong to. The majority of crystal occurrences, however, are not part of well-formed single crystals but are found as crystals grown together in aggregates. Examples of some descriptive terms for such aggregations are given here: granular, an intergrowth of mineral grains of approximately the same size; lamellar, flat, platelike individuals arranged in layers; bladed, elongated crystals flattened like a knife blade; fibrous, an aggregate of slender fibres, parallel or radiating; acicular, slender, needlelike crystals; radiating, individuals forming starlike or circular groups; globular, radiating individuals forming small spherical or hemispherical groups; dendritic, in slender divergent branches, somewhat plantlike; mammillary, large smoothly rounded, masses resembling mammae, formed by radiating crystals; botryoidal, globular forms resembling a bunch of grapes; colloform, spherical forms composed of radiating individuals without regard to size (this includes botryoidal, reniform, and mammillary forms); stalactitic, pendent cylinders or cones resembling icicles; concentric, roughly spherical layers arranged about a common centre, as in agate and in geodes; geode, a partially filled rock cavity lined by mineral material (geodes may be banded as in agate owing to successive depositions of material, and the inner surface is often covered with projecting crystals); and oolitic, an assemblage consisting of small spheres resembling fish roe.

Cleavage and Fracture

Both these properties represent the reaction of a mineral to an external force. Cleavage is breakage along planar surfaces, which are parallel to possible external faces on the crystal. It results from the tendency of some minerals to split in certain directions that are structurally weaker than others. Some crystals exhibit well-developed cleavage, as seen by the planar cleavage in mica; perfect cleavage of this sort is characterized by smooth, shiny surfaces. In other minerals, such as quartz, cleavage is absent. Quality and

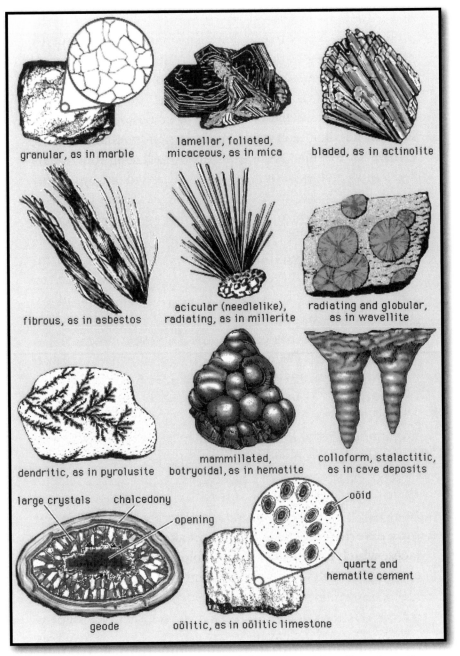

Common crystal aggregations and habits. Copyright Encyclopædia Britannica, Inc.; rendering for this edition by Rosen Educational Services

direction are the general characteristics used to describe cleavage. Quality is expressed as perfect, good, fair, and so forth; cleavage directions of a crystal are consistent with its overall symmetry.

Some crystals do not usually break in any particular direction, reflecting roughly equal bond strengths throughout the crystal structure. Breakage in such minerals is known as fracture. The term *conchoidal* is used to describe fracture with smooth, curved surfaces that resemble the interior of a seashell; it is commonly observed in quartz and glass. Splintery fracture is breakage into elongated fragments like splinters of wood, while hackly fracture is breakage along jagged surfaces.

LUSTRE

The term *lustre* refers to the general appearance of a mineral surface in reflected light. The main types of lustre, metallic and nonmetallic, are distinguished easily by the human eye after some practice, but the difference between them cannot be quantified and is rather difficult to describe. Metallic refers to the lustre of an untarnished metallic surface such as gold, silver, copper, or steel. These materials are opaque to light; none passes through even at thin edges. Pyrite (FeS_2), chalcopyrite ($CuFeS_2$), and galena (PbS) are common minerals that have metallic lustre. Nonmetallic lustre is generally exhibited by light-coloured minerals that transmit light, either through thick portions or at least through their edges. The following terms are used to distinguish the lustre of nonmetallic minerals: vitreous, having the lustre of a piece of broken glass (this is commonly seen in quartz and many other nonmetallic minerals); resinous, having the lustre of a piece of resin (this is common in sphalerite [ZnS]); pearly, having the lustre of mother-of-pearl (i.e., an iridescent pearl-like lustre characteristic of mineral surfaces that are parallel to well-developed cleavage planes; the cleavage surface of talc [$Mg_3Si_4O_{10}(OH)_2$] may show pearly lustre); greasy, having the appearance of being covered with a thin layer of oil (such lustre results from the scattering of light by a microscopically rough surface; some nepheline [$(Na, K)AlSiO_4$] and milky quartz may exhibit this); silky, descriptive of the lustre of a skein of silk or a piece of satin and characteristic of some minerals in fibrous aggregates (examples are fibrous gypsum [$CaSO_4 \cdot 2H_2O$], known as satin spar, and chrysotile asbestos [$Mg_3Si_2O_5(OH)_4$]); and adamantine, having the brilliant lustre of diamond, exhibited by minerals with a high refractive index comparable to diamond and which as such refract light as strongly as the latter (examples are cerussite [$PbCO_3$] and anglesite [$PbSO_4$]).

COLOUR

Minerals occur in a great variety of colours. Because colour varies not only from one mineral to another but also within the same mineral (or mineral group), the observer must learn in which minerals it is a constant property and can thus be relied on as a distinguishing criterion. Most minerals that have a metallic lustre vary little in colour, but nonmetallic minerals can demonstrate wide variance. Although the colour of a freshly broken surface of a metallic mineral is often highly diagnostic, this same mineral may become tarnished with time. Such a tarnish may dull minerals such as galena (PbS), which has a bright bluish lead-gray colour on a fresh surface but may become dull upon long exposure to air. Bornite (Cu_5FeS_4), which on a freshly broken surface has a brownish bronze colour, may be so highly tarnished on an older surface that it shows variegated purples and blues; hence, it is called peacock ore. In other words, in the identification of minerals with a metallic lustre, it is important for the observer to have a freshly broken surface for accurate determination of colour.

A few minerals with nonmetallic lustre display a constant colour that can be used as a truly diagnostic property. Examples are malachite, which is green; azurite, which is blue; rhodonite, which is pink; turquoise, which gives its name to the colour turquoise, a greenish blue to blue-green; and sulfur, which is yellow. Many nonmetallic minerals have a relatively narrow range of colours, although some have an unusually wide range. Members of the plagioclase feldspar series range from almost pure white in albite through light gray to darker gray toward the anorthite end-member. Most common garnets show various shades of red to red-brown to brown. Members of the monoclinic pyroxene group range from almost white in pure diopside to light green in diopside containing a small amount of iron as a substitute for magnesium in the structure through dark green in hedenbergite to almost black in many augites. Members of the orthopyroxene series (enstatite to orthoferrosilite) range from light beige to darker brown. On the other hand, tourmaline may show many colours (red, blue, green, brown, and black) as well as distinct colour zonation, from colourless through pink to green, within a single crystal. Similarly, numerous gem minerals such as corundum, beryl, and quartz occur in many colours; the gemstones cut from them are given varietal names. In short, in nonmetallic minerals of various kinds, colour is a helpful, though not a truly diagnostic (and therefore unique), property.

HARDNESS

Hardness (H) is the resistance of a mineral to scratching. It is a property by which minerals may be described relative to a standard scale of 10 minerals known as the Mohs scale of hardness. The degree of hardness is determined by observing the comparative ease or difficulty with which one mineral is scratched by another or by a steel tool.

MOH'S HARDNESS SCALE AND OBSERVATIONS ON HARDNESS OF SOME ADDITIONAL MATERIALS			
MINERAL	**MOHS HARDNESS**	**OTHER MATERIALS**	**OBSERVATIONS ON THE MINERALS**
talc	1		very easily scratched by the fingernail; has a greasy feel
gypsum	2	~2.2 fingernail	can be scratched by the fingernail
calcite	3	~3.2 copper penny	very easily scratched with a knife and just scratched with a copper coin
fluorite	4		very easily scratched with a knife but not as easily as calcite
apatite	5	~5.1 pocketknife ~5.5 glass plate	scratched with a knife with difficulty
orthoclase	6	~6.5 steel needle	cannot be scratched with a knife, but scratches glass with difficulty
quartz	7	~7.0 streak plate	scratches glass easily
topaz	8		scratches glass very easily
corundum	9		cuts glass
diamond	10		used as a glass cutter

Source: Modified from C. Klein, *Minerals and Rocks: Exercises in Crystallography, Mineralogy, and Hand Specimen Petrology*. Copyright 1989 John Wiley & Sons. Reprinted by permission of John Wiley & Sons, Inc.

For measuring the hardness of a mineral, several common objects that can be used for scratching are helpful, such as a fingernail, a copper coin, a steel pocketknife, glass plate or window glass, the steel of a needle, and a streak plate.

Because there is a general link between hardness and chemical composition, these generalizations can be made:

1. Most hydrous minerals are relatively soft (H < 5).
2. Halides, carbonates, sulfates, and phosphates also are relatively soft (H < 5½).
3. Most sulfides are relatively soft (H < 5), with marcasite and pyrite being examples of exceptions (H < 6 to 6½).
4. Most anhydrous oxides and silicates are hard (H > 5½).

Because hardness is a highly diagnostic property in mineral identification, most determinative tables use relative hardness as a sorting parameter.

TENACITY

Several mineral properties that depend on the cohesive force between atoms (and ions) in mineral structures are grouped under tenacity. A mineral's tenacity can be described by the following terms: malleable, capable of being flattened under the blows of a hammer into thin sheets without breaking or crumbling into fragments (most of the native elements show various degrees of malleability, but particularly gold, silver, and copper); sectile, capable of being severed by the smooth cut of a knife (copper, silver, and gold are sectile); ductile, capable of being drawn into the form of a wire (gold, silver, and copper exhibit this property); flexible, bending easily and staying bent after the pressure is removed (talc is flexible); brittle, showing little or no resistance to breakage, and as such separating into fragments under the blow of a hammer or when cut by a knife (most silicate minerals are brittle); and elastic, capable of being bent or pulled out of shape but returning to the original form when relieved (mica is elastic).

SPECIFIC GRAVITY

Specific gravity (G) is defined as the ratio between the weight of a substance and the weight of an equal volume of water at 4 °C (39 °F). Thus a mineral with a specific gravity of 2 weighs twice as much as the same volume of water. Since it is a ratio, specific gravity has no units.

The specific gravity of a mineral depends on the atomic weights of all its constituent elements and the manner in which the atoms (and ions) are packed together. In mineral series whose species have essentially identical structures, those composed of elements with higher atomic weight have higher specific gravities. If two minerals (as in the two polymorphs of carbon, namely graphite and diamond) have the same chemical composition, the difference in specific gravity reflects variation in internal packing of the atoms or ions (diamond, with a G of 3.51, has a more densely packed structure than graphite, with a G of 2.23).

Measurement of the specific gravity of a mineral specimen requires the use of a special apparatus. An estimate of the value, however, can be obtained by simply testing how heavy a specimen feels. Most people, from everyday experience, have developed a sense of relative weights for even such objects as nonmetallic and metallic minerals. For example, borax (G = 1.7) seems light for a nonmetallic mineral, whereas anglesite (G = 6.4) appears heavy. Average specific gravity reflects what a nonmetallic or metallic mineral of a given size should weigh. The average specific gravity for nonmetallic minerals falls between 2.65 and 2.75, which is seen in the range of values for quartz (G = 2.65), feldspar (G = 2.60 to 2.75), and calcite (G = 2.72). For metallic minerals, graphite (G = 2.23) feels light, while silver (G = 10.5) seems heavy. The average specific gravity for metallic minerals is approximately 5.0, the value for pyrite. With practice using specimens of known specific gravity, a person can develop the ability to distinguish between minerals that have comparatively small differences in specific gravity by merely lifting them.

Although an approximate assessment of specific gravity can be obtained by the hefting of a hand specimen of a specific monomineral, an accurate measurement can only be achieved by using a specific gravity balance. An example of such an instrument is the Jolly balance, which provides numerical values for a small mineral specimen (or fragment) in air as well as in water. Such accurate measurements are highly diagnostic and can greatly aid in the identification of an unknown mineral sample.

MAGNETISM

Only two minerals exhibit readily observed magnetism: magnetite (Fe_3O_4), which is strongly attracted to a hand magnet, and pyrrhotite ($Fe_{1-x}S$), which typically shows a weaker magnetic reaction. *Ferromagnetic* is a term that refers to materials that exhibit strong magnetic attraction when subjected to a magnetic field. Materials that show only a weak magnetic response in a strong applied magnetic field are known as paramagnetic. Those materials that are repelled by an applied magnetic force are known as diamagnetic. Because minerals display a wide range of slightly different magnetic properties, they can be separated from each other by an electromagnet. Such magnetic separation is a common procedure both in the laboratory and on a commercial scale.

Fluorescence

Some minerals, when exposed to ultraviolet light, will emit visible light during irradiation; this is known as fluorescence. Some minerals fluoresce only in shortwave ultraviolet light, others only in longwave ultraviolet light, and still others in either situation. Both the colour and intensity of the emitted light vary significantly with the wavelengths of ultraviolet light. Due to the unpredictable nature of fluorescence, some specimens of a mineral manifest it, while other seemingly similar specimens, even those from the same geographic area, do not. Some minerals that may exhibit fluorescence are fluorite, scheelite, calcite, scapolite, willemite, and autunite. Specimens of willemite and calcite from the Franklin district of New Jersey in the United States may show brilliant fluorescent colours.

Solubility in Hydrochloric Acid

The positive identification of carbonate minerals is aided greatly by the fact that the carbon-oxygen bond of the CO_3 group in carbonates becomes unstable and breaks down in the presence of hydrogen ions (H^+) available in acids. This is expressed by the reaction $2H^+ + CO_3^{2-} \rightarrow H_2O + CO_2$, which is the basis for the so-called fizz test with dilute hydrochloric acid (HCl). Calcite, aragonite, witherite, and strontianite, as well as copper carbonates, show bubbling, or effervescence, when a drop of dilute hydrochloric acid is placed on the mineral. This "fizz" is due to the release of carbon dioxide (CO_2). Other carbonates such as dolomite, rhodochrosite, magnesite, and siderite will show slow effervescence when acid is applied to powdered minerals or moderate effervescence only in hot hydrochloric acid.

Radioactivity

Minerals containing uranium (U) and thorium (Th) continually undergo decay reactions in which radioactive isotopes of uranium and thorium form various daughter elements and also release energy in the form of alpha and beta particles and gamma radiation. The radiation produced can be measured in the laboratory or in the field using a Geiger counter or a scintillation counter. A radiation counter therefore is helpful in identifying uranium- and thorium-containing minerals, such as uraninite, pitchblende, thorianite, and autunite.

Several rock-forming minerals contain enough radioactive elements to permit the determination of the time elapsed since the radioactive material was incorporated into the mineral.

CHAPTER 2
MINERAL CLASSIFICATION AND ASSOCIATIONS

S ince the middle of the 19th century, minerals have been classified on the basis of their chemical composition. Under this scheme, they are divided into classes according to their dominant anion or anionic group (e.g., halides, oxides, and sulfides). Different minerals also appear together within a rock matrix. As a result, the science of petrology, which focuses on the composition of rocks, is also concerned with mineral classification. Minerals and rocks alike are collections of chemical compounds, and these compounds undergo phase changes as the conditions of the surroundings change. Such phase changes may affect how one mineral behaves in the presence of another. Consequently, the concept of phase equilibrium between solid, liquid, and gaseous states of a given mineral or between different minerals that come in contact with one another is an important part of mineralogy and petrology.

CLASSIFICATION OF MINERALS

Several reasons justify use of a mineral's chemical composition as the distinguishing factor at the highest level of mineral classification. First, the similarities in properties of minerals with identical anionic groups are generally more pronounced than those with the same dominant cation. For example, carbonates have stronger resemblance to one another than do copper minerals. Secondly, minerals that have identical dominant anions are likely to be found in the same or similar geologic environments. Therefore, sulfides tend to occur together in vein or replacement deposits, while silicate-bearing rocks make up much of the Earth's crust. Third, current chemical practice employs a nomenclature and classification scheme for inorganic compounds based on similar principles.

Investigators have found, however, that chemical composition alone is insufficient for classifying minerals. Determination of internal structures, accomplished through the use of X-rays, allows a more complete appreciation of the nature of minerals. Chemical composition and internal structure together constitute the essence of a mineral and determine its physical properties; thus, classification should rely on both. Crystallochemical principles—i.e., those relating to both chemical composition and crystal structure—were first applied by the British physicist W. Lawrence Bragg and the Norwegian mineralogist Victor Moritz Goldschmidt in the study of silicate minerals. The silicate group was subdivided in part on the basis of composition but mainly according to internal structure. Based on the topology of the SiO_4 tetrahedrons, the subclasses include framework, chain, and sheet silicates, among others. Such mineral classifications are logical and well-defined.

The broadest divisions of the classification used in the present discussion are (1) native elements, (2) sulfides, (3) sulfosalts, (4) oxides and hydroxides, (5) halides, (6) carbonates, (7) nitrates, (8) borates, (9) sulfates, (10) phosphates, and (11) silicates.

NATIVE ELEMENTS

Apart from the free gases in the Earth's atmosphere, some 20 elements occur in nature in a pure (i.e., uncombined) or nearly pure form. Known as the native elements, they are partitioned into three families: metals, semimetals, and nonmetals The most common native metals, which are characterized by simple crystal structures, make up three groups: the gold group, consisting of gold, silver, copper, and lead; the platinum group, composed of platinum, palladium, iridium, and osmium; and the iron group, containing iron and nickel-iron. Mercury, tantalum, tin, and zinc are other metals that have been found in the native state. The native semimetals are divided into two isostructural groups (those whose members share a common structure type): (1) antimony, arsenic, and bismuth, with the latter two being more common in nature, and (2) the rather uncommon selenium and tellurium. Carbon, in the form of diamond and graphite, and sulfur are the most important native nonmetals.

WHAT IS A NATIVE ELEMENT?

A native element is a chemical element that may occur in nature uncombined with other elements. The group of native elements does not include those that occur as atmospheric gasses, however.

Of the 92 chemical elements found in nature only 19 are known to occur as minerals. These native elements are commonly divided into three groups—namely, metals (platinum, iridium, osmium, iron, zinc, tin, gold, silver, copper, mercury, lead, chromium); semimetals (bismuth, antimony, arsenic, tellurium, selenium); and nonmetals (sulfur, carbon). In metals the mineral structure is usually either cubic close-packed or hexagonal close-packed. The semimetals and nonmetals have more complex structures. Several native elements (e.g., carbon) have one or more polymorphic forms whose occurrence depends on the conditions of formation.

It is virtually impossible to make generalizations as to the occurrence of the native elements. They form under greatly contrasting physicochemical conditions and in all types of rocks. Even a single native element can occur in widely diverse environments. Native iron (kamacite), for example, is found primarily in meteorites. The iron meteorites called hexahedrites are almost completely composed of kamacite, and in those called octahedrites it is the principal constituent. Although terrestrial native iron is a great rarity, it has been found in igneous rocks (basalts), in carbonaceous sedimentary rocks, and in petrified wood.

Many of the other metals and certain non-metals are sufficiently abundant to form deposits of commercial importance. Native gold and silver, for example, are the principal ores of these metals.

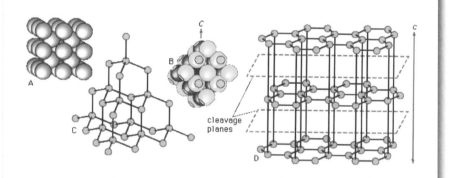

Structures of some native elements. (A) Close-packed model of simple cubic packing of equal spheres, as shown by iron. Each sphere is surrounded by eight closest neighbours. (B) Close-packed model of the structure of arsenic and antimony. Flat areas represent overlap between adjoining atoms. (C) Partial representation of the structure of diamond. (D) The structure of graphite with sheets perpendicular to the c axis. Copyright Encyclopædia Britannica, Inc.; rendering for this edition by Rosen Educational Services

NAME	COLOUR	LUSTRE	MOHS HARDNESS	SPECIFIC GRAVITY	HABIT OR FORM
NATIVE ELEMENTS					
alle-montite	tin-white; reddish gray	metallic	3–4	5.8–6.2	kidneylike masses
Amalgam					
gold-amalgam	yellowish	metallic		15.5	lumps or grains
moschel-lands-bergite	silver-white	bright metallic	3½	13.5–13.7	dodecahedrons; massive
potarite	silver-white	bright metallic	3½	13.5–16.1	grains or nuggets
antimony	tin-white	metallic	3–3½	6.6–6.7	massive
arsenic	tin-white, tarnishing to dark gray	nearly metallic on fresh surfaces	3½	5.6–5.8	granular massive; concentric nodules
arsenol-amprite	lead-gray	brilliant metallic	2	5.3–5.5	massive
bismuth	silver-white, with red-dish hue; tarnishes iridescent	metallic	2–2½	9.7–9.8	network or treelike crystal groups

NAME	COLOUR	LUSTRE	Mohs HARDNESS	SPECIFIC GRAVITY	HABIT OR FORM
Carbon					
diamond	pale to deep yellow or brown; white to blue-white; sometimes variable	ada-mantine to greasy	10	3.5	flattened octahedrons; dodecahedrons
graphite	black to dark steel-gray	metallic	1–2	2.1–2.2	platy or flaky massive
cohenite	tin-white, tarnishes to light bronze or gold-yellow		5½–6	7.2–7.7	elongated tabular crystals
copper	light rose, tarnishes quickly to copper-red and brown	metallic	2½–3	8.95	plates and scales; wirelike, treelike crystal groups; twisted bands; malformed crystals
gold	gold-yellow (when pure); silver-white to orange-red	metallic	2½–3	19.3	elongated or flattened crystals; wirelike, treelike, or spongy forms

NAME	COLOUR	LUSTRE	MOHS HARDNESS	SPECIFIC GRAVITY	HABIT OR FORM
iridos-mine	tin-white to light steel-gray	metallic	6–7	19.0–21.0	flakes or flattened grains
iron	steel-gray to iron-black	metallic	4	7.3–7.9	small blisters or large masses (terrestrial); plates and lamellar masses intergrown with nickel-iron (meteoritic)
lead	lead-gray; gray-white on fresh surfaces	dull; metallic on fresh surfaces	1½	11.4	rounded masses; thin plates
mercury	tin-white	very brilliant metallic		13.596	isolated drops; occasionally in larger liquid masses
nickel-iron	silver- to grayish-white	metallic	5	7.8–8.2	pebbles, grains, fine scales (terrestrial); intergrown with or bordering meteoritic iron (meteoritic)
palla-dium	whitish steel-gray	metallic	4½–5	11.9	grains

NAME	COLOUR	LUSTRE	MOHS HARDNESS	SPECIFIC GRAVITY	HABIT OR FORM
plati- niridium	yellowish silver-white; gray on fresh surfaces	metallic	6–7	22.6– 22.8	rounded or angular grains
platinum	whitish steel-gray to dark gray	metallic	4–4½	14–19	grains or scales; sometimes in lumps or nuggets
sch- reiber- site	silver- to tin-white; tarnishes to brass-yellow or brown	highly metallic	6½–7	7.0–7.3	plates; rods or needles
selenium	gray	metallic	2	4.8	crystals, often hollow or tube-like; glassy drops
silver	silver-white; tarnishes gray to black	metallic	2½–3	10.1– 11.1 (10.5 pure)	crystals, often in elongated, wire-like, or treelike groups; mas-sive as scales or coating
Sulfur					
rhombic (alpha-sulfur)	sulfur-, straw- to honey-yellow; yellowish brown or gray, green-ish, reddish	resin-ous to greasy	1½–2½	2.07	transparent to translucent tabular crystals; spherical or kid-neylike masses; crusts; powder

NAME	COLOUR	LUSTRE	MOHS HARDNESS	SPECIFIC GRAVITY	HABIT OR FORM
mono-clinic (beta-sulfur)	light yellow: nearly colourless; brownish due to included organic matter		slightly greater than alpha-sulfur	1.958, 1.982	thick tabular or elongated crystals
nacre-ous (gamma-sulfur)	light yellow; nearly colourless	ada-mantine	low	less than alpha-sulfur	minute transparent crystals
tantalum	grayish yellow	bright	6–7	11.2	minute crystals; fine grains
tellu-rium	tin-white	metallic	2–2½	6.1–6.3	columnar to fine granular massive; minute crystals
tin	tin-white	metallic	2	7.3	irregular rounded grains; natural crystals unknown
zinc	slightly grayish white	metallic	2	6.9–7.2	

NAME	FRACTURE OR CLEAVAGE	REFRACTIVE INDEX OR POLISHED SECTION DATA	CRYSTAL SYSTEM	REMARKS
alle-montite	one perfect cleavage	fine graphic intergrowth of allemontite with arsenic or antimony	hexago-nal	
Amalgam				
gold-amalgam	conchoidal fracture		isometric	
mos-chel-lands-bergite	two distinct cleavages		isometric	
potarite		intergrowth of "potarite groundmass" (white, iso-tropic, high reflectivity) and "potarite inclusions" (light gray; anisotropic)	isometric	
anti-mony	one perfect cleavage; two less so	brilliant white; very strong reflectivity	hexago-nal	

NAME	FRACTURE OR CLEAVAGE	REFRACTIVE INDEX OR POLISHED SECTION DATA	CRYSTAL SYSTEM	REMARKS
arsenic	one perfect cleavage	white; strong reflectivity; anisotropic	hexago-nal	
arsenol-amprite	one perfect cleavage			may be either impure native arsenic or a distinct modification
bismuth	one perfect and one good cleavage	brilliant creamy white, tarnish-ing yellow; anisotropic	hexago-nal	sectile; when heated, somewhat malleable
Carbon				
diamond	one perfect cleavage; conchoidal fracture	$n = 2.4175$	isometric	triboelec-tric; strong dispersion
graphite	one perfect cleavage	pleochroism and birefrin-gence extreme	hexago-nal	electrical con-ductor; greasy feel; thermo-electrically negative; thin fragments transparent and deep blue
cohenite	three cleavages		ortho-rhombic	strongly magnetic

NAME	FRACTURE OR CLEAVAGE	REFRACTIVE INDEX OR POLISHED SECTION DATA	CRYSTAL SYSTEM	REMARKS
copper	no cleavage; hackly fracture	rose-white; isotropic; strong reflectivity	isometric	highly ductile and malleable
gold	no cleavage; hackly fracture	brilliant gold-yellow; isotropic; high reflectivity	isometric	very ductile and malleable
iridosmine	one perfect cleavage	slightly yellowish white	hexagonal	slightly malleable; forms solid solution with siserskite, (Os, Ir), ranging from 77% Ir to almost 80% Os
iron	one cleavage; hackly fracture	white; isotropic	isometric	magnetic; malleable
lead	no cleavage	fresh surfaces gray-white, isotropic, high reflectivity; quickly dulled	isometric	very malleable; somewhat ductile
mercury			hexagonal (at -39 °C)	liquid at normal temperatures

NAME	FRACTURE OR CLEAVAGE	REFRACTIVE INDEX OR POLISHED SECTION DATA	CRYSTAL SYSTEM	REMARKS
nickel-iron	no cleavage		isometric	strongly magnetic; malleable; flexible
palla-dium	no cleavage	white; high reflectivity; isotropic	isometric	ductile; malleable
plati-nirid-ium	hackly fracture		isometric	somewhat malleable
plati-num	no cleav-age; hackly fracture	white; isotropic	isometric	malleable; ductile; sometimes magnetic
sch-reiber-site	one perfect cleavage		tetrago-nal	strongly magnetic
selenium	one good cleavage	fairly high reflectivity; creamy white; pleochroic; very strongly anisotropic	hexago-nal	electrical conductor; thin frag-ments transparent and red

NAME	FRACTURE OR CLEAVAGE	REFRACTIVE INDEX OR POL- ISHED SECTION DATA	CRYSTAL SYSTEM	REMARKS
silver	no cleavage; hackly fracture	brilliant silver-white; greatest reflectivity known; isotropic	isometric	ductile and malleable
Sulfur				
rhombic (alpha-sulfur)	three imperfect cleavages; conchoidal to uneven fracture	$n = 1.957$	ortho-rhombic	electrical nonconductor; negatively charged by friction
mono-clinic (beta-sulfur)	two cleavages	$n = 2.038$	mono-clinic	
nacre-ous (gamma-sulfur)	no observed cleavage		mono-clinic	reverts slowly to alpha-sulfur at room temperature
tanta-lum			isometric	
tellu-rium	one perfect cleavage	strongly aniso-tropic; white; very strongly reflective	hexago-nal	

NAME	FRACTURE OR CLEAVAGE	REFRACTIVE INDEX OR POLISHED SECTION DATA	CRYSTAL SYSTEM	REMARKS
tin	hackly fracture		tetrago-nal	ductile; malleable
zinc	one perfect cleavage		hexago-nal	though reported, existence in native form is doubtful

METALS

Gold, silver, and copper are members of the same group (column) in the periodic table of elements and therefore have similar chemical properties. In the uncombined state, their atoms are joined by the fairly weak metallic bond. These minerals share a common structure type, and their atoms are positioned in a simple cubic closest-packed arrangement. Gold and silver both have an atomic radius of 1.44 angstroms (Å), which enables complete solid solution to take place between them. The radius of copper is significantly smaller (1.28 Å), and as such copper substitutes only to a limited extent in gold and silver. Likewise, native copper contains only trace amounts of gold and silver in its structure.

Owing to their similar crystal structure, the members of the gold group display similar physical properties. All are rather soft, ductile, malleable, and sectile; gold, silver, and copper serve as excellent conductors of electricity and heat and exhibit metallic lustre and hackly fracture. These properties are attributable to their metallic bonding. The gold-group minerals crystallize in the isometric system and have high densities as a consequence of cubic closest packing.

In addition to the elements listed above, the platinum group also includes rare mineral alloys such as iridosmine. The members of this group are harder than the metals of the gold group and also have higher melting points.

The iron-group metals are isometric and have a simple cubic packed structure. Its members include pure iron, which is rarely found on the surface of the Earth, and two species of nickel-iron (kamacite and taenite), which have been identified as common constituents of meteorites. Native iron has been found in basalts of Disko Island, Greenland, and nickel-iron in Josphine and Jackson counties, Ore. The atomic radii of iron and nickel are both approximately 1.24 Å, and so nickel is a frequent substitute for iron. The terrestrial core is thought to be composed largely of such iron-nickel alloys.

SEMIMETALS

The semimetals antimony, arsenic, and bismuth have a structure type distinct from the simple-packed spheres of the metals. In these semimetals, each atom is positioned closer to three of its neighbouring atoms than to the rest. The structure of antimony and arsenic is composed of spheres that intersect along flat circular areas.

The covalent character of the bonds joining the four closest atoms is linked to the electronegative nature of the semimetals, reflected by their position in the periodic table. Members of this group are fairly brittle, and they do not conduct heat and electricity nearly as well as the native metals. The bond type suggested by these properties is intermediate between metallic and covalent; it is consequently stronger and more directional than pure metallic bonding, resulting in crystals of lower symmetry.

METALLIC SUBSTANCES

Metals are substances characterized by high electrical and thermal conductivity as well as by malleability, ductility, and high reflectivity of light.

Approximately three-quarters of all known chemical elements are metals. The most abundant varieties in the Earth's crust are aluminum, iron, calcium, sodium, potassium, and magnesium. The vast majority of metals are found in ores (mineral-bearing substances), but a few such as copper, gold, platinum, and silver frequently occur in the free state because they do not readily react with other elements.

Metals are usually crystalline solids. In most cases, they have a relatively simple crystal structure distinguished by a close packing of atoms and a high degree of symmetry. Typically, the atoms of metals contain less than half the full complement of electrons in their outermost shell. Because of this characteristic, metals tend not to form compounds with each other. They do, however, combine more readily with non-metals (e.g., oxygen and sulfur), which generally have more than half the maximum number of valence electrons. Metals differ widely in their chemical reactivity. The most reactive include lithium, potassium, and radium, whereas those of low reactivity are gold, silver, palladium, and platinum.

The high electrical and thermal conductivities of the simple metals (i.e., the non-transition metals of the periodic table) are best explained by reference to the free-electron theory. According to this concept, the individual atoms in such metals have lost their valence electrons to the entire solid, and these free electrons that give rise to conductivity move as a group throughout the solid. In the case of the more complex metals (i.e., the transition elements), conductivities are better explained

Block of metallic gold. © Jupiterimages Corporation

by the band theory, which takes into account not only the presence of free electrons but also their interaction with so-called *d* electrons.

The mechanical properties of metals, such as hardness, ability to resist repeated stressing (fatigue strength), ductility, and malleability, are often attributed to defects or imperfections in their crystal structure. The absence of a layer of atoms in its densely packed structure, for example, enables a metal to deform plastically, and prevents it from being brittle.

NONMETALS

The native nonmetals diamond, fullerene, graphite, and sulfur are structurally distinct from the metals and semimetals. The structure of sulfur (atomic radius = 1.04 Å), usually orthorhombic in form, may contain limited solid solution by selenium (atomic radius = 1.16 Å).

The polymorphs of carbon—graphite, fullerene, and diamond—display dissimilar structures, resulting in their differences in hardness and specific gravity. In diamond, each carbon atom is bonded covalently in a tetrahedral arrangement, producing a strongly bonded and exceedingly close-knit but not closest-packed structure. The carbon atoms of graphite, however, are arranged in six-membered rings in which each atom is surrounded by three close-by neighbours located at the vertices of an equilateral triangle. The rings are linked to form sheets that are separated by a distance exceeding one atomic diameter. Van der Waals forces act perpendicular to the sheets, offering a weak bond, which, in combination with the wide spacing, leads to perfect basal cleavage and easy gliding along the sheets. Fullerenes, a newly discovered polymorph of carbon, are found in meta-anthracite, in fulgurites, and in clays from the Cretaceous-Tertiary boundary in New Zealand, Spain, and Turkmenistan as well as in organic-rich layers near the Sudbury nickel mine of Canada.

SULFIDES

This important class includes most of the ore minerals. The similar but rarer sulfarsenides are grouped here as well. Sulfide minerals consist of one or more metals combined with sulfur; sulfarsenides contain arsenic replacing some of the sulfur.

Sulfides are generally opaque and exhibit distinguishing colours and streaks. (Streak is the colour of a mineral's powder.) The nonopaque varieties (e.g., cinnabar, realgar,

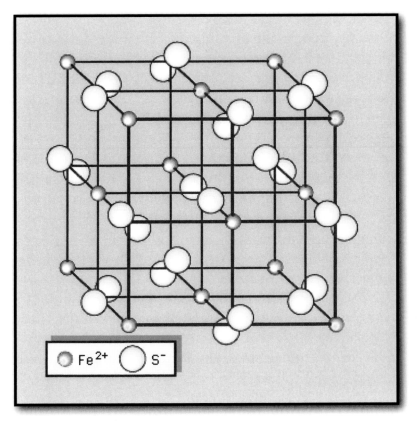

Schematic representation of the structure of pyrite, FeS_2, as based on a cubic array of ferrous iron cations (Fe^{2+}) and sulfur anions (S^-). Copyright Encyclopædia Britannica, Inc.; rendering for this edition by Rosen Educational Services

and orpiment) possess high refractive indices, transmitting light only on the thin edges of a specimen.

Few broad generalizations can be made about the structures of sulfides, although these minerals can be classified into small groups according to similarities in structure. Ionic and covalent bonding are found in many sulfides, while metallic bonding is apparent in others as evidenced by their metal properties. The simplest and most symmetric sulfide structure is based on the architecture of the sodium chloride structure. A common sulfide mineral that crystallizes in this manner is the ore mineral of lead, galena. Its highly symmetric form consists of cubes modified by octahedral faces at their corners. The structure of the common sulfide pyrite (FeS_2) also is modeled after the sodium chloride type; a disulfide grouping is located in a position of coordination with six surrounding ferrous iron atoms. The high symmetry of this structure is reflected in the external morphology of pyrite. In another sulfide structure, sphalerite (ZnS), each zinc atom is surrounded by four sulfur atoms in a tetrahedral coordinating arrangement. In a derivative of this structure type, the chalcopyrite ($CuFeS_2$) structure, copper and iron ions can be thought of as having been regularly substituted in the zinc positions of the original sphalerite atomic arrangement.

Arsenopyrite (FeAsS) is a common sulfarsenide that occurs in many ore deposits. It is the chief source of the element arsenic.

SULFOSALTS

There are approximately 100 species constituting the rather large and very diverse sulfosalt class of minerals. The sulfosalts differ notably from the sulfides and sulfarsenides with regard to the role of semimetals, such as arsenic (As) and antimony (Sb), in their structures. In the sulfarsenides, the semimetals substitute for some of the sulfur in the structure, while in the sulfosalts they are found instead in the metal site. For example, in the sulfarsenide arsenopyrite (FeAsS), the arsenic replaces sulfur in a marcasite- (FeS_2-) type structure. In contrast, the sulfosalt enargite (Cu_3AsS_4) contains arsenic in the metal position, coordinated to four sulfur atoms. A sulfosalt such as Cu_3AsS_4 may also be thought of as a double sulfide, $3Cu_2S \cdot As_2S_5$.

OXIDES AND HYDROXIDES

These classes consist of oxygen-bearing minerals; the oxides combine oxygen with one or more metals, while the hydroxides are characterized by hydroxyl $(OH)^-$ groups.

The oxides are further divided into two main types: simple and multiple. Simple oxides contain a single metal combined with oxygen in one of several possible metal:oxygen ratios (X:O): XO, X_2O, X_2O_3, etc. Ice, H_2O, is a simple oxide of the X_2O type that incorporates hydrogen as the cation. Although SiO_2 (quartz and its polymorphs) is the most commonly occurring oxide, it is discussed below in the section on silicates because its structure more closely resembles that of other silicon-oxygen compounds. Two nonequivalent metal sites (X and Y) characterize multiple oxides, which have the form XY_2O_4.

Unlike the minerals of the sulfide class, which exhibit ionic, covalent, and metallic bonding, oxide minerals generally display strong ionic bonding. They are relatively hard, dense, and refractory.

Oxides minerals generally occur in small amounts in igneous and metamorphic rocks and also as preexisting grains in sedimentary rocks. Several oxides have great economic value, including the principal ores of iron (hematite and magnetite), chromium (chromite), manganese (pyrolusite, as well as the hydroxides, manganite and romanechite), tin (cassiterite), and uranium (uraninite).

Members of the hematite group are of the X_2O_3 type and have structures based on hexagonal closest packing of the oxygen atoms with octahedrally coordinated (surrounded by and bonded to six atoms) cations between them. Corundum and hematite share a common hexagonal architecture. In the ilmenite structure, iron and titanium occupy alternate Fe-O and Ti-O layers.

The XO_2-type oxides are divided into two groups. The first structure type, exemplified by rutile, contains cations in octahedral coordination with oxygen. The second resembles fluorite (CaF_2); each oxygen is bonded to four cations located at the corners of a fairly regular tetrahedron, and each cation lies within a cube at whose corners

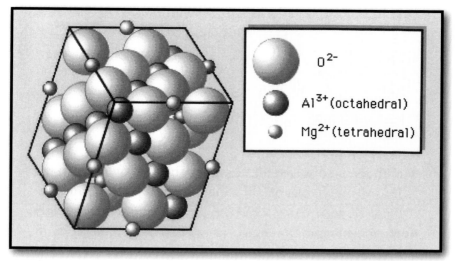

An oxygen layer in the spinel ($MgAl_2O_4$) structure. The large circles represent oxygen in approximate cubic closest packing; the cation layers on each side of the oxygen layer are also shown. Copyright Encyclopædia Britannica, Inc.; rendering for this edition by Rosen Educational Services

are eight oxygen atoms. This latter structure is exhibited by uranium, thorium, and cerium oxides, whose considerable importance arises from their roles in nuclear chemistry.

The spinel-group minerals have type XY_2O_4 and contain oxygen atoms in approximate cubic closest packing. The cations located within the oxygen framework are octahedrally (sixfold) and tetrahedrally (fourfold) coordinated with oxygen.

The $(OH)^-$ group of the hydroxides generally results in structures with lower bond strengths than in the oxide minerals. The hydroxide minerals tend to be less dense than the oxides and also are not as hard. All hydroxides form at low temperatures and are found predominantly as weathering products, as, for example, from alteration in hydrothermal veins. Some common hydroxides are brucite $[Mg(OH)_2]$, manganite $[MnO \cdot OH]$, diaspore $[a\text{-}AlO \cdot OH]$, and goethite $[a\text{-}FeO \cdot OH]$. The ore of aluminum, bauxite, consists of a mixture of diaspore, boehmite (γ-AlO $\cdot$ OH—a polymorph of diaspore), and gibbsite $[Al(OH)_3]$, plus iron oxides. Goethite is a common alteration product of iron-rich occurrences and is an iron ore in some localities.

HALIDES

Members of this class are distinguished by the large-sized anions of the halogens chlorine, bromine, iodine, and fluorine. The ions carry a charge of negative one and easily become distorted in the presence of strongly charged bodies. When associated with rather large, weakly polarizing cations of low charge, such as those of the alkali metals, both anions and cations take the form of nearly perfect spheres. Structures composed of these spheres exhibit the highest possible symmetry.

Pure ionic bonding is exemplified best in the isometric halides, for each spherical ion distributes its weak electrostatic charge over its entire surface. These halides manifest relatively low hardness and moderate-to-high melting points. In the solid state they are poor thermal and electric conductors, but when molten they conduct electricity well.

Halogen ions may also combine with smaller, more strongly polarizing cations than the alkali metal ions. Lower symmetry and a higher degree of covalent bonding prevail in these structures. Water and hydroxyl ions may enter the structure, as in atacamite $[Cu_2Cl(OH)_3]$.

The halides consist of about 80 chemically related minerals with diverse structures and widely varied origins. The most common are halite ($NaCl$), sylvite (KCl), chlorargyrite ($AgCl$), cryolite (Na_3AlF_6), fluorite (CaF_2), and atacamite. By the arrangement of the ions, it is evident that no molecules are present in the structure. Each cation and anion is in octahedral coordination with its six closest neighbours. The $NaCl$ structure is found in the crystals of many XZ-type halides, including sylvite (KCl) and chlorargyrite ($AgCl$). Some sulfides and oxides of XZ type crystallize in this structure type as well—for example, galena (PbS), alabandite (MnS), and periclase (MgO).

Several XZ_2 halides have the same structure as fluorite (CaF_2). In fluorite, calcium cations are positioned at the corners and face centres of cubic unit cells. (A unit cell is the smallest group of atoms, ions, or molecules from which the entire crystal structure can be generated by its repetition.) Each fluorine anion is in tetrahedral coordination with four calcium ions, while each calcium cation is in eightfold coordination with eight fluorine ions that form the corners of a cube around it.

Uraninite (UO_2) and thorianite (ThO_2) are two of the several oxides that have a fluorite-type structure.

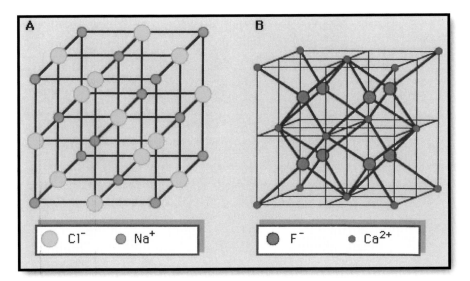

(A) The structure of halite, NaCl. (B) The structure of fluorite, CaF$_2$. Copyright Encyclopædia Britannica, Inc.; rendering for this edition by Rosen Educational Services

CARBONATES

The carbonate minerals contain the anionic complex $(CO_3)^{2-}$, which is triangular in its coordination—i.e., with a carbon atom at the centre and an oxygen atom at each of the corners of an equilateral triangle. These anionic groups are strongly bonded, individual units and do not share oxygen atoms with one another. The triangular carbonate groups are the basic building units of all carbonate minerals and are largely responsible for the properties particular to the class.

Carbonates are frequently identified using the effervescence test with acid. The reaction that results in the characteristic fizz, $2H^+ + CO_3^{2-} \rightarrow H_2O + CO_2$, makes use of the fact that the carbon-oxygen bonds of the CO_3 groups are not quite as strong as the corresponding carbon-oxygen bonds in carbon dioxide.

The common anhydrous carbonates are divided into three groups that differ in structure type: calcite, aragonite, and dolomite. The copper carbonates azurite and malachite are the only notable hydrous varieties.

Some members of the calcite group share a common structure type. It can be considered as a derivative of the NaCl structure in which CO_3 groups substitute for the chlorine ions and calcium cations replace the sodium cations. As a result of the triangular shape of the CO_3 groups, the structure is rhombohedral instead of isometric as in NaCl. The CO_3 groups are in planes perpendicular to the threefold c axis, and the calcium ions occupy alternate planes and are bonded to six oxygen atoms of the CO_3 groups.

Members of the calcite group exhibit perfect rhombohedral cleavage. The composition $CaCO_3$ most commonly occurs in two different polymorphs: rhombohedral calcite with calcium surrounded by six closest oxygen atoms and orthorhombic aragonite with calcium surrounded by nine closest oxygen atoms.

When CO_3 groups are combined with large divalent cations (generally with ionic radii greater than 1.0 Å), orthorhombic structures result. This is known as the aragonite structure type. Members of this group include those with large cations: $BaCO_3$, $SrCO_3$, and $PbCO_3$. Each cation is surrounded by nine closest oxygen atoms.

The aragonite group displays more limited solid solution than the calcite group. The type of cation present in aragonite minerals is largely responsible for the differences in physical properties among the members of the group. Specific gravity, for example, is roughly proportional to the atomic weight of the metal ions.

Dolomite [$CaMg(CO_3)_2$], kutnahorite [$CaMn(CO_3)_2$], and ankerite [$CaFe(CO_3)_2$] are three isostructural members of the dolomite group. The dolomite structure can be considered as a calcite-type structure in which magnesium and calcium cations occupy the metal sites in alternate layers. The calcium (Ca^{2+}) and magnesium (Mg^{2+}) ions differ in size by 33 percent, and this produces cation ordering with the two cations occupying specific and separate levels in the structure. Dolomite has a calcium-to-magnesium ratio of approximately 1:1, which gives it a composition intermediate between $CaCO_3$ and $MgCO_3$.

NITRATES

The nitrates are characterized by their triangular $(NO_3)^-$ groups that resemble the $(CO_3)^{2-}$ groups of the carbonates, making the two mineral classes similar in structure. The nitrogen cation (N^{5+}) carries a high charge and is strongly polarizing like the carbon cation (C^{4+}) of the CO_3 group. A tightly knit triangular complex is created by the three nitrogen-oxygen bonds of the NO_3 group; these bonds are stronger than all others in the crystal. Because the nitrogen-oxygen bond has greater strength than the corresponding carbon-oxygen bond in carbonates, nitrates decompose less readily in the presence of acids.

Nitrate structures analogous to those of the calcite group result when NO_3 combines in a 1:1 ratio with monovalent cations whose radii can accommodate six closest oxygen neighbours. For example, nitratite ($NaNO_3$), also called soda nitre, and calcite exhibit the same structure, crystallography, and cleavage. The two minerals differ in that nitratite is softer and melts at a lower temperature owing to its lesser charge; also, sodium has a lower atomic weight than calcium, causing nitratite to have a lower specific gravity as well. Similarly, nitre (KNO_3), also known as saltpetre, is an analogue of aragonite. These are two examples of only seven known naturally occurring nitrates.

BORATES

Minerals of the borate class contain boron-oxygen groups that can link together, in a phenomenon known as polymerization, to form chains, sheets, and isolated multiple groups. The silicon-oxygen (SiO_4) tetrahedrons of the silicates polymerize in a manner similar to the $(BO_3)^{3-}$ triangular groups of the borates. A single oxygen atom is shared between two boron cations (B^{3+}), thereby linking the BO_3 groups into extended units such as double triangles, triple rings, sheets, and chains. The oxygen atom is able to accommodate two boron atoms because the small boron cation has a bond strength to each oxygen that is exactly one-half the bond energy of the oxygen ion.

Although boron is usually found in triangular coordination with three oxygens, it also occurs in fourfold

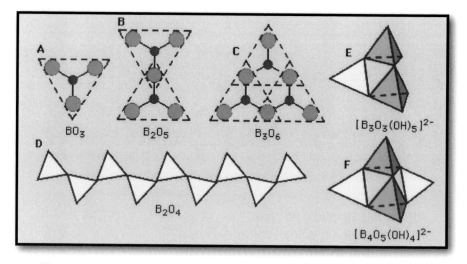

Various possible linkages of (A) BO₃ triangles to form (B,C) multiple groups and (D) chains in borates. Complex (E) triangle and (F) quadrangle groups are also shown. The group depicted in (F) occurs in borax. Copyright Encyclopædia Britannica, Inc.; rendering for this edition by Rosen Educational Services

coordination in tetrahedral groups. In addition, boron may exist as part of complex anionic groups such as $[B_3O_3(OH)_3]^{2-}$, consisting of one triangle and two tetrahedrons. Complex infinite chains of tetrahedrons and triangles are found in the structure of colemanite $[CaB_3O_4(OH)_3 \cdot H_2O]$; a complex ion composed of two tetrahedrons and two triangles, $[B_4O_5(OH)_4]^{2-}$, is present in borax $[Na_2B_4O_5(OH)_4 \cdot 8H_2O]$.

SULFATES

This class is composed of a large number of minerals, but relatively few are common. The most frequently occurring sulfates are anhydrite, gypsum, and members of the barite group (barite, celestite, and anglesite). All contain anionic $(SO_4)^{2-}$ groups in their structures. These anionic complexes are formed through the tight bonding of a central S^{6+} ion to four neighbouring oxygen atoms in a tetrahedral arrangement around the sulfur. This closely knit group is incapable of sharing any of its apical oxygen atoms with other SO_4 groups; as such the tetrahedrons occur as individual, unlinked groups in sulfate mineral structures.

Members of the barite group constitute the most important and common anhydrous sulfates. They have orthorhombic symmetry with large divalent cations bonded to the sulfate ion. In barite $(BaSO_4)$, each barium ion is surrounded by 12 closest oxygen ions belonging to seven distinct SO_4 groups.

Anhydrite $(CaSO_4)$ exhibits a structure very different from that of barite since the ionic radius of Ca^{2+} is considerably smaller than Ba^{2+}. Each calcium cation can only fit eight oxygen atoms around it from neighbouring SO_4 groups.

Gypsum $(CaSO_4 \cdot 2H_2O)$ is the most important and abundant hydrous sulfate.

PHOSPHATES

Although this mineral class is large (with almost 700 known species), most of its members are quite rare. Of the common phosphates, only apatite [$Ca_5(PO_4)_3(F, Cl, OH)$], the most important and abundant, can be considered as truly common. The members of this group are characterized by tetrahedral anionic $(PO_4)^{3-}$ complexes, which are analogous to the $(SO_4)^{2-}$ groups of the sulfates. The phosphorus ion, with a valence of positive five, is only slightly larger than the sulfur ion, which carries a positive six charge. Arsenates and vanadates are similar to phosphates.

SILICATES

The silicates, owing to their abundance on the Earth, constitute the most important mineral class. Approximately 25 percent of all known minerals and 40 percent of the most common ones are silicates; the igneous rocks that make up more than 90 percent of the Earth's crust are composed of virtually all silicates.

The fundamental unit in all silicate structures is the silicon-oxygen $(SiO_4)^{4-}$ tetrahedron. It is composed of a central silicon cation (Si^{4+}) bonded to four oxygen atoms that are located at the corners of a regular tetrahedron. The terrestrial crust is held together by the strong silicon-oxygen bonds of these tetrahedrons. Approximately 50 percent ionic and 50 percent covalent, the bonds develop from the attraction of oppositely charged ions as well as the sharing of their electrons.

The positive charge (+4) of each silicon cation is satisfied by its four bonds to oxygen atoms. Each oxygen ion (O^{2-}), however, contributes only one-half of its total bonding energy to a silicon-oxygen bond, so it is capable of also bonding to the silicon cation of another tetrahedron.

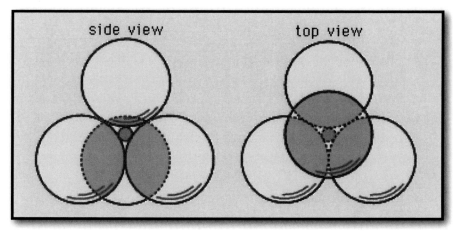

Two views of a closest-packed representation of the silicon-oxygen tetrahedron. Copyright Encyclopædia Britannica, Inc.; rendering for this edition by Rosen Educational Services

The SiO_4 tetrahedrons thereby become linked by shared oxygen atoms; this is referred to as polymerization. The degree and manner of polymerization are the bases for the variety present in silicate structures.

The silicates can be divided into groups according to structural configuration, which arises from the sharing of one, two, three, or all oxygen ions of a tetrahedron. Nesosilicates have isolated groups of SiO_4, while sorosilicates contain pairs of SiO_4 tetrahedrons linked into Si_2O_7 groups. Ring silicates, also known as cyclosilicates, are closed, ringlike silicates; the sixfold variety has composition Si_6O_{18}. Silicates that are composed of infinite chains of tetrahedrons are called inosilicates; single chains have a unit composition of SiO_3 or Si_2O_6, whereas double chains contain a silicon to oxygen ratio of 4:11. Phyllosilicates, or sheet silicates, are formed when three oxygen atoms are shared with adjoining tetrahedrons. The resulting infinite flat sheets have unit composition Si_2O_5. In structures where tetrahedrons share all their oxygen ions, an infinite three-dimensional network is created with an SiO_2 unit composition. Minerals of this type are called framework silicates or tectosilicates.

As a major constituent of the Earth's crust, aluminum follows only oxygen and silicon in importance. The radius of aluminum, slightly larger than that of silicon, lies close to the upper bound for allowable fourfold coordination in crystals. As a result, aluminum can be surrounded with four oxygen atoms arranged tetrahedrally, but it can also occur in sixfold coordination with oxygen. The ability to maintain two roles within the silicate structure makes aluminum a unique constituent of these minerals. The tetrahedral AlO_4 groups are approximately equal in size to SiO_4 groups and therefore can become incorporated into the silicate polymerization scheme. Aluminum in sixfold coordination may form ionic bonds with the SiO_4 tetrahedrons. Thus, aluminum may occupy tetrahedral sites as a replacement for silicon and octahedral sites in solid solution with elements such as magnesium and ferrous iron.

Several ions may be present in silicate structures in octahedral coordination with oxygen: Mg^{2+}, Fe^{2+}, Fe^{3+}, Mn^{2+}, Al^{3+}, and Ti^{4+}. All cations have approximately the same dimensions and thus are found in equivalent atomic sites, even though their charges range from positive two to positive four. Solid solution involving ions of different charge is accomplished through coupled substitutions, thereby maintaining neutrality of the structures.

NESOSILICATES

The silicon-oxygen tetrahedrons of the nesosilicates are not polymerized; they are linked to one another only by ionic bonds of the interstitial cations. As a result of the isolation of the tetrahedral groups, the crystal habits of these minerals are typically equidimensional so that prominent cleavage directions are not present. The size and charge of the interstitial cations largely determine the structural form of the nesosilicates. The relatively high specific gravity and hardness that are characteristic of this group arise from the dense packing of the atoms within the structure. Substitution of aluminum for silicon is normally quite low.

SOROSILICATES

These minerals contain sets of two SiO_4 tetrahedrons joined by one shared apical oxygen. A silicon-to-oxygen ratio of 2:7 is consequently present in their structures. More than 70 minerals belong to the sorosilicate group, although most are rare. Only the members of the epidote group and vesuvianite are common. Both independent $(SiO_4)^{4-}$ and double $(Si_2O_7)^{6-}$ groups are incorporated into the epidote structure, as is reflected in its formula: $Ca_2(Al, Fe)Al_2O(SiO_4)(Si_2O_7)(OH)$.

CYCLOSILICATES

Silicon-oxygen tetrahedrons are linked into rings in cyclosilicate structures, which have an overall Si:O ratio of 1:3. There are three closed cyclic configurations with the following formulas: Si_3O_9, Si_4O_{12}, and Si_6O_{18}. The rare titanosilicate benitoite ($BaTiSi_3O_9$) is the only mineral that is built with the simple Si_3O_9 ring. Axinite [(Ca, Fe, Mn)$_3Al_2(BO_3)(Si_4O_{12})(OH)$] contains Si_4O_{12} rings, along with BO_3 triangles and OH groups. The two common and important cyclosilicates, beryl ($Be_3Al_2Si_6O_{18}$) and tourmaline (which has an extremely complex formula), are based on the Si_6O_{18} ring.

INOSILICATES

This class is characterized by its one-dimensional chains and bands created by the linkage of SiO_4 tetrahedrons. Single chains may be formed by the sharing of two oxygen atoms from each tetrahedron, resulting in a structure with an Si:O ratio of 1:3. Two such chains that are aligned side by side with alternate tetrahedrons sharing an additional oxygen atom form bands of double chains. These structures have an Si:O ratio of 4:11. There are a number of silicate minerals, pyroxenoids, which have a similar Si:O ratio as pyroxene, but with structures that are not identical as the chains of silicon tetrahedra do not infinitely repeat. Two significant rock-forming mineral families display these structure types: the single-chain pyroxenes and the double-chain amphiboles.

The amphiboles and pyroxenes share the same cations and have many similar crystallographic, chemical, and physical properties: the colour, lustre, and hardness of analogous species are alike. A distinguishing factor between the two groups, the presence of the hydroxyl radical in the amphiboles, generally gives the double-chain members lower specific gravities and refractive indices than their single-chain analogues. Their crystal habits also are different: amphiboles exhibit needlelike or fibrous crystals, while pyroxenes take the form of stubby prisms. In addition, the different chain structures of the two groups result in different cleavage angles.

Pyroxenes occur in high-temperature igneous and metamorphic rocks. They crystallize at higher temperatures than their amphibole counterparts. A pyroxene formed early in the cooling of an igneous melt or in a metamorphic fluid may later combine with water at a lower temperature to form amphibole.

PHYLLOSILICATES

These minerals display a two-dimensional framework of infinite sheets of SiO_4 tetrahedrons. An Si:O ratio of 2:5 results from the sharing of three oxygen atoms in each tetrahedron. Sixfold symmetry is exhibited in undistorted sheets. The silicate sheet framework is largely responsible for the following properties of the phyllosilicates: platy or flaky habit, single pronounced cleavage, low specific gravity, softness, and possible flexibility and elasticity of cleavage layers. Most minerals of this group contain hydroxyls positioned in the middle of the sixfold rings of tetrahedrons.

Many soil constituents, produced through rock weathering, possess a sheet structure. Phyllosilicate properties contribute greatly to the ability of soils to release and retain plant food, to reserve water from wet to dry seasons, and to accommodate organisms and atmospheric gases.

The phyllosilicate class includes several important mineral groups.

TECTOSILICATES

Almost 75 percent of the Earth's crust is composed of minerals with the three-dimensional framework of the tectosilicates. All oxygen atoms of the SiO_4 tetrahedrons of members of this class are shared with nearby tetrahedrons, creating a strongly bound structure with an Si:O ratio of 1:2. Other than the zeolite group, which can accommodate water owing to the open nature of its structure, all members listed in the table are anhydrous.

MINERAL ASSOCIATIONS AND PHASE EQUILIBRIUM

The preceding sections provided an overview of major mineral groups but did not treat minerals as part of assemblages in rock types nor discuss the experimental study of minerals and rock occurrences. Petrology, the scientific study of rocks, is concerned largely with identifying individual minerals in rocks, along with their abundance, grain size, and texture, because rocks typically consist of a variety of minerals. Such information is essential to an understanding of the history of any rock.

Petrological research requires a strong understanding of the principles of mineralogy and mineral identification and a thorough familiarity with the theoretical and experimental studies of rock origins. The present section focuses on phase equilibrium, upon which the link between the study of minerals and the study of rocks is largely based.

A phase is a homogeneous substance that has a fixed composition and uniform chemical and physical properties. Only a mineral that displays no solid solution may therefore be considered a phase. Quartz (SiO_2), for example, is a low-temperature phase in the $Si-O_2(SiO_2)$ system, and kyanite (Al_2SiO_5) is a high-pressure phase in the $Al_2O_3-SiO_2(Al_2SiO_5)$ system. The term *phase region* is used when a mineral exhibits compositional variation, as in the solid-solution series between forsterite and fayalite. A phase may exist as a solid, liquid, or gas: H_2O, for example, occurs in the form of ice (solid), water (liquid), and steam (gas).

Equilibrium refers to the stable coexistence of two or more phases and is established relative to time. If two phases in a mixture of water and ice coexist so that the amount of each is fixed indefinitely, they are said to be in equilibrium. The minerals of some rocks have existed together since their formation for periods of several million years, yet one cannot always ascertain if these rock constituents are in equilibrium or are still undergoing changes.

A determining factor of the equilibrium state of minerals is the presence (or absence) of a reaction rim, which is a region separating two or more minerals consisting of the products of a reaction between them. The absence of any observable reaction rims between minerals that physically touch each other suggests that they were in equilibrium at the time when the rock formed. Additional chemical data regarding elemental distribution between the minerals is necessary to verify this assumption. In contrast, the presence of megascopically or microscopically visible rims indicates that some minerals were not in equilibrium. Garnet, for example, may react with coexisting biotite to produce a chlorite rim between them, revealing that the two minerals were not always in equilibrium. An experimental petrologist must assign some period of time after which the absence of further changes between phases will indicate that equilibrium has been reached. The time period is variable, depending on the speed of the reactions involved and in part on the patience of the investigator; it may range from a few hours to several years.

Components are the minimum number of independent chemical species that are necessary to describe the compositions of all the phases present in a system. The compound H_2O is generally used as the sole component defining the H_2O system, although H_2 and O_2 define the chemical system as well. In examinations of the stability fields of $MgSiO_3$ (enstatite), $MgSiO_3$ is normally used as the component rather than the three elements, Mg, Si, and O, or the two oxides, MgO and SiO_2. The three components generally used in the pyroxene system CaO-MgO-FeO-SiO_2 are $CaSiO_3$-$MgSiO_3$-$FeSiO_3$.

ASSEMBLAGE AND THE PHASE RULE

In the early stages of the study of a rock, the constituent minerals of the rock must be identified. Orthoclase, albite, quartz, and biotite may be found in an igneous granite. By examining the granite's texture, one may conclude that the four minerals crystallized at approximately the same elevated temperature and that orthoclase-albite-quartz-biotite is its mineral assemblage. The term *assemblage* is frequently applied to all minerals included in a rock but more appropriately should be used for those minerals that are in equilibrium (and are known more specifically as the equilibrium assemblage). The granite discussed above may display surficial cavities that are lined by several clay minerals and limonite (a hydrous iron oxide). The original high-temperature granite was altered to form the low-temperature clay minerals and limonite; there are consequently two distinct assemblages present in the rock: the high-temperature orthoclase-albite-quartz-biotite assemblage and the low-temperature assemblage of clay minerals and limonite.

Metamorphic rocks also may contain separate assemblages. A shale that at low temperatures was composed of a sericite-kaolin-dolomite-quartz-feldspar assemblage can become metamorphosed at higher temperatures to produce a garnet-sillimanite-biotite-feldspar assemblage.

An assemblage thus consists of minerals that formed under the same or quite comparable conditions of pressure and temperature. In practice, minerals that physically touch one another with no reaction rims or alteration products are included in the assemblage. It is likely that the minerals satisfying these conditions are in equilibrium, but additional chemical tests are commonly necessary to define the equilibrium assemblage without ambiguity.

Phase systems are governed by a phase rule, which defines the number of minerals that may coexist in equilibrium: $F = C - P + 2$, where F is the variance, or number of degrees of freedom, C is the number of independent components, and P is the number of phases. Applying this rule to a three-phase, three-component system, F is 2. This indicates that two parameters—e.g., pressure and temperature—may be varied independently of one another without altering the number of phases.

Phase Diagrams

Phase (or stability) diagrams are used to illustrate the conditions under which certain minerals are stable. The following are examples of phase diagrams employed in the study of igneous, metamorphic, and sedimentary rocks.

Use in Igneous Petrology

In the field of igneous petrology, the researcher commonly employs a phase equilibrium approach to compare the mineral assemblages found in naturally occurring and synthetic rocks. Much can be learned from studying the melting of an igneous rock and the reverse process, the crystallization of minerals from a melt (liquid phase). Graphic representations of systems with a liquid phase are called liquidus diagrams. The dashed contours on such diagrams, which are called isotherms, represent temperatures at which a mineral melts. They define what is known as a liquidus surface. As temperatures decrease, the minerals will crystallize in the manner defined by the arrows on the boundaries separating the different mineral phases. A careful study of the crystalline products formed upon the cooling of melts of specific compositions allows the igneous petrologist to compare such results with minerals observed in natural igneous rocks.

Use in Metamorphic Petrology

Pressure-temperature (P-T) phase diagrams are applied in the study of the conditions under which metamorphic rocks originate. They illustrate the equilibrium relationships among various mineral phases in terms of pressure and temperature. The minerals that are separated by a reaction curve may exist in equilibrium at the conditions occurring along the line. The reaction curves for Al_2SiO_5 and for muscovite + quartz $\longleftrightarrow$ potassium-feldspar + sillimanite + H_2O are significant in metamorphic rocks that have a high aluminum oxide (Al_2O_3) content as compared to other components (e.g., calcium oxide [CaO], magnesium oxide [MgO], and ferrous oxide [FeO]). Shales enriched in clay minerals contain a rather large amount of aluminum oxide, and during metamorphism of the shale mineral reactions and recrystallization occur. In their metamorphic form, shales appear as pelitic schists, and these may include significant amounts of sillimanite, muscovite, and quartz.

Theoretical calculations are combined with experimental observations to arrive at phase diagrams. In laboratory experiments conducted on the three polymorphs of Al_2SiO_5, chemicals of high purity are most often used as the starting materials, but extremely pure minerals may be substituted. A specimen of gem-grade kyanite that does not contain any inclusions may be reacted at high temperatures to form sillimanite. The placement of the reaction curve between the kyanite and sillimanite fields is determined by the first instance of sillimanite formation from kyanite and also the initial stage of the reverse reaction. X-ray powder diffraction and optical microscopic techniques are employed to estimate the conditions under which these reactions commence, but the experimental methods are subject to some degree of uncertainty. Therefore, the reaction curves, although commonly drawn as narrow lines, may actually represent wider reaction zones. Also, the naturally occurring system is more complex than the simplified version devised in the laboratory, and so difficulty arises when attempting to relate the two. A P-T diagram serves mainly as a tool in evaluating the conditions of metamorphism, such as pressure and temperature.

EH–PH DIAGRAMS

Eh–pH diagrams illustrate the fields of stability of mineral or chemical species in terms of the activity of hydrogen ions (pH) and the activity of electrons (Eh). Consequently, the reactions illustrated on Eh–pH diagrams involve either proton transfer (e.g., hydrolysis) or electron transfer (oxidation or reduction) or both. In natural environments, pH values extend from 1 to 9.5, and Eh values from -500 to +800 millivolts. Rarely are temperatures and pressures other than those normally encountered on the Earth's surface considered.

The area on an Eh–pH diagram that represents the range of these variables within which a particular mineral is stable is called the stability field of that mineral. Such a representation enables a geochemist to determine whether a mineral is in equilibrium with its surroundings or subject to chemical transformation.

USE IN SEDIMENTARY PETROLOGY

Phase diagrams can also be helpful in the assessment of physical and chemical conditions that prevailed during the deposition of a chemical sedimentary sequence. Atmospheric conditions are characterized by low temperatures and pressures, and under such conditions stability fields of minerals can often conveniently be expressed in terms of Eh (oxidation potential) and pH (the negative logarithm of the hydrogen ion concentration $[H^+]$; a pH of 0–7 indicates acidity, a pH of 7–14 indicates basicity, and neutral solutions have a pH of 7).

A high Eh value corresponds to a compound stable under oxidizing conditions, while a low Eh value indicates a mineral that occurs in reducing environments. For example, pyrite and pyrrhotite, two sulfide minerals, occur at low Eh values and at pH values of 4–9. Lines separating the fields of an Eh-pH diagram represent conditions under which the two minerals may exist in equilibrium. Hematite and magnetite, for example, are often found together in iron-bearing sediments. Eh-pH diagrams are valuable in providing information regarding the chemical and physical environments that existed during atmospheric weathering and during chemical sedimentation and diagenesis of sediments deposited by water at temperatures of 25 to about 100 °C (77 to 212 °F) and approximately one atmosphere pressure. The coexistence of hematite and magnetite common in Precambrian iron-bearing rocks (those formed from 4.6 billion to 542 million years ago) may enable investigators to estimate variables such as Eh and pH that prevailed in the original ancient sedimentary basin.

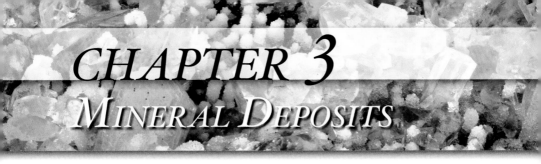

A mineral deposit is the name for an aggregate of a mineral in an unusually high concentration. About half of the known chemical elements possess some metallic properties. The term *metal*, however, is reserved for those chemical elements that possess two or more of the characteristic physical properties of metals (opacity, ductility, malleability, fusibility) and are also good conductors of heat and electricity. Approximately 40 metals are made available through the mining and smelting of the minerals in which they occur.

Certain kinds of mineral can be smelted more readily than others; these are commonly referred to as ore minerals. Ore minerals tend to be concentrated in small, localized rock masses that form as a result of special geologic processes, and such local concentrations are called mineral deposits. Mineral deposits are what prospectors seek. The terms *ore mineral* and *mineral deposit* were originally applied only to minerals and deposits from which metals are recovered, but present usage includes a few nonmetallic minerals, such as barite and fluorite, that are found in the same kinds of deposit as metallic minerals.

No deposit consists entirely of a single ore mineral. There are always admixtures of valueless minerals, collectively called gangue. The more concentrated an ore mineral, the more valuable the mineral deposit. For every mineral deposit there is a set of conditions, such as the level of concentration and the size of the deposit, that must be reached if the deposit is to be worked at a profit. A mineral deposit that is sufficiently rich to be worked at a profit is called an ore deposit, and in an ore deposit the assemblage of ore minerals plus gangue is called the ore.

All ore deposits are mineral deposits, but the reverse is not true. *Ore deposit* is an economic term, while *mineral deposit* is a geologic term. Whether a given mineral deposit is also an ore deposit depends on many factors other than the level of concentration and the size of the deposit; all factors that affect the mining, processing, and transporting of the ore must be considered as well. Among such factors are the shape of a deposit, its depth below the surface, its geographic remoteness, access to transportation, the political stability of the region, and market factors such as the price of the metal in world trade and the costs of borrowing the money needed to develop a mine. Because market factors change continually, a given mineral deposit may sometimes be an ore deposit, but at other times it may be uneconomic and hence not an ore deposit.

Mineral deposits have been found both in rocks that lie beneath the oceans and in rocks that form the continents, although the only deposits that actually have been mined are in the continental rocks. (The mining of ocean deposits lies in the future.) The continental crust averages 35–40 km (20–25 miles) in thickness, and below the crust lies the mantle. Mineral deposits may occur in the mantle, but with present technology it is not possible to discover them.

GEOCHEMICALLY ABUNDANT AND SCARCE METALS

Metals used in industrial and technological applications can be divided into two classes on the basis of their abundance in the Earth's crust. The geochemically abundant metals, of which there are five (aluminum, iron, magnesium, manganese, and titanium), constitute more than

0.1 percent by weight of the Earth's crust, while the geo-chemically scarce metals, which embrace all other metals (including such familiar ones as copper, lead, zinc, gold, and silver), constitute less than 0.1 percent. In almost every rock, at least tiny amounts of all metals can be detected by sensitive chemical analysis. However, there are important differences in the way the abundant and scarce metals occur in common rocks. Geochemically abundant metals tend to be present as essential con-stituents in minerals. For example, basalt, a common igneous rock, consists largely of the minerals olivine and pyroxene (both magnesium-iron silicates), feldspar (sodium-calcium-aluminum silicate), and ilmenite (iron-titanium oxide). Careful chemical analysis of a basalt will reveal the presence of most of the geochemically scarce metals too, but no amount of searching will reveal min-erals in which one or more of the scarce metals is an essential constituent.

Geochemically scarce metals rarely form minerals in common rocks. Instead, they are carried in the structures of common rock-forming minerals (most of them silicates) through the process of atomic substitution. This process involves the random replacement of an atom in a min-eral by a foreign atom of similar ionic radius and valence, without changing the atomic packing of the host min-eral. Atoms of copper, zinc, and nickel, for example, can substitute for iron and magnesium atoms in olivine and pyroxene. However, since substitution of foreign atoms produces strains in an atomic packing, there are limits to this process, as determined by temperature, pressure, and various chemical parameters. Indeed, the substitution limits for most scarce metals in common silicate minerals are low—in many cases only a few hundred substituting atoms for every million host atoms—but even these limits are rarely exceeded in common rocks.

One important consequence that derives from the way abundant and scarce metals occur in common rocks is that ore minerals of abundant metals can be found in many common rocks, while ore minerals of scarce metals can be found only where some special, restricted geologic process has formed localized enrichments that exceed the limits of atomic substitution.

ORE MINERALS

Two factors determine whether a given mineral is suitable to be an ore mineral. The first is the ease with which a mineral can be separated from the gangue and concentrated for smelting. Concentrating processes, which are based on the physical properties of the mineral, include magnetic separation, gravity separation, and flotation. The second factor is smelting—that is, releasing the metal from the other elements to which it is chemically bonded in the mineral. Smelting processes are discussed below, but of primary importance in this consideration of the suitability of an ore mineral is the amount of energy needed to break the chemical bonds and release the metal. In general, less energy is needed to smelt sulfide, oxide, or hydroxide minerals than is required to smelt a silicate mineral. For this reason, few silicate minerals are ore minerals. Because the great bulk of the Earth's crust (about 95 percent) is composed of silicate minerals, sulfide, oxide, and hydroxide ore minerals are at best only minor constituents of the Earth's crust—and in many cases they are very rare constituents. The preferred ore minerals of both geochemically abundant and geochemically scarce metals are native metals, sulfides, oxides, hydroxides, or carbonates. In a few cases, silicate minerals have to be used as ore minerals because the metals either do not form more desirable minerals or form desirable minerals that rarely occur in large deposits.

NATIVE METALS

Only two metals, gold and platinum, are found principally in their native state, and in both cases the native metals are the primary ore minerals. Silver, copper, iron, osmium, and several other metals also occur in the native state, and a few occurrences are large enough—and sufficiently rich—to be ore deposits. One example is the rich deposits of native copper in the Lake Superior area of Michigan in the United States. Here the copper occurs in interbedded conglomerates (a sedimentary rock consisting of pebbles and boulders) and basaltic lava flows, most of which are vesicular and have fragmental layers of basaltic rubble on top of each flow. In the basalt, the native copper and associated gangue minerals fill the vesicles and cavities in the rubble; in the conglomerate, the copper fills spaces between the pebbles and in part replaces some of the smaller rock fragments. Originally discovered and worked by native Americans who manufactured and traded ornaments of malleable copper, the great Michigan copper deposits were first mined in 1845 and continued in production for more than a century.

SULFIDES

The largest group of ore minerals consists of sulfides. Because the physical and chemical properties of telluride, selenide, and arsenide minerals are very similar to those of sulfide minerals, and because these minerals tend to occur together, it is convenient to use the term *sulfide* to embrace these similar minerals. Copper, lead, zinc, nickel, molybdenum, silver, arsenic, antimony, bismuth, cobalt, and mercury all form sulfide ore minerals. Gold and silver form tellurides under certain circumstances, and platinum forms an important arsenide ore mineral.

The principle of atomic substitution operates in all classes of minerals, and some of the rarest metals occur by atomic substitution in sulfide ore minerals of other scarce metals. For example, cadmium and indium are generally present in small amounts in the zinc sulfide sphalerite, the major ore mineral of zinc. In fact, most of the world's cadmium and indium is recovered as a by-product of the smelting of sphalerite concentrates to produce zinc.

OXIDES AND HYDROXIDES

Oxides and hydroxides are a large and diverse group of ore minerals. The major ore minerals of the geochemically abundant metals aluminum, iron, manganese, and titanium are either oxides or hydroxides, while the oxide-forming scarce metals are chromium, tin, tungsten, tantalum, niobium, and uranium. Vanadium is found mainly by atomic substitution in magnetite, a major oxide ore mineral of iron.

CARBONATES AND SILICATES

Carbonate minerals are widespread in the Earth's crust, but only a few are ore minerals. These are the carbonates of iron, manganese, magnesium, and the rare earths. The number of metals won from silicate ore minerals is small. Most important are beryllium, zirconium, and lithium, plus a certain amount of nickel recovered from the nickel silicate garnierite.

FORMATION OF MINERAL DEPOSITS

Mineral deposits form because some medium serves as a concentrating and transporting agent for the ore minerals, and some process subsequently causes the transporting agent to precipitate, or deposit, the minerals. Examples of concentrating and transporting agents are groundwater, seawater, and magma; examples of precipitating processes are boiling (as in a hot spring), the cooling of a hot solution, the crystallization of a magma, and a chemical reaction between a solution and the rocks through which it flows. The same kinds of concentrating and transporting agent and the same kinds of precipitating process are involved in the formation of deposits of both geochemically abundant and geochemically scarce metals.

There are six principal concentrating and transporting agents, together with the classes of deposit that they form.

MAGMATIC CONCENTRATION

Magma is molten rock, together with any suspended mineral grains and dissolved gases, that forms when temperatures rise and melting occurs in the mantle or crust. When magma rises to the Earth's surface through fissures and volcanic vents, it is called lava. Lava cools and crystallizes quickly, so that igneous rocks formed from lava tend to consist of tiny mineral grains. (Sometimes cooling can be so rapid that mineral grains cannot form and a glass results.) Underground magma, on the other hand, cools and crystallizes slowly, and the resulting igneous rocks tend to contain mineral grains at least 0.5 cm (about 0.2 inch) in diameter.

PEGMATITE DEPOSITS

The crystallization of magma is a complex process because magma is a complex substance. Certain magmas, such as those which form granites, contain several percent water dissolved in them. When a granitic magma cools, the first minerals to crystallize tend to be anhydrous (e.g., feldspar), so an increasingly water-rich residue remains. Certain rare chemical elements, such as lithium, beryllium, and niobium, that do not readily enter into atomic substitution in the main granite minerals (feldspar, quartz, and mica) become concentrated in the water-rich residual magma. If the crystallization process occurs at a depth of about 5 km (about 3 miles) or greater, the water-rich residual magma may migrate and form small bodies of igneous rock, satellitic to the main granitic mass, that are enriched in rare elements. Such small igneous bodies, called rare-metal pegmatites, are sometimes exceedingly coarse-grained, with individual grains of mica, feldspar, and beryl up to 1 metre (about 3 feet) across. Pegmatites have been discovered on all continents, providing an important fraction of the world's lithium, beryllium, cesium, niobium, and tantalum. Pegmatites also are the major source of sheet mica and important sources of gemstones, particularly tourmalines and the gem forms of beryl (aquamarine and emerald).

CARBONATITE DEPOSITS

Carbonatites are igneous rocks that consist largely of the carbonate minerals calcite and dolomite; they sometimes also contain the rare-earth ore minerals bastnaesite, parisite, and monazite, the niobium ore mineral pyrochlore, and (in the case of the carbonatite deposit at Palabora in South Africa) copper sulfide ore minerals. The origin of carbonatite magma is obscure. Most carbonatites occur close to intrusions of alkaline igneous rocks (those rich in potassium or sodium relative to their silica contents) or to the ultramafic igneous rocks (rocks with silica contents below approximately 50 percent by weight) known as kimberlites and lamproites. These associations suggest a common derivation, but details of the way that carbonatite magmas might concentrate geochemically scarce metals remain conjectural.

Carbonatites have been found on all continents; they also range widely in age, from deposits in the East African Rift Valley that were formed during the present geologic age to South African deposits dating from the early Proterozoic Eon (2.5 billion to 543 million years ago). Many carbonatites are mined or contain such large reserves that they will be mined someday. Among the most important are Mountain Pass, Calif., U.S., a major source of rare earths; the Loolekop Complex, Palabora, S.Af., mined for copper and apatite (calcium phosphate, used as a fertilizer), plus by-products of gold, silver, and other metals; Jacupiranga, Brazil, a major resource of rare earths; Oka, Que., Can., a niobium-rich body; and the Kola Peninsula of Russia, mined for apatite, magnetite, and rare earths.

MAGMATIC CUMULATES

Magmatic segregation is a general term referring to any process by which one or more minerals become locally concentrated (segregated) during the cooling and crystallization of a magma. Rocks formed as a result of magmatic segregation are called magmatic cumulates. While a magma may start as a homogeneous liquid, magmatic segregation during crystallization can produce an assemblage of cumulates with widely differing compositions. Extreme segregation can sometimes produce monomineralic cumulates; a dramatic example occurs in the Bushveld Igneous Complex of South Africa, where cumulus layers of chromite (iron-magnesium-chromium oxide, the only chromium ore mineral) are encased in cumulus layers of anorthite (calcium-rich feldspar).

Mineral deposits that are magmatic cumulates are only found in mafic and ultramafic igneous rocks (i.e., rocks that are low in silica). This is due to the control exerted by silica on the viscosity of a magma: the higher the silica content, the more viscous a magma and the more slowly segregation can proceed. Highly viscous magmas, such as those of granitic composition, tend to cool and crystallize faster than segregation can proceed. In low-silica (and, hence, low-viscosity) magmas such as gabbro, basalt, and komatiite, mineral grains can float, sink, or be moved so rapidly by flowing magma that segregation can occur before crystallization is complete.

As with most geologic processes that cannot be directly observed, a certain amount of uncertainty exists about how cumulates form. A mineral such as chromite, with a density considerably greater than the magma from which it crystallizes, will tend to sink as soon as it forms. As a result, geologists long held the opinion that cumulates of chromite and other dense minerals formed only by sinking. This simple picture was challenged in 1961 by E. Dale Jackson, a geologist employed by the U.S. Geological Survey, who studied chromite cumulates of the Stillwater Complex in Montana. The findings of Jackson and later workers suggested that cumulates can also be produced by such phenomena as in-place crystallization of monomineralic layers on the floor of a magma chamber or density currents carrying mineral grains from the walls and roof of a magma chamber to the floor. Opinion still remains open, but most geologists now agree that in-place crystallization and density currents are more important in the formation of magmatic cumulates than density sinking.

Three oxide ore minerals form magmatic cumulates: chromite, magnetite, and ilmenite. The world's largest chromite deposits are all magmatic cumulates; the largest and richest of these is in the Bushveld Complex of South Africa. Cumulus deposits of magnetite make poor iron ores, because cumulus magnetites invariably contain elements such as titanium, manganese, and vanadium by atomic substitution—although vanadiferous magnetites are important as a source of vanadium. In fact, much of the world's production of this metal comes from cumulus magnetites in the Bushveld Complex.

IMMISCIBLE MELTS

A different kind of magmatic segregation involves liquid immiscibility. A cooling magma will sometimes precipitate droplets of a second magma that has an entirely different composition. Like oil and water, the two magmas will not mix (i.e., they are immiscible). The chemical principle governing precipitation of an immiscible liquid is the same as that governing crystallization of a mineral from a magma: when the concentration of a particular mineral within a parent magma reaches saturation, precipitation occurs. If saturation is reached at a temperature above the melting point of the mineral, a drop of liquid precipitates instead of a mineral grain. The composition of this immiscible drop is not exactly that of the pure mineral, because the liquid tends to scavenge and concentrate many elements from the parent magma, and this process can lead to rich ore deposits.

Iron sulfide is the principal constituent of most immiscible magmas, and the metals scavenged by iron sulfide liquid are copper, nickel, and the platinum group. Immiscible sulfide drops can become segregated and form immiscible magma layers in a magma chamber in the same way that cumulus layers form; then, when layers of sulfide magma cool and crystallize, the result is a deposit of ore minerals of copper, nickel, and platinum-group metals in a gangue of an iron sulfide mineral. Among the ore deposits of the world formed in this way are the Merensky Reef of the Bushveld Complex, producer of a major fraction of the world's platinum-group metals; the Stillwater Complex, Montana, host to platinum-group deposits similar to the Merensky Reef; and the Norilsk deposits of Russia, containing large reserves of platinum-group metals.

Under suitable conditions, immiscible sulfide liquids can also become segregated from flowing lavas. An example is offered by the Kambalda nickel deposit in Western Australia. At Kambalda a nickel ore mineral, pentlandite, together with valuable by-product minerals of copper and platinum-group metals, crystallized in an iron-sulfide-rich gangue from a sulfide liquid that had become segregated from a magnesium-rich lava called a komatiite (named for the Komati River in South Africa).

A group of unique deposits formed by immiscible sulfide liquids is the Sudbury Igneous Complex in Ontario, Can., which formed about 1.85 billion years ago. Elliptical in outline (approximately 60 km [37 miles] long by 28 km [17 miles] wide), the complex has the shape of a funnel pointing down into the Earth. A continuous lower zone of a mafic rock called norite lies above a discontinuous zone of gabbro, some of which contains numerous broken fragments of the underlying basement rocks and some of which is rich in sulfide ore minerals of nickel, copper, and platinum-group metals. Many hypotheses have been suggested for the origin of the Sudbury Complex. Some consider it to be an intrusive igneous complex, and some consider it a combination of intrusive and extrusive igneous rocks, but the most widely held opinion derives from the work of the American scientist Robert S. Dietz, who in 1964 suggested that the Sudbury structure is an astrobleme, the site of a large meteorite impact. The complex's sulfide ore bodies are thought to be derived from immiscible magmas formed in the Earth's mantle as a result of the impact (and possibly mixed with meteorite material), while the uppermost layers are thought to be rock debris remaining from the impact.

A final and highly controversial group of deposits deserves mention because some geologists believe them to have formed from immiscible melts. These are magnetite deposits associated with volcanic rocks of dioritic affinity (i.e., igneous rocks intermediate in composition between granites and gabbros). There is no doubt that lava flows account for the presence of magnetite deposits in northern Chile, but there is great conjecture over whether magnetite bodies associated with these lavas formed as a result of a dioritic magma precipitating an immiscible oxide magma, as a magnetite lava formed through the melting of a previously formed sedimentary iron deposit, or as the source of a hydrothermal solution that deposited the magnetite. Many experts draw the latter conclusion. Considerable controversy also surrounds the origin of the famous Swedish iron ores at Kiruna and Gällivare. These magnetite-apatite bodies encased in volcanic rocks have been variously interpreted as having formed as immiscible oxide magmas, as iron-rich sediments that were subsequently metamorphosed, and as deposits arising from volcanic exhalations.

HYDROTHERMAL SOLUTION

Hydrothermal mineral deposits are those in which hot water serves as a concentrating, transporting, and depositing agent. They are the most numerous of all classes of deposit.

Hydrothermal deposits are never formed from pure water, because pure water is a poor solvent of most ore minerals. Rather, they are formed by hot brines, making it more appropriate to refer to them as products of hydrothermal solutions. Brines, and especially sodium-calcium chloride brines, are effective solvents of many sulfide and oxide ore minerals, and they are even capable of dissolving and transporting native metals such as gold and silver.

The water in a hydrothermal solution can come from any of several sources. It may be released by a crystallizing magma; it can be expelled from a mass of rock undergoing metamorphism; or it may originate at the Earth's surface as rainwater or seawater and then trickle down to great depths through fractures and porous rocks, where it will be heated, react with adjacent rocks, and become a hydrothermal solution. Regardless of the origin and initial composition of the water, the final compositions of all hydrothermal solutions tend to converge, owing to reactions between solutions and the rocks they encounter.

Hydrothermal solutions are sodium-calcium chloride brines with additions of magnesium and potassium salts, plus small amounts of many other chemical elements. The solutions range in concentration from a few percent to as much as 50 percent dissolved solids by weight. Existing hydrothermal solutions can be studied at hot springs, in subsurface brine reservoirs such as those in the Imperial Valley of California, the Cheleken Peninsula on the eastern edge of the Caspian Sea in Turkmenistan, in oil-field brines, and in submarine springs along the mid-ocean ridge. Fossil hydrothermal solutions can be studied in fluid inclusions, which are tiny samples of solution trapped in crystal imperfections by a growing mineral.

Because hydrothermal solutions form as a result of many processes, they are quite common within the Earth's crust. Hydrothermal mineral deposits, on the other hand, are neither common nor very large compared to other geologic features. It is apparent from this that most solutions eventually mix in with the rest of the hydrosphere and leave few obvious traces of their former presence. Those solutions that do form mineral deposits (and thereby leave obvious evidence of their former presence) do so because some process causes them to deposit their dissolved loads in a restricted space or small volume of porous rock. It is most convenient, therefore, to discuss hydrothermal mineral deposits in the context of their settings.

VEINS

The simplest hydrothermal deposit to visualize is a vein, which forms when a hydrothermal solution flows through an open fissure and deposits its dissolved load. A great many veins occur close to bodies of intrusive igneous rocks because the igneous rocks serve as heat sources that create convectively driven flows in hydrothermal solutions. Precipitation of the minerals is usually caused by cooling of the hydrothermal solution, by boiling, or by chemical reactions between the solution and rocks lining the fissure. Some famous deposits are the tin-copper-lead-zinc veins of Cornwall, Eng.; the gold-quartz veins of Kalgoorlie, W. Aus., Australia, and Kirkland Lake, Ont., Can.; the tin-silver veins of Llallagua and Potosí, Bol.; and the silver-nickel-uranium veins of the Erzgebirge, Ger., which were first described by Georgius Agricola in his book *De re metallica* (1556).

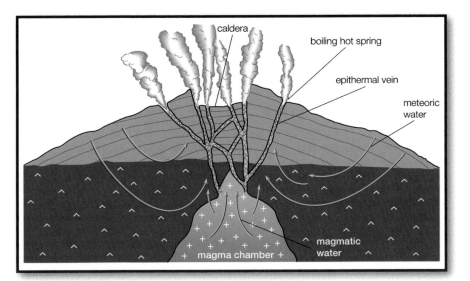

The relationship between hot springs and epithermal veins. Encyclopædia Britannica, Inc.

Hydrothermal deposits formed at shallow depths below a boiling hot spring system are commonly referred to as epithermal, a term retained from an old system of classifying hydrothermal deposits based on the presumed temperature and depth of deposition. Epithermal veins tend not to have great vertical continuity, but many are exceedingly rich and deserving of the term *bonanza*. Many of the famous silver and gold deposits of the western United States, such as Comstock in Nevada and Cripple Creek in Colorado, are epithermal bonanzas.

PORPHYRY DEPOSITS

Among the most distinctive hydrothermal deposits is a class known as porphyry copper deposits, so called because they are invariably associated with igneous intrusives that are porphyritic (meaning the rock is a mixture of coarse and fine mineral grains). Porphyry copper deposits (and their close relatives, porphyry molybdenum deposits) contain disseminated mineralization, meaning that a large volume of shattered rock contains a ramifying network of tiny quartz veins, spaced only a few centimetres apart, in which grains of the copper ore minerals chalcopyrite and bornite (or the molybdenum ore mineral molybdenite) occur with pyrite. The shattered rock serves as a permeable medium for the circulation of a hydrothermal solution, and the volume of rock that is altered and mineralized by the solution can be huge: porphyry coppers are among the largest of all hydrothermal deposits, with some giant deposits containing many billions of tons of ore. Although in most deposits the ore averages only between 0.5 and 1.5 percent copper by weight, the tonnages of ore mined are so large that more than 50 percent of all copper produced comes from porphyry coppers.

Porphyry coppers are often associated with stratovolcanoes. As a result of the volcanism that rings the Pacific

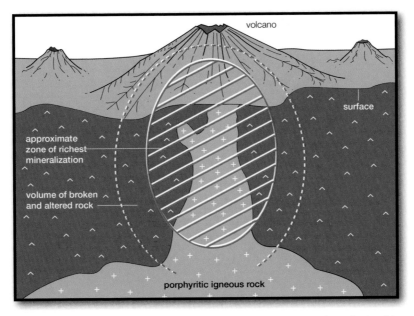

Idealized drawing of a porphyry copper deposit, showing the relationship between the porphyry body, the altered and mineralized rock, and the overlying volcano. Encyclopædia Britannica, Inc.

Ocean basin, porphyry coppers are conspicuous features of mineralization along the western borders of North and South America and in the Philippines. Among the major deposits are El Teniente, El Salvador, and Chuquicamata in Chile, Cananea in Mexico, and, in the United States, Bingham Canyon in Utah, Ely and Yerington in Nevada, and San Manuel in Arizona.

SKARNS

When a limestone or marble is invaded by a high-temperature hydrothermal solution, the carbonate minerals calcite and dolomite react strongly with the slightly acid solution to form a class of mineral deposit called a skarn. Because solutions tend to have high temperatures close to a magma chamber, most skarns are found immediately adjacent to intrusive igneous rocks. The solutions introduce silica and iron, which combine with the calcium and magnesium in the parent rock to form silicate minerals such as diopside, tremolite, and andradite. The hydrothermal solutions may also deposit ore minerals of iron, copper, zinc, tungsten, or molybdenum.

The mining of magnetite from a skarn deposit at Cornwall, Penn., U.S., commenced in 1737 and continued for two and a half centuries. Copper skarns are found at many places, including Copper Canyon in Nevada and Mines Gaspé in Quebec, Can. Tungsten skarns supply much of the world's tungsten from deposits such as those at Sangdong, Korea; King Island, Tas., Australia; and Pine Creek, Calif., U.S.

Volcanogenic Massive Sulfides

Wherever volcanism occurs beneath the sea, the potential exists for seawater to penetrate the volcanic rocks, become heated by a magma chamber, and react with the enclosing rocks—in the process concentrating geochemically scarce metals and so forming a hydrothermal solution. When such a solution forms a hot spring on the seafloor, it can suddenly cool and rapidly deposit its dissolved load. Mineral deposits formed by this process, which are called volcanogenic massive sulfide (VMS) deposits, are known in ancient seafloor rocks of all geologic ages. In addition, deposits forming today as a result of submarine hot-spring activity have been discovered at a number of places along the oceanic ridge (the most volcanically active zone on Earth), and in back-arc basins associated with subduction zones.

VMS deposits constitute some of the richest deposits of copper, lead, and zinc known. Some of the most famous, found in Japan and called *kuroko* deposits, yield ores that contain as much as 20 percent combined copper, lead, and zinc by weight, plus important amounts of gold and silver. Other famous VMS deposits are the historic copper deposits of Cyprus and, in Canada, the Kidd Creek deposit in Ontario and the Noranda deposits of Quebec.

MISSISSIPPI VALLEY TYPE

The central plains of North America, running from the Appalachian Mountains on the east to the Rocky Mountains on the west, are underlain by nearly flat sedimentary rocks that were laid down on a now-covered basement of igneous and metamorphic rocks. The cover of sedimentary rocks, which have been little changed since they were deposited, contains numerous strata of limestone, and within the limestones near the bottom of the pile is found a distinctive class of mineral deposit. Because the central plains coincide closely with the drainage basin of the Mississippi River, this class of deposit has come to be called the Mississippi Valley type (MVT).

MVT deposits are always in limestones and are generally located near the edges of sedimentary basins or around the edges of what were islands or high points in the seafloor when the limestone was deposited. The

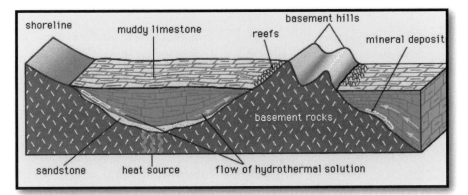

The relationship between Mississippi Valley-type deposits, the edges of sedimentary basins, and the flow of hydrothermal solutions. Copyright Encyclopædia Britannica, Inc.; rendering for this edition by Rosen Educational Services

hydrothermal solutions that introduced the ore minerals (principally the lead mineral galena and the zinc mineral sphalerite) apparently flowed through the sandstones and conglomerates that commonly underlie the limestones. Where they met a barrier to flow, such as a basement high or a basin edge, the solutions moved and reacted with the limestone, depositing ore minerals.

Among the many famous MVT deposits are the great zinc deposits of Pine Point in Canada's Northwest Territories; the Tri-State zinc district centred on Joplin, Mo., U.S.; the Viburnum Trend of southeast Missouri; deposits in Cumberland, Eng., and in Trepča, Serbia; and the lead-zinc deposits of the central Irish plains.

STRATIFORM DEPOSITS

A final class of hydrothermal deposit is called stratiform because the ore minerals are always confined within specific strata and are distributed in a manner that resembles particles in a sedimentary rock. Because stratiform deposits so closely resemble sedimentary rocks, controversy surrounds their origin. In certain cases, such as the White Pine copper deposits of Michigan, the historic Kupferschiefer deposits of Germany and Poland, and the important copper deposits of Zambia, research has demonstrated that the origin is similar to that of MVT deposits—that is, a hydrothermal solution moves through a porous aquifer at the base of a pile of sedimentary strata and, at certain places, deposits ore minerals in the overlying shales. The major difference between stratiform deposits and MVT deposits is that, in the case of stratiform deposits, the host rocks are generally shales (fine-grained, clastic sedimentary rocks) containing significant amounts of organic matter and fine-grained pyrite.

Several of the world's largest and most famous lead-zinc deposits are stratiform; they also are among the most

METASOMATIC REPLACEMENT

Metasomatic replacement is the process of simultaneous solution and deposition whereby one mineral replaces another. It is an important process in the formation of epigenetic mineral deposits (those formed after the formation of the host rock), in the formation of high- and intermediate-temperature hydrothermal ore deposits, and in supergene sulfide enrichment (enriched by generally downward movement). Metasomatic replacement is the method whereby wood petrifies (silica replaces the wood fibres), one mineral forms a pseudomorph of another, or an ore body takes the place of an equal volume of rock.

Replacement occurs when a mineralizing solution encounters minerals unstable in its presence. The original mineral is dissolved and almost simultaneously exchanged for another. The exchange does not occur molecule for molecule, but volume for volume; hence, fewer molecules of a less dense mineral will replace those of a more dense mineral. Replacement takes place first along major channels in a host rock through which the hydrothermal solutions flow. Smaller openings, even those of capillary size, eventually are altered, the smallest by diffusion at the very front of the exchange where solutions cannot flow.

Early-formed replacement minerals are themselves replaced, and definite mineral successions have been established. The usual sequence among the commoner hypogene (deposited by generally ascending solutions) metallic sulfide minerals is pyrite, enargite, tetrahedrite, sphalerite, chalcopyrite, bornite, galena, and pyrargyrite.

Although replacement can occur at any temperature or pressure, it is most effective at elevated temperatures, at which chemical activity is enhanced. Replacement by cold circulating waters mostly is confined to soluble rocks, such as limestone. These may be replaced by iron oxides, manganese oxides, or calcium phosphates; vast surface deposits of copper and zinc carbonates have also formed where limestones were replaced, and valuable deposits have occurred where supergene sulfide enrichment occurs. With higher temperatures, replacement increases until, at high temperatures, hardly any rock may resist. Solutions at intermediate temperatures form simple sulfides and sulfosalts for the most part, and those at higher temperatures form sulfides and oxides. Replacement deposits are the largest and most valuable of all metallic ore deposits except those of iron.

controversial in origin because there are no obvious aquifers underlying the mineralized strata. Three examples are in Australia: Broken Hill in New South Wales, Mount Isa in Queensland, and McArthur River in the Northern Territory. Another example is the famous Canadian lead-zinc deposit at Sullivan, B.C. At Broken Hill, metamorphism has almost completely obscured the original geologic environment, but in the other three cases evidence suggests that hydrothermal fluids moved upward along a fault from deeper within a sedimentary basin, then reacted with a shale while it was still a mud on the seafloor. Details of the actual processes involved remain controversial.

GROUNDWATER

Groundwater is that part of subsurface water that is below the water table—that is, water in the zone of saturation. For the purpose of the present discussion, the difference between groundwater and hydrothermal solutions is that groundwater retains many of its original chemical characteristics and remains within 1 km (0.6 mile) or less of the surface. Such waters form two important classes of deposit.

ROLL-FRONT DEPOSITS

Uranium occurs in two valence states, U^{4+} and U^{6+}. Weathering of rocks converts uranium into the +6 state, in which state it forms the uranyl ion $(UO_2)^{2+}$. Uranyl compounds tend to be soluble in groundwater, whereas U^{4+} compounds are not. So long as the groundwater remains oxidizing, uranyl ions are stable and uranium can be transported by groundwater; however, when uranyl ions encounter a reducing agent such as organic matter, U^{4+} uranium is precipitated as uraninite and coffinite.

Because groundwater flowing through an aquifer and meeting a reducing zone will deposit a zone, or front, of uraninite, and because the front tends to move slowly forward through the aquifer, dissolving as the oxidizing groundwater moves in and precipitating at the front of the zone, deposits formed in this fashion are known as roll-front uranium deposits. Such deposits have been extensively mined in the western United States, notably in Colorado, Wyoming, Utah, and Texas.

CALICHE DEPOSITS

A second class of uranium-bearing groundwater deposits forms in dry land areas where evaporation of groundwater during summer months is an important process. Evaporation causes precipitation of dissolved solids, and the most abundant dissolved solid in dry land groundwater is calcium carbonate. When deposited, this mineral forms a hard, calcareous cement known as caliche. If uranium is present in the groundwater, uranium minerals such as carnotite will also be precipitated and thus form a uraniferous caliche deposit. Extensive deposits of this kind have been identified in the Namib Desert in southwestern Africa and in desert areas of Western Australia.

SEAWATER OR LAKE WATER

When either sea or lake waters evaporate, salts are precipitated. These salts include sodium chloride, potassium and magnesium chlorides, borax, and sodium carbonate. Such salts are important economically, but they are not used for the recovery of metals and thus do not warrant discussion here. One very important class of metallic mineral deposit, though, is also formed by precipitation from lake or seawater. This class of deposit comprises compounds of iron or manganese and is known as a chemical sediment, because the mineral constituents are transported in solution and then precipitated to form a sediment as a result of chemical reaction.

IRON DEPOSITS

By far the most important metal from an economic and technical point of view is iron. Sedimentary iron deposits, from which almost all iron is obtained, can therefore be viewed as one of the world's great mineral treasures. There are two major types of deposit. The first, and by far the most important, is banded iron formations (BIFs), so called because they are finely layered alternations of cherty silica and an iron mineral, generally hematite, magnetite, or siderite.

BIFs can be divided into two kinds. The first, and quantitatively most important, is found in sequences of sedimentary rocks deposited in the shallow waters of continental shelves or in ancient sedimentary basins. These deposits are typified by the vast BIFs around Lake Superior and are called Lake Superior-type deposits. Their individual sediment layers can be as thin as 0.5 mm (0.02 inch) or as thick as 2.5 cm (1 inch), but the alternation of a siliceous band and an iron mineral band is invariable. Several points about Lake Superior-type deposits are remarkable. First, individual thin bands have enormous continuity. During the 1980s, A.F. Trendall, working for the Geological Survey of Western Australia, studied deposits in the Hamersley Basin and found that individual thin layers could be traced for more than 100 km (about 60 miles). Such continuity suggests that evaporation played a major role in precipitating both the iron minerals and the silica. A second remarkable feature of Lake Superior-type deposits is that they only formed between 2.7 and 1.8 billion years ago. Such a narrow time frame suggests that the chemistry of the oceans and atmosphere at the time of formation differed greatly from that of the present (in today's ocean, iron is virtually insoluble because the oxidizing atmosphere causes the precipitation of insoluble ferric iron compounds).

Lake Superior-type BIFs are known and mined on all continents. Among the most famous are the Lake Superior deposits of Michigan and Minnesota, the Labrador Trough deposits of Canada, Serra dos Carajas in Brazil, the Transvaal Basin deposits of South Africa, and the Hamersley Basin of Australia.

A second kind of BIF, known as an Algoma type, formed over a much wider time range than the Lake Superior type (from 3.8 billion to a few hundred million years ago). Algoma-type BIFs are also finely layered intercalations of silica and an iron mineral, generally hematite or magnetite, but the individual layers lack the lateral continuity of Lake Superior-type BIFs. Algoma-type BIFs are found within rock sequences containing a significant proportion of submarine volcanic rocks, and for this reason it is generally accepted that such deposits formed as a result of submarine volcanism. Such a conclusion is supported by two simple observations: first, that many volcanogenic massive sulfide deposits, such as those in New Brunswick, Can., are found in the same stratigraphic horizons as Algoma-type iron deposits and, second, that in the modern ocean iron-rich, chemically precipitated siliceous layers can sometimes be observed surrounding seafloor hot springs. Important iron deposits of the Algoma type are also exploited in Western Australia and Liberia.

Historically, a great deal of iron was mined from a second major type of chemically precipitated marine iron deposit. Containing pinhead-sized ooliths (small, rounded, accretionary masses formed by repeated deposition of thin layers of an iron mineral), these oolitic iron deposits have been largely supplanted in importance by BIFs, but they once formed the backbone of the iron and steel industries in western Europe and North America. European oolitic iron deposits, commonly called Minette-type deposits, contain ooliths of siderite, a siliceous iron mineral known as chamosite, and goethite. The deposits were formed in shallow, near-shore marine environments and are most extensively developed in England, the Lorraine area of France, Belgium, and Luxembourg. In North America oolitic iron deposits contain ooliths of hematite, siderite, and chamosite and are called Clinton-type deposits. The geologic setting of Clinton-type deposits is very similar to Minette types, the most obvious difference being the presence of goethite in the Minettes and hematite in the Clintons. Clinton-type deposits are found in the Appalachians from Newfoundland to Alabama, and they are several hundred million years older than the Minette-type deposits. Because goethite dehydrates slowly and spontaneously to hematite, it is probable that the major difference between the two deposit types is age.

MANGANESE DEPOSITS

Manganese is very similar to iron in chemistry and in the way it is distributed and concentrated in rocks. Such is the case because manganese, like iron, has two important valence states, Mn^{2+} and Mn^{4+}. In the +2 state, manganese forms soluble compounds and can be transported in solution. In the +4 state, however, it forms insoluble compounds, and any solution containing Mn^{2+} in solution will, on meeting an oxidizing environment, quickly precipitate a +4 compound such as pyrolusite, MnO_2.

Manganese forms chemical sediment deposits analogous to the Minette-type iron deposits; that is, the deposits form in shallow, near-shore environments and are oolitic. The most important of such deposits were formed just north of the Black Sea about 35 million years ago during the Oligocene Epoch. Named Chiatura and Nikopol after two cities in Georgia and Ukraine, they contain an estimated 70 percent of the world's known resources of high-grade manganese.

Manganese deposits similar to Algoma-type iron deposits are widespread. Generally considered to have formed as a result of submarine volcanism, most are too poor to mine, but, where weathering has caused secondary enrichment (discussed below), small but very rich ore deposits have formed. Such deposits are mined in Brazil, Mexico, Gabon, and Ghana.

RAINWATER

Each of the deposit-forming processes discussed above involves the transport and deposition of ore minerals from solution. But solutions can also form deposits by dissolving and removing valueless material, leaving a residuum of less-soluble ore minerals. Deposits developed as residues from dissolution are called residual deposits. They occur most prominently in warm tropical regions subjected to high rainfall.

LATERITES

Soils developed in warm tropical climates tend to be leached of all soluble material. Such soils are called laterites, and the insoluble residues remaining in them are hydroxide minerals of iron and aluminum. Most laterites are such intimate mixtures of iron and aluminum minerals that beneficiation to produce a pure concentrate of one or the other is not possible, but some residual deposits are naturally enriched in one metal or the other and under such circumstances are viable ores.

Most iron-rich laterites are of little interest, because BIFs are much more desirable ores. However, aluminum-rich laterites, called bauxites, are of considerable interest and are the principal ores of aluminum. Bauxites develop either on rocks that are initially low in iron or on iron-rich rocks under circumstances in which organic matter or some other special factor renders iron sufficiently soluble to be separated from the aluminum minerals. Bauxites that are currently forming in tropical regions in Australia, Brazil, West Africa, and elsewhere all contain gibbsite ($Al[OH]_3$) as the ore mineral. Older bauxites contain boehmite and diaspore (both $HAlO_2$), which form as a result of the slow, spontaneous dehydration of gibbsite.

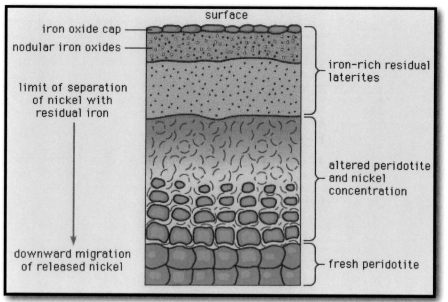

Lateritic weathering releases nickel from atomic substitution in nickeliferous peridotite. Migrating downward, the nickel is redeposited as the mineral garnierite. Copyright Encyclopædia Britannica, Inc.; rendering for this edition by Rosen Educational Services

When mafic igneous rocks such as gabbros and peridotites are subjected to lateritic weathering, nickel released from atomic substitution in the primary igneous silicate minerals can be redeposited at and below the water table as the mineral garnierite, $H_4Ni_3Si_2O_9$. Although garnierite is a silicate mineral (the most difficult type to smelt), an efficient method has been discovered to recover its nickel content, and it is therefore an excellent ore mineral. The most famous nickeliferous laterites are those of New Caledonia, which have been mined for many years. Other important deposits are known in Australia and Cuba.

SECONDARY ENRICHMENT

An especially important class of residual deposit is formed by both the removal of valueless material in solution and the solution and redeposition of valuable ore minerals. Because solution and redeposition can produce highly enriched deposits, the process is known as a secondary enrichment.

Secondary enrichment can affect most classes of ore deposit, but it is notably important in three circumstances. The first circumstance arises when gold-bearing rocks—even rocks containing only traces of gold—are subjected to lateritic weathering. Under such circumstances, the gold can be secondarily enriched into nuggets near the base of the laterite. The importance of secondary enrichment of gold in lateritic regions was realized only during the gold boom of the 1980s, especially in Australia.

The second circumstance involves mineral deposits containing sulfide minerals, especially copper sulfides, that are subjected to weathering under desert conditions. Sulfide minerals are oxidized at the surface and produce sulfuric acid, and acidified rainwater then carries the copper, as copper sulfate, down to the water table. Below the water table, where sulfide minerals remain unoxidized, any iron sulfide grains present will react with the copper sulfate solution, putting iron into solution and precipitating a copper mineral. The net result is that copper is transferred from the oxidizing upper portion of the deposit to that portion at and just below the water table. Secondary enrichment of porphyry copper deposits in the southwestern United States, Mexico, Peru, and Chile is an important factor in making those deposits ores. Lead, zinc, and silver deposits are also subject to secondary enrichment under conditions of desert weathering.

The third circumstance in which secondary enrichment is important involves BIFs and sedimentary manganese deposits. A primary BIF may contain only 25 to 30 percent iron by weight, but, when subjected to intense weathering and secondary enrichment, portions of the deposit can be enriched to as high as 65 percent iron. Some primary BIFs are now mined and beneficiated under the name taconite, but in essentially all of these deposits mining actually commenced in the high-grade secondary-enrichment zone. Sedimentary manganese deposits, especially those formed as a result of submarine volcanism, must also be secondarily enriched before they become ores.

FLOWING SURFACE WATER

When mineral grains of different density are moved by flowing water, the less dense grains will be most rapidly moved, and a separation of high-density and low-density grains can be effected. Mineral deposits formed as a result of gravity separation based on density are called placer deposits.

For effective concentration, placer minerals must not only have a high density (greater than about 3.3 grams per cubic cm [1.9 ounces per cubic inch]), they must also possess a high degree of chemical resistance to dissolution or reaction with surface water and be mechanically durable. The common sulfide ore minerals do not form placers, because they rapidly oxidize and break down. Ore minerals having suitable properties for forming placers are the oxides cassiterite (tin), chromite (chromium), columbite (niobium), ilmenite and rutile (titanium), magnetite (iron), monazite and xenotime (rare-earth metals), and zircon (zirconium). In addition, native gold and platinum have been mined from placers, and several gemstone minerals—in particular, diamond, ruby, and sapphire— also concentrate in placers.

ALLUVIAL PLACERS

After a mineral-bearing soil reaches the bottom of a slope, it can be moved by stream water so that stream or alluvial placers form. Alluvial placers have played an especially important historical role in the production of gold. Indeed, more than half of the gold ever mined has come from placers, since the giant Witwatersrand gold deposits in South Africa are fossil placers more than two billion years old. Other fossil placers (i.e., deposits whose stream waters have long disappeared) have been discovered at Serra de Jacobina in Brazil (gold) and Blind River, Ont., Can. (uranium), but nowhere has a deposit been found equal to Witwatersrand. Just why and how such an extraordinarily large concentration of gold occurred there is a matter of continuing scientific controversy.

PLACER DEPOSITS

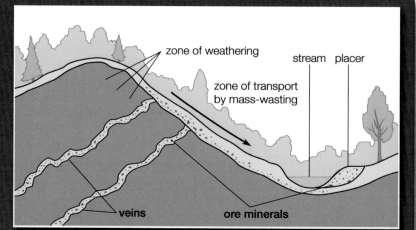

Chemically resistant minerals weather from a vein deposit, move downhill by mass-wasting, and are concentrated by flowing water into a stream placer. Encyclopædia Britannica, Inc.

Natural concentrations of heavy minerals that result from the effect of gravity on moving particles are called placer deposits. When heavy, stable minerals are freed from their matrix by weathering processes, they are slowly washed downslope into streams that quickly winnow the lighter matrix. Thus the heavy minerals become concentrated in stream, beach, and lag (residual) gravels and constitute workable ore deposits. Minerals that form placer deposits have high specific gravity, are chemically resistant to weathering, and are durable; such minerals include gold, platinum, cassiterite, magnetite, chromite, ilmenite, rutile, native copper, zircon, monazite, and various gemstones.

There are several varieties of placer deposits: stream, or alluvial, placers; eluvial placers; beach placers; and eolian placers. Stream placers, by far the most important, have yielded the most placer gold, cassiterite, platinum, and gemstones. Primitive mining probably began with such deposits, and their ease of mining and sometime great richness have made them the cause of some of the world's greatest gold and diamond "rushes." Stream placers depend on swiftly flowing water for their concentration. Because the ability to transport solid material varies approximately as the square of the velocity, the flow rate plays an important part; thus, where the velocity decreases, heavy minerals are deposited much more quickly than the light ones. Examples of stream placers include the rich gold deposits of Alaska and the Klondike, the platinum placers of the Urals, the tin (cassiterite) deposits of Malaysia, Thailand, and Indonesia, and the diamond placers of Congo (Kinshasa) and Angola.

BEACH PLACERS

When wave trains impinge obliquely on a beach, a net flow of water, called a longshore drift, occurs parallel to the beach. Such a current can produce a beach placer. Beach placers are a major source of ilmenite, rutile, monazite, and zircon. They have been extensively mined in India, Australia, Alaska (U.S.), and Brazil.

METALLOGENIC PROVINCES AND EPOCHS

Mineral deposits are not distributed uniformly through the Earth's crust. Rather, specific classes of deposit tend to be concentrated in particular areas or regions called metallogenic provinces. These groupings of deposits occur because deposit-forming processes, such as the emplacement of magma bodies and the formation of sedimentary basins, are themselves controlled by larger processes that shape the face of the Earth. The shape and location of such features as continents and oceans, volcanoes, sedimentary basins, and mountain ranges are controlled, either directly or indirectly, through the process known as plate tectonics—the lateral motion of segments of the lithosphere, the outermost 100-km- (60-mile-) thick layer of the Earth. For example, the distribution of hydrothermal mineral deposits, which form as a result of volcanism, is controlled by plate tectonics because most of the Earth's volcanism occurs along plate margins. In addition, porphyry copper deposits are formed as a result of volcanism along a subduction zone (i.e., the zone where one plate descends beneath another); this gives rise to metallogenic provinces parallel to subduction plate edges. Evidence indicates that plate tectonics has operated for at least two billion years, so that the locations and features of most metallogenic provinces formed over this period can be explained, at least in part, by this geologic process. Factors controlling the distribution of deposits formed more than two billion years ago are still a matter for research, but they too may have been linked to plate tectonics.

Metallogenic epochs are units of geologic time during which conditions were particularly favourable for the formation of specific classes of mineral deposit. One conspicuous example of a metallogenic epoch is the previously mentioned 900-million-year period, from 2.7 to 1.8 billion years ago, when all of the great Lake Superior-type BIFs were formed. Because the iron in these deposits was deposited from seawater (an impossibility today, since the atmosphere is too oxidizing to allow seawater to transport iron), it is probable that a specific composition of the atmosphere and ocean peculiar to that period defined the BIF metallogenic epoch. Another great deposit-forming period occurred between about 2.8 and 2.65 billion years ago, when a large number of volcanogenic massive sulfide deposits formed; the probable cause of this metallogenic epoch was a period of extremely active submarine volcanism.

CHAPTER 4
THE SILICATES

The silicates make up about 95 percent of the Earth's crust and upper mantle, occurring as the major constituents of most igneous rocks and in appreciable quantities in sedimentary and metamorphic varieties as well. They also are important constituents of lunar samples, meteorites, and most asteroids. In addition, planetary probes have detected their occurrence on the surfaces of Mercury, Venus, and Mars. Of the approximately 600 known silicate minerals, only the feldspars, amphiboles, pyroxenes, micas, olivines, feldspathoids, and zeolites are significant in rock formation.

The basic structural unit of all silicate minerals is the silicon tetrahedron in which one silicon atom is surrounded by and bonded to (i.e., coordinated with) four oxygen atoms, each at the corner of a regular tetrahedron. These SiO_4 tetrahedral units can share oxygen atoms and be linked in a variety of ways, which results in different structures. The topology of these structures forms the basis for silicate classification. For example, sorosilicates are silicate minerals consisting of double tetrahedral groups in which one oxygen atom is shared by two tetrahedrons. Inosilicates show a single-chain structure wherein each tetrahedron shares two oxygen atoms. Phyllosilicates have a sheet structure in which each tetrahedron shares one oxygen atom with each of three other tetrahedrons. Tectosilicates show a three-dimensional network of tetrahedrons, with each tetrahedral unit sharing all of its oxygen atoms.

Details of the linkage of tetrahedrons became known early in the 20th century when X-ray diffraction made the determination of crystal structure possible. Prior to this, the classification of silicates was based on chemical and physical similarities, which often proved to be ambiguous. Although many properties of a silicate mineral group are determined by tetrahedral linkage, an equally important factor is the type and location of other atoms in the structure.

Silicate minerals can be thought of as three-dimensional arrays of oxygen atoms that contain void spaces (i.e., crystallographic sites) where various cations can enter. Besides the tetrahedral (4-fold coordination) sites, 6-fold, 8-fold, and 12-fold sites are common. A correlation exists between the size of a cation (a positively charged ion) and the type of site it can occupy: the larger the cation, the greater the coordination, because large cations have more surface area with which the oxygen atoms can make contact. Tetrahedral sites are generally occupied by silicon and aluminum; 6-fold sites by aluminum, iron, titanium, magnesium, lithium, manganese, and sodium; 8-fold sites by sodium, calcium, and potassium; and 12-fold sites by potassium. Elements of similar ionic size often substitute for one another. An aluminum ion, for example, is only slightly larger than a silicon ion, allowing substitution for silicon in both tetrahedral and 6-fold sites.

SILICATE MINERALS				
NAME	COLOUR	LUSTRE	MOHS HARD-NESS	SPECIFIC GRAVITY
Tectosilicates (three-dimensional networks)				
feldspar (for other examples, see feldspar)				
orthoclase	flesh-red, white to pale yellow, red, green	vitreous	6–6½	2.6

NAME	COLOUR	LUSTRE	MOHS HARD-NESS	SPECIFIC GRAVITY
feldspathoid (for other examples, see feldspathoid)				
nepheline	light-coloured; reddish, green-ish, brownish	vitreous to greasy	5½–6	2.6–2.7
silica (for other examples, see silica mineral)				
quartz	variable	vitreous to greasy (coarse-grained); waxy to dull (fine-grained)	7 (a hard-ness standard)	2.65
zeolite (for other examples, see zeolite)				
chabazite	white; flesh-red	vitreous	4½	2.0–2.1
Phyllosilicates (sheet structures)				
clay (for other examples, see clay mineral)				
chlorite	green	vitreous or pearly	2–3	2.6–3.0
smectite				2.2–2.7
mica (for other examples, see mica)				
apophyllite	colourless, white, pink, pale yellow, or green	pearly iridescent	4½–5	2.3–2.4
muscovite	commonly white or colourless; light shades of green, red, or brown	vitreous to silky or pearly	2–2½	2.8–3.0

NAME	COLOUR	LUSTRE	MOHS HARD-NESS	SPECIFIC GRAVITY
prehnite	pale green to gray, white, or yellow	vitreous	6–6½	2.9–3.0
pyrophyl-lite	white and various pale colours	dull and glistening	1–2	2.6–2.9
talc	colourless; white; pale or dark green; brown	pearly	1 (a hardness standard)	2.6–2.8
Inosilicates (chain structures)				
amphibole (for other examples, see amphibole)				
common hornblende	pale to dark green	glassy	5–6	3.0–3.4
mullite	white			3.0
pyroxene (for other examples, see pyroxene)				
augite	brown, green, black	vitreous	5½–6	3.2–3.5
rhodonite	pink to brownish red	vitreous	5½–6½	3.6–3.8
wollas-tonite	white; also colourless, gray, or very pale green	vitreous	4½–5	2.9–3.1
Cyclosilicates (ring structures)				
axinite	clove- or lilac-brown; pearl-gray; yellowish	highly glassy	6½–7	3.3–3.4

NAME	COLOUR	LUSTRE	MOHS HARD-NESS	SPECIFIC GRAVITY
beryl	various greens; variable, including deep-green (emerald), blue-green (aquamarine), pink (morganite), yellow (heliodore)	vitreous	7½–8	2.7–2.8
cordierite	various blues	vitreous	7	2.5–2.8
tourmaline	extremely variable	vitreous to resinous	7–7½	3.0–3.2
Sorosilicates (double tetrahedral structures)				
hemimor-phite	white, sometimes tinted bluish or greenish; yellow to brown	vitreous	5	3.4–3.5
melilite	colourless; grayish green; brown	vitreous to resinous	5–6	
gehlenite				3.1
åkerman-ite				2.9
Nesosilicates (independent tetrahedral structures)				
andalusite	pink, white, or rose-red; also variable	vitreous	6½–7½	3.1–3.2
chryso-colla	green, bluish green	vitreous	2–4	2.0–2.8
datolite	colourless or white; also various pale tints	vitreous	5–5½	2.9–3.0

NAME	COLOUR	LUSTRE	MOHS HARD-NESS	SPECIFIC GRAVITY
epidote	yellowish green to dark green	vitreous	6–7	3.3–3.5
garnet	variable	vitreous to resinous	6–7½	
almandine				4.3
andradite				3.9
grossula-rite				3.6
pyrope				3.6
spessartite				4.2
uvarovite				3.9
kyanite	blue; white; also variable	vitreous to pearly	4–7 (variable)	3.5–3.7
olivine (for other examples, see olivines)				
forsterite-fayalite series	various greens and yellows	vitreous	6½–7	3.2 (forsterite) to 4.4 (fayalite)
phenacite	colourless; also wine-yellow, pale rose, brown	vitreous	7½–8	3.0
sillimanite	colourless or white; also various browns and greens	vitreous to subadamantine	6½–7½	3.2–3.3
sphene	colourless, yellow, green, brown, black	adamantine to resinous	5	3.4–3.6
staurolite	dark red-brown; yellow-brown; brown-black	subvitreous to resinous	7–7½	3.7–3.8

NAME	COLOUR	LUSTRE	MOHS HARD-NESS	SPECIFIC GRAVITY
thorite	black; also orange-yellow (orangite)		4½–5	4.5–5.0; 5.2–5.4 (orangite)
topaz	straw- or wine-yellow; white; grayish, greenish, bluish, reddish	vitreous	8 (a hard-ness standard)	3.5–3.6
vesuvianite	yellow, green, brown	vitreous	6–7	3.3–3.4
willemite	white or green-ish yellow	vitreous to resinous	5½	3.9–4.2
zircon	reddish brown, yellow, gray, green, or colourless	adamantine	7½	4.6–4.7
zoisite	white; gray; green-brown; pink (thulite)	vitreous	6–6½	3.2–3.4

SILICATE MINERALS				
NAME	HABIT	FRAC-TURE OR CLEAVAGE	REFRAC-TIVE INDICES	CRYSTAL SYSTEM
Tectosilicates (three-dimensional networks)				
feldspar (for other examples, see feldspar)				
orthoclase	twinned crystals	two good cleav-ages of 90 degrees	alpha = 1.518–1.529 beta = 1.522–1.533 gamma = 1.522–1.539	monoclinic

NAME	HABIT	FRAC-TURE OR CLEAVAGE	REFRAC-TIVE INDICES	CRYSTAL SYSTEM
feldspathoid (for other examples, see feldspathoid)				
nepheline	small glassy crystals or grains	poor cleavage	omega = 1.529–1.546 epsilon = 1.526–1.542	hexagonal
silica (for other examples, see silica mineral)				
quartz	prismatic and rhombohedral crystals; massive	conchoidal fracture	omega = 1.544 epsilon = 1.553	hexagonal
zeolite (for other examples, see zeolite)				
chabazite	single, cubelike rhombohedrons	poor cleavage	omega = 1.470–1.494 epsilon = 1.470–1.494	hexagonal
Phyllosilicates (sheet structures)				
clay (for other examples, see clay mineral)				
chlorite	large crystalline blocks; fine-grained, flaky aggregates	platy cleavage	alpha = 1.57–1.64 gamma = 1.575–1.645	monoclinic or triclinic
smectite	broad undulating mosaic sheets that break into irregular fluffy masses of minute particles		alpha = 1.480–1.590 gamma = 1.515–1.630	

NAME	HABIT	FRAC-TURE OR CLEAVAGE	REFRAC-TIVE INDICES	CRYSTAL SYSTEM
mica (for other examples, see mica)				
apophyllite	tabular, prismatic, or granular crystals; prisms and bipyramids when well-formed	one perfect, one poor cleavage	omega = 1.534–1.535 epsilon = 1.535–1.537	tetragonal
muscovite	large tabular blocks (called books); pseudohexagonal crystals; fine-grained aggregates	one perfect, platy cleavage	alpha = 1.552–1.574 beta = 1.582–1.610 gamma = 1.587–1.616	
prehnite	rosettes of small radiating crystals; tabular or prismatic crystals; lamellar or botryoidal massive	one good cleavage	alpha = 1.611–1.632 beta = 1.615–1.642 gamma = 1.632–1.665	ortho-rhombic
pyrophyllite	lamellar massive; granular to compact massive	one perfect cleavage	alpha = 1.534–1.556 beta = 1.586–1.589 gamma = 1.596–1.601	monoclinic
talc	compact foliated masses	one perfect cleavage	alpha = 1.539–1.553 beta = 1.589–1.594 gamma = 1.589–1.600	monoclinic

NAME	HABIT	FRAC-TURE OR CLEAVAGE	REFRAC-TIVE INDICES	CRYSTAL SYSTEM
Inosilicates (chain structures)				
amphibole (for other examples, see amphibole)				
common horn-blende	massive	one good cleavage of 56 degrees	alpha = 1.615–1.705 beta = 1.618–1.714 gamma = 1.632–1.730	monoclinic
mullite	elongated prismatic crystals; melts	one distinct cleavage	alpha = 1.642–1.653 beta = 1.644 gamma = 1.654–1.679	ortho-rhombic
pyroxene (for other examples, see pyroxene)				
augite	short, thick, tabular crystals	one good cleavage of 87 degrees	alpha = 1.671–1.735 beta = 1.672–1.741 gamma = 1.703–1.761	monoclinic
rhodonite	rounded tabular crystals; cleavable to compact massive; embedded grains	two perfect cleavages	alpha = 1.711–1.738 beta = 1.715–1.741 gamma = 1.724–1.751	triclinic
wollas-tonite	cleavable, fibrous, or compact massive; tabular crystals	one perfect, two good cleavages	alpha = 1.616–1.640 beta = 1.628–1.650 gamma = 1.631–1.653	triclinic

NAME	HABIT	FRAC-TURE OR CLEAVAGE	REFRAC-TIVE INDICES	CRYSTAL SYSTEM
Cyclosilicates (ring structures)				
axinite	broad, sharp-edged, wedge-shaped crystals; lamellar massive	one good cleavage	alpha = 1.674–1.693 beta = 1.681–1.701 gamma = 1.684–1.704	triclinic
beryl	long hexagonal crystals	conchoidal to uneven fracture	omega = 1.569–1.598 epsilon = 1.565–1.590	hexagonal
cordierite	short prismatic crystals; embed-ded grains; compact massive	one dis-tinct cleavage	alpha = 1.522–1.558 beta = 1.524–1.574 gamma = 1.527–1.578	ortho-rhombic
tourmaline	parallel or radi-ating groups of striated, elon-gated hexagonal prisms, often rounded or barrel-shaped; massive	subcon-choidal to uneven fracture	omega = 1.635–1.675 epsilon = 1.610–1.650	hexagonal
Sorosilicates (double tetrahedral structures)				
hemimor-phite	sheaflike crystal aggregates	one perfect cleavage	alpha = 1.614 beta = 1.617 gamma = 1.636	ortho-rhombic

NAME	HABIT	FRAC-TURE OR CLEAVAGE	REFRAC-TIVE INDICES	CRYSTAL SYSTEM
melilite	short prismatic crystals; tablets	one distinct cleavage		tetragonal
gehlenite			omega = 1.669 epsilon = 1.658	
åkerman-ite			omega = 1.632 epsilon = 1.640	
Nesosilicates (independent tetrahedral structures)				
andalusite	coarse prisms; massive	one good cleavage of 89 degrees	alpha = 1.629–1.640 beta = 1.633–1.644 gamma = 1.638–1.650	ortho-rhombic
chryso-colla	crusts; botryoi-dal masses	conchoidal fracture	omega = 1.46 epsilon = 1.54	ortho-rhombic?
datolite	tabular or short prismatic crys-tals; botryoidal and globular or divergent and radiating massive	conchoidal to uneven fracture	alpha = 1.622–1.626 beta = 1.649–1.654 gamma = 1.666–1.670	monoclinic

NAME	HABIT	FRAC-TURE OR CLEAVAGE	REFRAC-TIVE INDICES	CRYSTAL SYSTEM
epidote	striated elongated crystals; fibrous or granular massive; disseminated	one perfect cleavage	alpha = 1.712–1.756 beta = 1.720–1.789 gamma = 1.723–1.829	monoclinic
garnet	crystals; irregular embedded grains; compact, granular, or lamellar massive	subconchoidal fracture		isometric
almandine			$n = 1.830$	
andradite			$n = 1.887$	
grossularite			$n = 1.734$	
pyrope			$n = 1.714$	
spessartite			$n = 1.800$	
uvarovite			$n = 1.86$	
kyanite	elongated tabular, bladed crystals	one good, one perfect cleavage	alpha = 1.712–1.718 beta = 1.719–1.723 gamma = 1.727–1.734	triclinic
olivine (for other examples, see olivines)				
forsterite-fayalite series	flattened crystals; compact or granular massive; embedded grains	one indistinct cleavage	alpha = 1.631–1.827 beta = 1.651–1.869 gamma = 1.670–1.879	ortho-rhombic

NAME	HABIT	FRAC- TURE OR CLEAVAGE	REFRAC- TIVE INDICES	CRYSTAL SYSTEM
phenacite	rhombohedral crystals	one distinct cleavage	omega = 1.654 epsilon = 1.670	hexagonal
sillimanite	vertically striated, square prisms; long, slender parallel crystal groups to fibrous or columnar massive	one perfect cleavage	alpha = 1.654–1.661 beta = 1.658–1.670 gamma = 1.673–1.684	ortho- rhombic
sphene	wedge-shaped crystals, often twinned; compact massive	one good cleavage	alpha = 1.843–1.950 beta = 1.870–2.034 gamma = 1.943–2.110	monoclinic
staurolite	cruciform twins	one distinct cleavage	alpha = 1.739–1.747 beta = 1.744–1.754 gamma = 1.750–1.762	monoclinic
thorite	square prismatic crystals; small masses	one distinct cleavage	omega = 1.8	tetragonal
topaz	prismatic crystals	one perfect cleavage	alpha = 1.606–1.629 beta = 1.609–1.631 gamma = 1.616–1.638	ortho- rhombic

NAME	HABIT	FRAC-TURE OR CLEAVAGE	REFRAC-TIVE INDICES	CRYSTAL SYSTEM
vesuvianite	prismatic crystals; massive	subconchoidal to uneven fracture	omega = 1.703–1.752 epsilon = 1.700–1.746	tetragonal
willemite	hexagonal prismatic crystals; disseminated grains; fibrous massive	one easy cleavage	omega = 1.691–1.714 epsilon = 1.719–1.732	hexagonal
zircon	square prismatic crystals; irregular forms; grains	conchoidal fracture	omega = 1.923–1.960 epsilon = 1.968–2.015	tetragonal
zoisite	striated prismatic crystals; columnar to compact massive	one perfect cleavage	alpha = 1.685–1.705 beta = 1.688–1.710 gamma = 1.697–1.725	ortho-rhombic

AMPHIBOLES

Amphiboles are found principally in metamorphic and igneous rocks. They occur in many metamorphic rocks, especially those derived from mafic igneous rocks (those containing dark-coloured ferromagnesian minerals) and siliceous dolomites. Amphiboles also are important constituents in a variety of plutonic and volcanic igneous rocks that range in composition from granitic to gabbroic. Amphibole, from the Greek *amphibolos*, meaning "ambiguous," was named by the famous French crystallographer and mineralogist René-Just Haüy (1801) in allusion to the great variety of composition and appearance shown by this mineral group. There are 5 major groups of amphibole leading to 76 chemically defined end-member amphibole compositions according to the British mineralogist Bernard E. Leake. Because of the wide range of chemical substitutions permissible in the crystal structure, amphiboles can crystallize in igneous and metamorphic rocks with a wide range of bulk chemistries. Typically amphiboles form as long prismatic crystals, radiating sprays, and asbestiform (fibrous) aggregates; however, without the aid of chemical analysis, it is difficult to megascopically identify all but a few of the more distinctive end-member amphiboles. The combination of prismatic form and two diamond-shaped directions of cleavage at about 56° and 124° is the diagnostic feature of most members of the amphibole group.

CHEMICAL COMPOSITION

The complex chemical composition of members of the amphibole group can be expressed by the general formula $A_{0-1}B_2C_5T_8O_{22}(OH, F, Cl)_2$, where A = Na, K; B = Na, Zn, Li, Ca, Mn, Fe^{2+}, Mg; C = Mg, Fe^{2+}, Mn, Al, Fe^{3+}, Ti, Zn, Cr; and T = Si, Al, Ti. Nearly complete substitution may take place between sodium and calcium and among magnesium, ferrous iron, and manganese (Mn). There is limited substitution between ferric iron and aluminum and between titanium and other C-type cations. Aluminum can partially substitute for silicon in the tetrahedral (T) site. Partial substitution of fluorine (F), chlorine, and oxygen for hydroxyl (OH) in the hydroxyl site is also common. The complexity of the amphibole formula has given rise to numerous mineral names within the amphibole group. In 1997 Leake presented a precise nomenclature of 76 names that encompass the chemical variation within this group. The mineral nomenclature of the amphiboles is divided into four principal subdivisions based on B-group cation occupancy: (1) the iron-magnesium-manganese amphibole group, (2) the calcic amphibole group, (3) the sodic-calcic amphibole group, and (4) the sodic amphibole group.

Numerous common amphiboles can be represented within the $Mg_7Si_8O_{22}(OH)_2$ (magnesio-anthophyllite)–$Fe_7Si_8O_{22}(OH)_2$ (grunerite)–"$Ca_7Si_8O_{22}(OH)_2$" (hypothetical pure calcium amphibole) compositional field. This diagram is commonly referred to as the amphibole quadrilateral. Complete substitution extends from tremolite $[Ca_2Mg_5Si_8O_{22}(OH)_2]$ to ferro-actinolite $[Ca_2Fe_5Si_8O_{22}(OH)_2]$. Actinolite is the intermediate member of the tremolite-ferro-actinolite series. The compositional range from about 0.9 $Mg_7Si_8O_{22}(OH)_2$ to about $Fe_2Mg_5Si_8O_{22}(OH)_2$ is represented by the orthorhombic amphibole known as anthophyllite. The monoclinic cummingtonite-grunerite series exists from about $Fe_2Mg_2Si_8O_{22}(OH)_2$ to $Fe_7Si_8O_{22}(OH)_2$. Intermediate amphibole compositions do not exist between anthophyllite and the tremolite-actinolite series. Compositional gaps also exist between the cummingtonite-grunerite series and other calcic amphiboles. Consequently, coexisting pairs of anthophyllite-tremolite and grunerite-ferroactinolite are found together in some rocks. Sodium-bearing amphiboles are represented by the glaucophane $[Na_2Mg_3Al_2Si_8O_{22}(OH)_2]$–riebeckite $[Na_2Fe^{2+}{}_{/3}Fe^{3+}{}_{/3}Si_8O_{22}(OH)_2]$ series. Additional sodium is contained in the A site of the structure of arfvedsonite $[NaNa_2Fe^{2+}{}_{/4}Fe^{3+}Si_8O_{22}(OH)_2]$. For amphiboles that are not precisely characterized by their chemistry, it is not possible to assign a specific name. Hornblende is the general name used for calcic amphiboles identified only by physical or optical properties.

The amphiboles differ chemically from the pyroxenes in two major respects. Amphiboles have hydroxyl groups in their structure and are considered to be hydrous silicates that are stable only in hydrous environments where water can be incorporated into the structure as $(OH)^-$. The second major compositional difference is the presence of the A site in amphiboles that contains the large alkali elements, typically sodium cations and at times potassium cations. The pyroxenes do not have an equivalent site that can accommodate potassium. The presence of hydroxyl groups in the structure of amphiboles decreases their thermal stability relative to the more refractory (heat-resistant) pyroxenes. Amphiboles decompose to anhydrous minerals (mainly pyroxenes) at elevated temperatures.

CRYSTAL STRUCTURE

The fundamental building block of all silicate mineral structures is the silicon-oxygen tetrahedron $(SiO_4)^{4-}$. It consists of a central silicon atom surrounded by four oxygen atoms in the shape of a tetrahedron. The essential characteristic of the amphibole structure is a double chain of corner-linked silicon-oxygen tetrahedrons that extend indefinitely parallel to the c crystallographic axis, the direction of elongation. The tetrahedrons alternately share two and three oxygen atoms to produce a silicon-to-oxygen ratio of 4:11. The double chains repeat along their length at intervals of approximately 5.3 angstroms (Å), or 2.1×10^{-9} inch, and this defines the ideal c axis of the unit cell. The double chains are separated from other double chains and bonded to each other laterally by planes of cations and hydroxyl ions. The figure on page 130 illustrates the double chains as well as the octahedral strips to which they are bonded. The structure contains, besides the tetrahedral sites that constitute the chains, additional cation

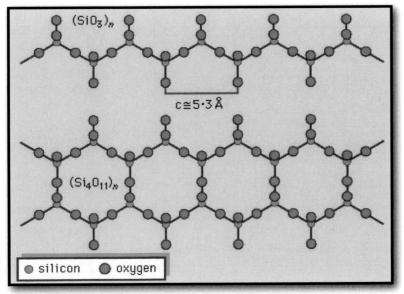

Illustration of pyroxene single-chain silicon-oxygen tetrahedral structure $(SiO_3)n$ and amphibole double-chain structure $(Si_4O_{11})n$. Copyright Encyclopædia Britannica, Inc.; rendering for this edition by Rosen Educational Services

sites labeled A, $M4$, $M3$, $M2$, and $M1$. The A site contains the large alkali ions, mainly sodium, and is bonded to 10 to 12 oxygen and hydroxyl ions. The A site is filled to the extent necessary to maintain electrical neutrality, but typically the available A sites are not completely occupied. The $M1$, $M2$, and $M3$ octahedrons contain the C-type cations and share edges to form octahedral bands parallel to the c crystallographic direction. $M1$ and $M3$ bond to four oxygen atoms and two hydroxyl anions. $M2$ is coordinated by six oxygen atoms. $M4$ has sixfold to eightfold coordination and accommodates the B-type cations. The $M4$ site is most similar to the $M2$ site in pyroxene and accommodates Ca^{2+}, as does the $M2$ site in pyroxene. Amphiboles have two each of the $M1$, $M2$, and $M4$ sites and one $M3$ site, giving a total of seven octahedral cations in the unit cell. The tetrahedral-octahedral-tetrahedral (t-o-t) strips,

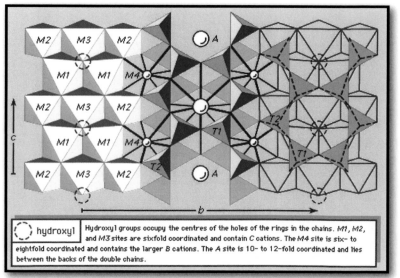

Hydroxyl groups occupy the centres of the holes of the rings in the chains. M1, M2, and M3 sites are sixfold coordinated and contain C cations. The M4 site is six- to eightfold coordinated and contains the larger B cations. The A site is 10- to 12-fold coordinated and lies between the backs of the double chains.

Projection of the crystal structure of a monoclinic amphibole as viewed down the a axis. Copyright Encyclopædia Britannica, Inc.; rendering for this edition by Rosen Educational Services

also known as I beams, are approximately twice as wide in the *b* direction as the equivalent t-o-t strips in pyroxenes because of the doubling of the chains in the amphiboles. The structure ruptures around the stronger I beams and produces the characteristic 56° and 124° amphibole cleavage angles.

The similarity between the crystal structures of the major layer silicates (clays and micas) and the chain silicates (pyroxenes and amphiboles) has long been recognized. The structures of all of these silicates can be considered as consisting of combinations of two structural units, the pyroxene I beams and the mica sheets. Both structures contain a band of octahedrons sandwiched between two oppositely pointing chains of tetrahedrons. Combinations of these two basic structural units, or "modules," can produce all other minerals in the layer silicate and chain silicate groups. The term *biopyribole* has been used to describe any mineral that has both I beams and sheetlike

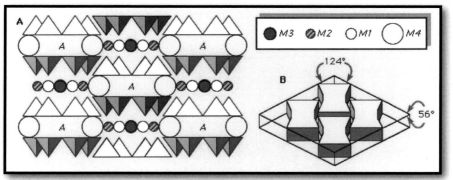

(A) Schematic projection of the monoclinic amphibole structure on a plane perpendicular to the c axis. (B) Control of cleavage angles by I beams in the amphibole structure. Copyright Encyclopædia Britannica, Inc.; rendering for this edition by Rosen Educational Services

structures. The name comes from *bio*tite (mica), *pyr*oxene, and amph*ibole*. Biopyriboles have chain widths and repeat sequences like pyroxenes (single-chain repeats), amphiboles (double-chain repeats), and triple-chain repeats. The latter are intermediate between an amphibole I beam and the sheet structure of mica. Pyribole refers to any member of the biopyribole group, excluding the sheet silicates (i.e., the pyroxenes and amphiboles together).

PHYSICAL PROPERTIES

Long prismatic, acicular, or fibrous crystal habit, Mohs hardness between 5 and 6, and two directions of cleavage intersecting at approximately 56° and 124° generally suffice to identify amphiboles in hand specimens. The specific gravity values of amphiboles range from about 2.9 to 3.6. Amphiboles yield water when heated in a closed tube and fuse with difficulty in a flame. Their colour ranges extensively from colourless to white, green, brown, black, blue, or lavender and is related to composition, principally the iron content. Magnesium-rich amphiboles such as anthophyllite, cummingtonite, and tremolite are colourless or light in colour. The tremolite-ferroactinolite series ranges from white to dark green with increasing iron content. The finely fibrous and massive variety of actinolite-tremolite known as nephrite jade ranges from green to black. Common hornblende is typically black. Glaucophane and riebeckite are usually blue. Anthophyllite is gray to various shades of green and brown. The cummingtonite-grunerite series occurs in various shades of light brown. Iron-free varieties of tremolite containing manganese can have a lavender colour.

The common crystallographic habit of amphiboles is acicular or prismatic; however, most of the amphiboles are also known to crystallize in the asbestiform habit. The asbestiform variety of riebeckite is called crocidolite or blue asbestos. Amosite is a rare asbestiform variety of grunerite, named from the company Amos (Asbestos Mines of South Africa). The most important commercial asbestos material is chrysotile, the asbestiform variety of serpentine.

In thin sections, amphiboles are distinguished by several properties, including two directions of cleavage at

Riebeckite (of the crocidolite variety) from South Africa. © Rodolfo Crespi

approximately 56° and 124°, six-sided basal cross sections, characteristic colour, and pleochroism (colour variance with the direction of light propagation). Orthorhombic amphiboles exhibit less intense pleochroism than the monoclinic amphiboles.

ORIGIN AND OCCURRENCE

Exhibiting an extensive range of possible cation sub-stitutions, amphiboles crystallize in both igneous and metamorphic rocks with a broad range of bulk chemical compositions. Because of their relative instability to chem-ical weathering at the Earth's surface, amphiboles make up only a minor constituent in most sedimentary rocks.

IGNEOUS ROCKS

Calcic amphiboles are characteristically contained in igneous rocks. Igneous amphiboles are intermediate in composition between tremolite, tschermakite, edenite, and pargasite end-members. Typically, these amphiboles of intermediate composition are called hornblende. Hornblende occurs in various plutonic igneous rocks, including diorites, quartz diorites, and granodiorites. It also occurs as phenocrysts in andesite lavas that contained enough water for amphiboles to form. Hastingsite is found in granites and alkali-rich intrusives such as syenites. The alkali amphiboles riebeckite and arfvedsonite are found most commonly in granites, syenites, nepheline syenites, and related pegmatites. Richterite occurs as a hydrother-mal product and in veins in alkaline igneous rocks.

CONTACT METAMORPHIC ROCKS

Amphiboles occur in contact metamorphic aureoles around igneous intrusions. (An aureole is the zone sur-rounding an intrusion, which is a mass of igneous rock that solidified between other rocks located within the Earth.) The contact aureoles produced in siliceous limestones and dolomites, called skarns or calc-silicate rocks, characteristically contain metamorphic amphiboles such as tremolite or actinolite. The presence of tremolite implies a relatively low grade of metamorphism as tremolite breaks down to form the pyroxene diopside in the presence of calcite and quartz at elevated temperatures. Richterite-winchite occurs in hydrothermally metamorphosed limestones. Magnesium-rich anthophyllites are found along contact zones of granitic dikes intruding ultramafic rocks (those rich in iron and magnesium).

REGIONAL METAMORPHIC ROCKS

Many different amphiboles may be contained in regional metamorphic rocks. Commonly several amphiboles may coexist with one another in the same sample, depending on the bulk chemistry of the rock and on the pressure and temperature of metamorphism. The amphiboles typically occur with plagioclase feldspar, quartz, and biotite, as well as with chlorite and oxide minerals. In magnesium-rich rocks, tremolite, anthophyllite, and hornblende may exist together. Gedrite and cummingtonite coexist with garnet in rocks enriched in aluminum and iron. Rocks containing cummingtonite or grunerite are characteristic of metamorphosed iron formations associated with iron oxides, iron-rich sheet silicates, carbonates, and quartz. Glaucophane occurs only in such metamorphic rocks as schist, eclogite, and marble. Glaucophane associated with jadeite, lawsonite, and calcite or aragonite is the characteristic assemblage found in high-pressure, low-temperature metamorphic rocks called blueschists, which have a blue colour imparted by the glaucophane. Blueschists have basaltic bulk compositions and may also contain riebeckite. The latter also may occur in regional metamorphic schists. Tremolite-actinolite and the sheet-silicate chlorite are the principal minerals in the low-to-moderate temperature and pressure greenschist metamorphic rocks. Hornblende is characteristic of some medium-grade metamorphic rocks known as amphibolites, in which hornblende and plagioclase are the major constituents.

Dehydration of amphiboles in the lower crust or mantle may be an important source of water that aids in the generation of magmas from partial melting processes.

FELDSPARS

Feldspars constitute a group of aluminosilicate minerals that contain calcium, sodium, or potassium. Feldspars make up more than half the Earth's crust, and professional literature about them constitutes a large percentage of the literature of mineralogy.

Of the more than 3,000 known mineral species, less than 0.1 percent make up the bulk of the Earth's crust and mantle. These and an additional score of minerals serve as the basis for naming most of the rocks exposed on the Earth's surface.

Each of the common rock-forming minerals can be identified on the basis of its chemical composition and its crystal structure (i.e., the arrangement of its constituent atoms and ions). The nonopaque minerals can also be identified by their optical properties. Fairly expensive equipment and sophisticated procedures, however, are required for such determinations. Therefore, it is fortunate that macroscopic examination, along with one or more tests, are sufficient to identify these minerals as they occur in most rocks. The following descriptions include basic chemical and structural data and the properties used in macroscopically based identifications.

Optical data, which are not included in these descriptions, are available in mineralogy books.

Two important rock-forming materials that are not minerals are major components of a few rocks. These are glass and macerals. Glass forms when magma (molten rock material) is quenched—i.e., cooled so rapidly that the constituent atoms do not have time to arrange themselves into the regular arrays characteristic of minerals. Natural glass is the major constituent of a few volcanic rocks—e.g., obsidian. Macerals are macerated bits of organic matter, primarily plant materials; one or more of the macerals are the chief original constituents of all the diverse coals and several other organic-rich rocks such as oil shales.

In the classification of igneous rocks of the International Union of Geological Sciences (IUGS), the feldspars are treated as two groups: the alkali feldspars and the plagioclase feldspars. The alkali feldspars include orthoclase, microcline, sanidine, anorthoclase, and the two-phase intermixtures called perthite. The plagioclase feldspars include members of the albite-anorthite solid-solution series. Strictly speaking, however, albite is an alkali feldspar as well as a plagioclase feldspar.

CHEMICAL COMPOSITION

All the rock-forming feldspars are aluminosilicate minerals with the general formula AT_4O_8 in which A = potassium, sodium, or calcium (Ca); and T = silicon (Si) and aluminum (Al), with a Si:Al ratio ranging from 3:1 to 1:1. Microcline and orthoclase are potassium feldspars ($KAlSi_3O_8$), usually designated Or in discussions involving their end-member composition. Albite ($NaAlSi_3O_8$—usually designated Ab) and anorthite ($CaAl_2Si_2O_8$—An) are end-members of the plagioclase series. Sanidine, anorthoclase, and the perthites are alkali feldspars whose chemical compositions lie between Or and Ab.

As is apparent from the preceding statements, solid solution plays an important role in the rock-making feldspars. (Members of solid-solution series are single crystalline phases whose chemical compositions are inter-mediate to those of two or more end-members.) The alkali (Or-Ab) series exhibits complete solid solution at high temperatures but only incomplete solid solution at low temperatures; substitution of potassium for sodium is involved. The plagioclase (Ab-An) series exhibits essentially complete solid solution at both high and low temperatures; coupled substitution of sodium and silicon by calcium and aluminum occurs. The An-Or system has only limited solid-solution tendencies.

The most obvious differences between the high- and low-temperature diagrams are along the alkali-feldspar (Or-Ab) join (the boundary line between the phases). As indicated, sanidine and anorthoclase are high-temperature alkali feldspars, and perthite is their low-temperature ana-logue. Sanidine is a single-phase alkali feldspar; although frequently described chemically by the formula (K, Na) $AlSi_3O_8$, most analyzed specimens of sanidine range between Or_{50} and Or_{80}. (This designation is used to specify the fractions of the constituents. For example, Or_{80} indi-cates that the mineral is composed of 80 percent $KAlSi_3O_8$ and 20 [i.e., 100 - 80] percent $NaAlSi_3O_8$.) Anorthoclase is a variously used name that is most often applied to apparently homogeneous alkali feldspar masses, at least some of which consist of submicroscopic lamellae (layers) of albite and orthoclase; their bulk compositions typically range between Or_{25} and Or_{60}. Perthite consists of intimate intermixtures of a potassium feldspar—either microcline or orthoclase— and a sodium-rich plagioclase that occurs as microscopic to macroscopic masses within the potassium feldspar host.

Many perthites are formed when high-temperature potassium-sodium feldspars of appropriate compositions are cooled in such a manner that the original solid-solution phase exsolves (i.e., unmixes, so that a homogeneous mineral separates into two or more different minerals) to form intermixtures — sometimes termed intergrowths — of two phases.

Some perthites, however, appear to have been formed as a result of partial replacement of original potassium feldspars by sodium-bearing fluids. In any case, perthite is the name properly applied to intimate mixtures in which the potassium feldspar component predominates over the plagioclase constituent, whereas antiperthite is the name given to intimate mixtures in which the plagioclase constituent is predominant. Perthites are common, whereas antiperthites are relatively rare.

The plagioclase series is essentially continuous at both high and low temperatures. The names of members of the series designate relative proportions of the end-members. Although plagioclase grains in some rocks are essentially homogeneous, those in many rocks are zoned—i.e., different parts of individual grains have different Ab and An contents. One explanation for zoning in plagioclases formed from magmas can be implied from information known about the Ab-An system. Upon cooling, the first crystals that form from a melt with the composition X (= An_{50}) will have the composition Y (approximately An_{83}). With further cooling, in some cases the first and subsequently formed crystals will react continuously with the remaining liquid, thereby maintaining equilibrium; when the liquid becomes totally crystallized, the system will consist of homogeneous plagioclase crystals. In cases in which such equilibrium is not maintained during cooling, the early and subsequently formed feldspars have different An contents. For example, zoned crystals may form with differing An contents arranged one on top of another so that their margins are relatively sodium-rich as compared to their earlier-formed, more calcium-rich cores. The resulting zoning may be gradational or well-defined or may assume some combination of these characteristics.

Many elements other than those required for the Or, Ab, and An end-member compositions have been recorded in analyses of feldspars. Those that have been recorded to occur as substitutions within the feldspar structures include lithium (Li), rubidium (Rb), cesium (Cs), magnesium (Mg), strontium (Sr), barium (Ba), yttrium (Y), ferrous iron (Fe^{2+}), thallium (Tl), lead (Pb), lanthanum (La) and other rare earth elements, and ammonium (NH_4) in the A position; and titanium (Ti), ferric (Fe^{3+}) and ferrous (Fe^{2+}) iron, boron (B), gallium (Ga), germanium (Ge), and phosphorus (P) in the T position. Of these, substitution of some barium for potassium and some titanium or ferric iron or both for aluminum are especially common in alkali feldspars. Several other elements also have been recorded as traces in feldspar analyses; it seems very likely, however, that some of these elements may reside in impurities— i.e., within unrecognized microscopic or submicroscopic inclusions of other minerals.

CRYSTAL STRUCTURE

Sanidine and orthoclase are monoclinic or nearly so; the plagioclase feldspars are triclinic. All, however, have the same fundamental structure: it consists of a continuous, negatively charged, three-dimensional framework that is made up of corner-sharing SiO_4 and AlO_4 tetrahedrons (each tetrahedron consists of a central silicon or aluminum atom bonded to four oxygen atoms) and positively charged cations (e.g., the potassium, sodium, and/or calcium) that occupy relatively large interstices within the framework. Although the framework is sufficiently elastic to adjust itself to the different sizes of the *A* cations, the relatively large potassium cations give structures that have a monoclinic or only slightly off-monoclinic symmetry, whereas the smaller sodium and calcium cations lead to distorted structures that have triclinic symmetry.

One aspect of the feldspar—especially the potassium feldspar—structures that is of particular interest is termed ordering. This phenomenon is indicative of the conditions under which the feldspar was formed and its subsequent thermal history. Ordering in feldspars is based on the distributional pattern of silicon and aluminum within the different tetrahedrons. It can be characterized as follows: silicon and aluminum have a random distribution within the tetrahedrons of sanidine, an arrangement termed disordered; they have a regular distribution within the constituent tetrahedrons of microcline, an arrangement

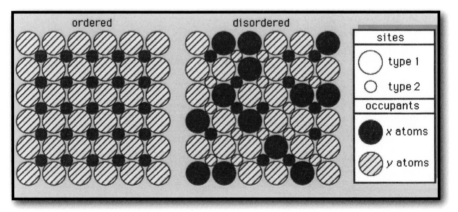

Schematic diagram showing ordered (left) and disordered (right) arrays within a structure having two kinds of sites (type 1 and type 2) and two types of occupants (x atoms and y atoms). In the ordered structure all x atoms are distributed uniformly in the spaces between the y atoms, whereas in the disordered structure no regular arrangement obtains. Copyright Encyclopædia Britannica, Inc.; rendering for this edition by Rosen Educational Services

termed ordered; and they are distributed within the tetrahedrons of orthoclase in a manner usually characterized as only partly ordered. The disordered structure of sanidine reflects formation at high temperatures followed by rapid cooling; the high degree of ordering of microcline reflects either growth at low temperatures or very slow cooling from higher temperatures; the partial ordering of orthoclase indicates either formation at intermediate temperatures or formation at high temperatures followed by fairly slow cooling. With regard to this phenomenon, it is also noteworthy that all plagioclase feldspars are more nearly ordered than their associated potassium feldspars regardless of the temperatures that prevailed when they were formed.

Crystals of all the common rock-forming feldspars tend to look alike; megascopic examination of crystal form typically cannot be used to distinguish between feldspars. The angle between the face that intersects the *b* axis

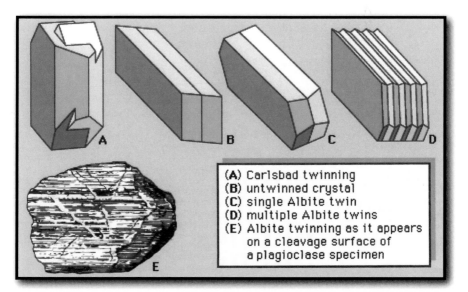

(A) Carlsbad twinning
(B) untwinned crystal
(C) single Albite twin
(D) multiple Albite twins
(E) Albite twinning as it appears on a cleavage surface of a plagioclase specimen

Twinning in feldspars. Copyright Encyclopædia Britannica, Inc.; rendering for this edition by Rosen Educational Services

and is parallel to *a* and *c* and the face that intersects the *c* axis and is parallel to *a* and *b* is 90° for the monoclinic feldspars and ranges from about 86° to roughly 89°30′ for the triclinic feldspars; the deviations from 90° are not readily discernible with the naked eye. In any case, feldspar crystals are relatively rare; almost all occur in miarolitic cavities, in pegmatite masses, or as phenocrysts within porphyries. (A porphyry is an igneous rock containing conspicuous crystals, called phenocrysts, surrounded by a matrix of finer-grained minerals or glass or both.) In most rocks, both alkali and plagioclase feldspars occur as irregularly shaped grains with only a few or no crystal faces. This general absence of crystal faces reflects the fact that crystallization of these feldspars was interfered with by previously formed minerals within the same mass.

ALKALI FELDSPARS

Alkali feldspars are common silicate minerals that often occur as variously coloured, glassy crystals. They are used in the manufacture of glass and ceramics; transparent, highly coloured, or iridescent varieties are sometimes used as gemstones. The alkali feldspars are primarily important as constituents of rocks; they are very widespread and abundant in alkali and acidic igneous rocks (particularly syenites, granites, and granodiorites), in pegmatites, and in gneisses. The alkali feldspars may be regarded as mixtures of sodium aluminosilicate ($NaAlSi_3O_8$) and potassium aluminosilicate ($KAlSi_3O_8$). Both the sodium and potassium aluminosilicates have several distinct forms, each form with a different structure. The form stable at high temperatures is sanidine (a sodium aluminosilicate), which has a random distribution of aluminum and silicon atoms in its crystal structure. Low-temperature forms include orthoclase, microcline, and adularia (all potassium aluminosilicates); these have an ordered arrangement of such atoms. If specimens of the high-temperature varieties are rapidly cooled, the random distribution is preserved. In the Earth's crust the alkali feldspars display a range of ordering from the fully random distribution of sanidine and orthoclase to the fully ordered distribution of microcline.

Both crystals and irregularly shaped grains of feldspars are commonly twinned. Some individual grains are twinned in two or more ways. Carlsbad twinning occurs in both monoclinic and triclinic feldspars; albite twinning occurs only in triclinic feldspars. Albite twinning, which is typically polysynthetic (i.e., multiple or repeated), can be observed as a set of parallel lines on certain crystal or cleavage surfaces of many plagioclase feldspars.

PHYSICAL PROPERTIES

It is important to be able to distinguish feldspar group minerals from other rock-forming minerals and from one another because their presence (versus absence), along with their relative quantities, serves as the basis for classifying and naming many rocks, especially those of igneous origin. In the laboratory, it is relatively easy to identify the feldspars by determining their chemical compositions, their structures, or their optical properties. In some cases, staining techniques are employed. Fortunately, most feldspar grains can also be identified rather easily on the basis of macroscopic examination in the field, using properties such as those described below.

COMMON PROPERTIES OF THE GROUP

As might be suspected on the basis of their similar chemical compositions and structures, all of the rock-forming feldspars have several similar properties. As indicated by the fact that they lack inherent colour, feldspars can be colourless, white, or nearly any colour if impure. In general, however, orthoclase and microcline have a reddish tinge that ranges from a pale, fleshlike pink to brick-red, whereas typical rock-forming plagioclases are white to dark gray. As a group, feldspars range from transparent to nearly opaque, have nonmetallic lustres—typically vitreous to subvitreous on fractures and pearly or porcelaneous on cleavage surfaces, exhibit two cleavages—one perfect, the other good—at or near 90° to each other, and have a Mohs hardness of approximately 6.

The presence of two cleavages at or near 90° distinguishes the feldspars from all other common rock-forming minerals except halite and the pyroxenes. The hardness (2½) and the salty taste of halite make that distinction clear. The gray to black streak of the common rock-forming pyroxenes, which contrasts markedly with the white or slightly tinted hues of the streaks of the feldspars—including those that are dark-coloured—affords a simple way to distinguish between these minerals, even those that are similar in appearance. (Streak is the colour of a mineral's powder, which can be produced readily by pounding or scratching the mineral with a geologic pick or hammer.)

IDENTIFICATION OF SPECIFIC FELDSPARS

Alkali feldspars can often be distinguished from plagioclase feldspars because most grains of the latter exhibit albite twinning, which is manifested by parallel lines on certain cleavage surfaces, whereas grains of alkali feldspars do not. This criterion is not, however, absolute; some plagioclase feldspars are not polysynthetically twinned. Furthermore, upon only cursory examination some perthitic textures may be mistaken for polysynthetic twinning. Fortunately, this resemblance is seldom confusing once one has thoroughly examined several examples of both features. The two features differ rather markedly: the traces of the polysynthetic twinning are straight, whereas the perthitic textures that are most likely to be mistaken for polysynthetic twinning have an interdigitated appearance.

Another property that is sometimes used to distinguish between alkali and plagioclase feldspars is their different specific gravity values. The ideal value for the potassium-rich alkali feldspars is 2.56, which is less than the lowest value for the plagioclases (namely, 2.62 for albite).

Sanidine is usually distinguished rather easily from the other alkali feldspars because it typically appears glassy— i.e., it tends to be colourless, and much of it is transparent. Microcline and orthoclase, by contrast, are characteristically white, light gray, or flesh- to salmon-coloured and subtranslucent. Except for its green variety, usually called amazonstone or amazonite, microcline can seldom be distinguished from orthoclase by macroscopic means. In the past, much microcline was misidentified as orthoclase because of the incorrect assumption that all microcline is green. Today, prudent geologists identify potassium feldspars other than sanidine simply as alkali, or in some cases potassium, feldspars when describing rocks on the basis of macroscopic examination. That is to say, they do not make a distinction between microcline and orthoclase until they have proved their identity by determining, for example, their optical properties. Upon macroscopic examination, an orthoclase is also generally identified merely as an alkali feldspar except by those who are acquainted with the rocks known to contain anorthoclase.

The rock-forming plagioclases can seldom be identified as to species by macroscopic means. Nevertheless, some rules of thumb can be employed: White or off-white plagioclase feldspars that exhibit a bluish iridescence (the so-called peristerites) have overall albite compositions, even though they are submicroscopic intergrowths of 70 percent An_2 and 30 percent An_{25}; and dark-coloured plagioclases that exhibit iridescence of such hues as blue, green, yellow, or orange are labradorites. In addition, the identities of associated minerals tend to indicate the approximate An-Ab contents of the plagioclase feldspars—for example, biotite most commonly accompanies albite or oligoclase; hornblende commonly occurs with andesine; and the pyroxenes, augite and/or hypersthene, typically accompany labradorite or bytownite. Additional characteristics for two of the feldspars are as follows: Microcline commonly exhibits "grid twinning." This combination of two kinds of twinning, although best seen by means of a microscope equipped to use doubly polarized light, is sometimes discernible macroscopically. (Polarized refers to light that vibrates in a single plane.) Plagioclase feldspars that constitute lamellar masses in complex pegmatites are albite; this variety is often referred to by the name cleavelandite.

Origin and Occurrence

Feldspars occur in all classes of rocks. They are widely distributed in igneous rocks, which indicates that they have formed by crystallization from magma. Physical weathering of feldspar-bearing rocks may result in sediments and sedimentary rocks that contain feldspars; however, this is a rare occurrence because in most environments the feldspars tend to be altered to other substances, such as clay minerals. They also may be found in many metamorphic rocks formed from precursor rocks that contained feldspars and/or the chemical elements required for their formation. In addition, feldspars occur in veins and pegmatites, in which they were apparently deposited by fluids, and within sediments and soils, in which they were probably deposited by groundwater solutions.

Uses

Feldspars are used widely in the glass and ceramics industries. Alkali feldspars are more commonly used commercially than plagioclase feldspars. Albite, or soda spar as it is known commercially, is used in ceramics. The feldspar-rich rocks larvikite and a few anorthosites are employed as both interior and exterior facing slabs.

In addition, several feldspars are used as gemstones. For example, varieties that show opalescence are sold as moonstone. Spectrolite is a trade name for labradorite with strong colour flashes. Sunstone (oligoclase or ortho-clase) is typically yellow to orange to brown with a golden sheen; this effect appears to be due to reflections from inclusions of red hematite. Amazonite, a green variety of microcline, is used as an ornamental material.

Sanidine occurs as phenocrysts (large noticeable crystals) in extrusive felsic igneous rocks such as rhyolite and trachyte. It indicates that the rocks cooled quickly after their eruption. Sanidine is also diagnostic of high-temperature contact metamorphism as an indicator of sanidinite hornfels or facies.

Orthoclase is a primary constituent of intrusive felsic igneous rocks such as granite, granodiorite, and syenites. It may also occur in some metamorphic pelitic schists and gneisses. Microcline, also found in granitic rocks and pegmatites, is present in sedimentary rocks such as sandstones and conglomerates. It can also occur in meta-morphic rocks.

Albite is found commonly in granites, syenites, rhyo-lites, and trachytes. Albite is common in pegmatites and may replace earlier formed microcline as cleavelandite. It is also common in low-grade metamorphic rocks ranging from zeolite to greenschist facies.

Oligoclase is characteristic of granodiorites and mon-zonites. It may also have a sparkle owing to inclusions of hematite, in which case it is called sunstone. Oligoclase is found in metamorphic rocks formed under moderate temperature conditions such as amphibolite facies.

Certain feldspars are somewhat less common. Anorthite is found only in gabbros, though it is common in certain high-grade metamorphic rocks such as granulite facies. Many metamorphosed limestones also contain anorthite. Bytownite is also only found in gabbros, whereas labradorite is found in gabbros, basalts, and anorthosites. Labradorite is often iridescent. This quality makes it desirable for interior and exterior building slabs. In contrast, andesine is rare except in andesites and diorites.

FELDSPATHOIDS

Feldspathoids make up a group of alkali aluminosilicate minerals similar to the feldspars in chemical composition but either having a lower silica-alkali ratio or containing chloride, sulfide, sulfate, or carbonate. They are considered to be the specific minerals of igneous rocks usually termed alkalic, which is the designation applied to igneous rocks whose alkali content (i.e., amount of sodium [Na] and/or potassium [K]) exceeds the amount required by the available silica to form one or more feldspars plus or minus mica. Minerals of the feldspathoid group whose silica contents are less than those of their feldspar analogues include nephelin, leucite, sodalite, and cancrinite.

CHEMICAL COMPOSITION AND CRYSTAL STRUCTURE

The feldspathoid group minerals are sodium, potassium, and calcium aluminosilicates, many of which resemble the feldspars in appearance. Like the feldspars, they have framework structures that consist of silica and alumina tetrahedrons. Unlike the feldspars, however, the arrangements of the tetrahedrons differ from species to species, and the interstices may contain water and/

or other simple or complex anions such as chlorine (Cl), carbonate (CO^{2-}_3), or sulfate (SO^{2-}_4), as well as sodium, potassium, and calcium. Consequently, different feldspathoids have somewhat different structures: some are isometric, others are hexagonal, and still others are tetragonal.

PHYSICAL PROPERTIES

The physical properties of the various feldspathoids differ from those of the feldspars and from one another. Properties of nepheline, leucite, sodalite, and cancrinite are summarized below.

Nepheline (hardness [H] 5½–6, specific gravity [G] 2.56–2.67) typically occurs as irregularly shaped, white, gray, or brownish, greasy- to waxy-appearing grains that may exhibit one rather poor cleavage. Simple hexagonal prisms occur as phenocrysts in some volcanic porphyries. On weathered exposures, nepheline grains are commonly weathered more than their associated minerals, thus leaving, for example, feldspar grains of nepheline syenites in relief. A simple test often used to help identify nepheline is based on the fact that it, as well as sodalite and cancrinite, reacts with acids to form gelatinous silica.

Leucite (H 5½–6, G 2.47–2.50) commonly occurs as white to light gray trapezohedrons. The crystal form represents the formation of leucite as an isometric mineral. However, the mineral can be shown to be tetragonal by methods such as optical studies. The crystal form of leucite indicates the conditions under which it was crystallized, and the tetragonal structure shows that it has undergone post-crystallization inversion.

Sodalite (H 5½–6, G 2.27–2.50) consists of a group of minerals. Different species of this group may exhibit different colours. The sodalite of most rocks occurs as irregularly shaped, translucent, bluish-coloured grains with a vitreous to greasy lustre.

Cancrinite (H 5–6, G 2.32–2.51) typically occurs as yellowish grains, some of which exhibit one perfect cleavage, that are closely associated with one or more of the other feldspathoids, most commonly nepheline.

ORIGIN AND OCCURRENCE

The feldspathoids are relatively rare. As noted previously, they are considered here primarily because they are the specific minerals used in naming alkalic igneous rocks. In this role, the feldspathoids, along with minerals of the melilite group, are referred to as foids in the IUGS classification of igneous rocks. Feldspathoids may occur along with feldspars in igneous rocks. They do not occur in igneous rocks containing original free silica—i.e., in rocks that contain quartz of the same generation. They are, in fact, incompatible with consanguineous quartz (that derived from the same parent magma), as is quite apparent from the following equations:

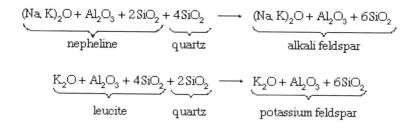

As can be seen from these equations, a feldspar would form in lieu of its feldspathoid chemical analogue in any silica-saturated magma.

Nepheline is the most common feldspathoid; it is a major constituent of many alkalic igneous rocks such as nepheline syenites. Feldspathoids also occur in a few other kinds of rocks—e.g., contact-metamorphic skarns.

USES

Nepheline is sometimes used as a source of soda, silica, and alumina in the manufacture of glass and ceramics. Leucite was formerly used in Italy for fertilizer. Sodalite, once treasured as the basic ingredient of ultramarine pigment, is still used as a gemstone and as the desired constituent of many of the blue rocks used as facing stones.

GARNETS

Garnets, favoured by lapidaries since ancient times and used widely as an abrasive, occur in rocks of each of the major classes. In most rocks, however, garnets occur in only minor amounts—i.e., they are accessory minerals. Nevertheless, as a consequence of their distinctive appearances, they are frequently recognized in hand specimens and become part of the name of the rock in which they are contained—e.g., garnet mica schist. Garnets may be colourless, black, and many shades of red and green.

CHEMICAL COMPOSITION

Garnets comprise a group of silicates with the general formula $A_3B_2(SiO_4)_3$, in which A = Ca, Fe^{2+}, Mg, Mn^{2+}; B = Al, Cr, Fe^{3+}, Mn^{3+}, Si, Ti, V, Zr; and Si may be replaced partly by Al, Ti, and/or Fe^{3+}. In addition, many analyses indicate the presence of trace to minor amounts of Na, beryllium (Be), Sr, scandium (Sc), Y, La, hafnium (Hf), niobium (Nb), molybdenum (Mo), cobalt (Co), nickel (Ni), copper (Cu), silver (Ag), Zn, cadmium (Cd), B, Ga, indium (In), Ge, tin (Sn), P, arsenic (As), F, and rare earth elements. Grossular is often recorded as having a composition containing water, but the true substitution seems to involve 4 H^+ for Si^{4+}; and a complete series appears to exist between grossular $[Ca_3Al_2(SiO_4)_3]$ and hydrogrossular $[Ca_3Al_2(SiO_4)_{3-x}(H_4O_4)x]$. Other hydrogarnets have been reported—e.g., hydroandradite and hydrospessartine; the general formula for hydrogarnets would be $A_3B_2(SiO_4)_{3-x}(H_4O_4)x$, and the general formula for an end-member hydrogarnet would be $A_3B_2(H_4O_4)_3$.

Nearly all natural garnets exhibit extensive substitution; solid-solution series—some complete, others only partial—exist between several pairs of the group. In practice, the name of the end-member that makes up the largest percentage of any given specimen is usually applied—e.g., a garnet with the composition $Al_{45}Py_{25}Sp_{15}Gr_9An_6$ would be called almandine.

Analyses of natural specimens suggest that the following solid-solution series exist: in the pyralspite subgroup, a complete series between almandine and both pyrope and spessartine; in the ugrandite subgroup, a continuous series between grossular and both andradite and uvarovite; less than a complete series between any member of the pyralspite subgroup and any member of the ugrandite subgroup; and an additional series between pyrope and andradite and one or more of the less common garnets (e.g., pyrope with knorringite $[Mg_3Cr_2(SiO_4)_3]$ and andradite with schorlomite $[Ca_3Ti_2(Fe_2, Si)O_{12}]$).

A few well-studied garnets from metamorphic rocks have been shown to be chemically zoned with layers of differing compositions. Most of the differences thus far described appear to reflect, for the most part, differences in occupants of the A structural positions.

CRYSTAL STRUCTURE

Garnets consist of groups of independent, distorted SiO_4 tetrahedrons, each of which is linked, by sharing corners, to distorted BO_6 (e.g., aluminum- and/or iron-centred) octahedrons, thus forming a three-dimensional framework. The interstices are occupied by A divalent metal ions (e.g., Ca, Fe^{2+}, Mg, and Mn), so that each one is surrounded by eight oxygen atoms that are at the corners of a distorted cube. Therefore, each oxygen is coordinated by two A, one B, and one silicon cation. The configuration of the array is such that garnets are isometric (cubic).

Garnets commonly occur as well-developed crystals. The typical forms of the crystals have 12 or 24 sides

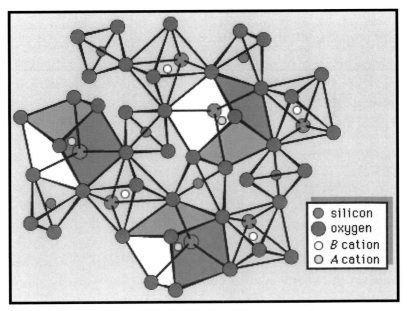

The structure of garnet. This schematic diagram of part of the garnet structure shows the distorted silicon-oxygen tetrahedrons and BO_6 octahedrons and the distorted cubes with central A cations. Copyright Encyclopædia Britannica, Inc.; rendering for this edition by Rosen Educational Services

Dodecahedron, a common crystal form of garnet. Miller Museum of Geology and Mineralogy, Queen's University at Kingston, Ont., Can.

and are called dodecahedrons and trapezohedrons, respectively, or they are combinations of such forms. All tend to be nearly equant. A few studies have led to the suggestion that these crystal habits can be correlated with chemical composition—i.e., that dodecahedrons are most likely to be grossular-rich; that trapezohedrons tend to be pyrope-, almandine-, or spessartine-rich; and that combinations are generally andradite-rich. In any case, many garnets have individual faces that are not well developed, and thus the crystals are roughly spherical. Garnet also occurs in fine to coarse granular masses.

Trapezohedron, a common crystal form of garnet. © Wendell E. Wilson

PHYSICAL PROPERTIES

The diverse garnets can be distinguished from other common rock-forming minerals rather easily since they do not physically resemble any of them. All garnets have vitreous to resinous lustres. Most are translucent, although they may range from transparent to nearly opaque. Garnets lack cleavage but tend to be brittle. They have Mohs hardness values of 6½ to 7½; their specific gravities, which vary with composition, range from about 3.58 (pyrope) to 4.32 (almandine). Their habits, also noteworthy, have already been described.

A garnet's predominant end-member constituent can only be defined absolutely by, for example, chemical analysis or differential thermal analysis (DTA), a method

Dodecahedron-trapezohedron combination, a common crystal form of garnet. Miller Museum of Geology and Mineralogy, Queen's University at Kingston, Ont., Can.

based on the examination of the chemical and physical changes resulting from the application of heat to a mineral. Nonetheless, in many rocks a garnet can be named tentatively as to its probable composition after only macroscopic examination if its colour is considered in conjunction with the identity of its associated minerals and geologic occurrence. This is true despite the fact that even individual garnet species may assume several different colours: almandine's colour range is deep red to dark brownish red; pyrope may be pink to purplish or deep red to nearly black; spessartine may be brownish orange, burgundy, or reddish brown; grossular may be nearly colourless, white, pale green, yellow, orange, pink, yellowish brown, or brownish red; and andradite may be honey yellow or greenish yellow, brown, red, or nearly black.

The availability of garnets of several colours, along with properties that make them rather durable and relatively easily worked, is responsible for their widespread use as gemstones.

ORIGIN AND OCCURENCE

The rock-forming garnets are most common in metamorphic rocks. A few occur in igneous rocks, especially granites and granitic pegmatites. Garnets derived from such rocks occur sporadically in clastic sediments and sedimentary rocks.

Garnets commonly contain many inclusions—i.e., fragments of other rocks and minerals. Pinwheel garnet and snowball garnet are designations sometimes applied to those garnets whose inclusions appear to have been rotated. These garnets occur sporadically in foliated metamorphic rocks. Although their presence in diverse rocks has been interpreted variously, present-day consensus appears to be that they represent rotation during

COMMON OCCURRENCES OF ROCK-FORMING GARNETS	
almandine	metamorphic rocks—especially mica schists, amphibolites, and granulites; granites, aplites, and granitic pegmatites
spessartine	granitic pegmatites; silica-rich skarns; metamorphosed manganese-bearing rocks
grossular	impure calcite and dolomite marbles, especially those in contact metamorphic zones; amphibolites; basic igneous rocks
andradite	large masses associated with tactites, some of which constitute ore deposits, in calcareous rocks of contact metasomatic origin
pyrope	ultramafic rocks such as pyroxenites and peridotites and serpentinites derived from them; eclogites (high-pressure metamorphic rocks)

growth under conditions of dynamic metamorphism that involved differential pressures.

Iron-rich garnets are frequently weathered to rusty masses that consist largely of limonite, and spessartine has weathered to masses of manganese oxide ores under tropical conditions (e.g., in India and Brazil). Garnets as a group, however, are relatively resistant to most weathering processes. Consequently, they occur in some sandy sediments and sandstones. Indeed, the red-coloured grains that are commonly found along some beaches are garnets.

USES

The hardness, lack of cleavage, and tendency to break into irregular grains have led to the recovery, crushing, and size-sorting of garnet for use in abrasives such as sandpaper. In addition, as previously mentioned, garnets are used as gemstones. Transparent red and reddish purple pyrope from the Middle East and from the former Czechoslovakia have been utilized in this capacity for centuries. Green andradite is cut, polished, and marketed as the highly prized stone demantoid. In addition, rhodolite is a pale rose-red garnet made up of two parts pyrope and one part almandine. Essonite, also called hessonite (cinnamon garnet), is a gem form of grossular. Synthetic garnets with certain compositions, many of which do not have natural representatives, serve important functions because they are ferrimagnetic or antiferromagnetic or because they possess properties particularly suitable for use in lasers.

JADE

Jade refers to either of two tough, compact, typically green gemstones that take a high polish. Jadeite and nephrite have been carved into jewelry, ornaments, small sculptures, and utilitarian objects from earliest recorded times. The more highly prized of the two jadestones is jadeite.

Jadeite and nephrite differ in both chemical composition and crystalline structure. Jadeite is a silicate of sodium and aluminum and is classed as a pyroxene. Nephrite is a silicate of calcium and magnesium belonging to the amphibole group of minerals and is properly regarded as tremolite. In both types, the microscopic crystals are tightly interlocked to form a compact aggregate. Both jadestone types may be white or colourless, but colours such as red, green, violet, and gray may occur owing to the presence of iron, chromium, or manganese impurities, respectively. The most highly prized variety is jadeite of an emerald-green hue.

The two different types of jade, when worked and polished, can usually be distinguished by their appearance alone. The fine lustre of polished nephrite is oily rather than vitreous (glassy), while that of jadeite is the reverse.

Uncut (left) *and cut jadeite.* Runk/Schoenberger— Grant Heilman

Some colours are also peculiar to one stone or the other; for example, the popular apple- and emerald-green jewelry jades are invariably jadeite. There are also wide variations of translucency in both stones. The area around the city of Mogaung in northern Myanmar (Burma) has long been the main source of gem-quality jadeite. Occurrences of nephrite are more numerous and geographically more widespread.

Over the course of history, jade has been successively cut and shaped with sandstone, slate, and quartz sand (as an abrasive); by tools made of bronze; by tools of iron, using manually operated lathes; and finally, beginning in the 19th century, by machine-powered lathes, steel saws, and diamond-pointed drills. Carborundum and diamond dust have replaced crushed garnets and corundum (emery) as abrasives.

Both jadestones were worked into implements by Neolithic peoples in many parts of the world. The best-known finds are from the lake dwellings of Switzerland, western France, Central America, Mexico, and China. Jade is hard, tough, and heavy, and it takes and keeps a good edge, while its fine colours and warm polish must have greatly appealed to Neolithic craftsmen. When the stone-based Neolithic cultures were succeeded by ones using bronze and iron, however, jade gradually lost its industrial value and fell from favour as a gemstone in all but a few regions.

Jade and jade carving are associated preeminently with China, since in no other region of the world has this obdurate material been worked with such skill in such a long and unbroken tradition. For millennia the jade carved by the Chinese consisted of nephrite from the region of Ho-t'ien (Khotan) and Yarkand in what is now Sinkiang. Jadeite does not appear to have been worked by them until the 18th century CE, when large quantities of that jadestone began entering the country from Myanmar via Yunnan province.

As early as the Neolithic period the Chinese were carving jade into tools and simple cult objects in the form of flat disks with circular orifices at their centre. During the Shang dynasty (18th–12th century BCE), they began making small ornamental plaques with decorative designs of animals incised on them in low relief. From the later part of the Chou dynasty (about 500 BCE), the intro-duction of iron tools made more accomplished carvings possible, and jade began to be made into a wide variety of utilitarian and luxury objects, such as belt hooks and ornaments, sword and scabbard accoutrements, hollow vessels, and, most importantly, sculpture in the round. The craft of jade carving in China attained maturity toward the close of the Chou dynasty in 255 BCE, with designs of unsurpassed excellence and beauty, and the tradition continued for the next 2,000 years.

The reign (1735–96) of the great Ch'ing-dynasty emperor Ch'ien-lung was a particularly important period for jade carving. Under his patronage and in those times of exceptional prosperity and luxury, thousands of carved jades were added to the imperial collections, and the mate-rial was applied to countless new decorative, ceremonial, and religious uses in the Forbidden City at Peking and in the homes of nobles and officials. Greater quantities of jade were entering China than ever before, and emerald-green jadeite from Myanmar became as highly esteemed as the finest nephrite from Sinkiang. Fabulous prices were paid for high-quality carvings of people, animals, and plants; bottles, urns, vases, and other vessels; and all sorts of personal accessories.

The Aztecs, Mayas, and other pre-Columbian Indian peoples of Mexico and Central America carved jadeite for use as ornaments, amulets, and badges of rank. Nearly all of these Mesoamerican jades are of various shades of green, with emerald green the most highly prized colour among the Aztecs; their jade carvings comprise plaques, figurines, small masks, pendants, and implements. The appreciation of jade died out in Mesoamerica after the Spanish conquest in the 16th century, however. The source for all Mesoamerican jade is the Motagua Valley in Guatemala.

Until the landing of Europeans there in the 18th century, the Maoris of New Zealand were entirely ignorant of metals, and the most highly prized of their industrial stones was nephrite, from which they made axes, knives, chisels, adzes, and the short swords, or *mere,* of their chiefs. These jade swords served not only as weapons but as symbols of authority and were usually worked from stone of specially fine colour or distinctive marking.

Several varieties of the mineral serpentine superficially resemble nephrite and are sometimes fraudulently sold as such, but they can be distinguished by their relative softness. Another deceptive practice is that of dyeing colourless pieces of jade green to simulate high-quality stone. The most successful imitations of jadeite are completely artificial and consist of a heavy lead glass that has been cleverly tinted to imitate jadeite's distinctive apple-green colour.

OLIVINES

Olivines make up a group of common magnesium, iron silicate minerals. They are an important rock-forming mineral group. Magnesium-rich olivines are abundant in low-silica mafic and ultramafic igneous rocks and are believed to be the most abundant constituent of the Earth's upper mantle. Olivine also occurs in high-temperature metamorphic rocks, lunar basalts, and some meteorites.

The name olivine derives from the unusual yellow-green to deep bottle-green colour of the magnesium-iron olivine series. Typically the name olivine is given to members of the forsterite-fayalite solid-solution series. In addition to these magnesium and ferrous iron end-members, the olivine group contains manganese (tephroite), calcium-manganese (glaucochroite), calcium-magnesium (monticellite), and calcium-iron (kirschsteinite) end-members. Gem-quality forsterite olivine is known as peridot. Because of its high melting point and resistance to chemical reagents, magnesium olivine is an important refractory material—i.e., it can be used in furnace linings and in kilns when other materials are subjected to heat and chemical processes.

CHEMICAL COMPOSITION

The composition of most olivines can be represented in the system Ca_2SiO_4-Mg_2SiO_4-Fe_2SiO_4. The most abundant olivines occur in the system from forsterite (Mg_2SiO_4) to fayalite (Fe_2SiO_4). Most of the naturally occurring olivines are intermediate in composition to these two end-members and have the general formula $(Mg, Fe)_2SiO_4$. Members of the series monticellite ($CaMgSiO_4$) to kirschsteinite ($CaFeSiO_4$) are rare. Minor elements such as aluminum, nickel, chromium, and boron can substitute in olivine.

The name forsterite is restricted to those species with no more than 10 percent iron substituting for magnesium; fayalite (from Fayal Island in the Azores, where it was believed to occur in a local volcanic rock but probably was obtained from slag brought to the island as ship's ballast) is restricted to species with no more than 10 percent magnesium substituting for iron. Compositions intermediate to these series end-members are identified by Fo_xFa_y, which is an expression of the molar percentage of each compound. For example, $Fo_{70}Fa_{30}$ denotes a composition of olivine that is 70 percent forsterite. The notation is shortened to Fo_{70}.

The continuity in the forsterite-fayalite series has been verified experimentally. At the magnesium-rich end of the solid-solution series, natural crystals may contain very small amounts of calcium, nickel, and chromium; the iron-rich members near the other end of the series may incorporate small amounts of manganese and calcium. Apart from ferrous iron, the crystalline structure of the olivines is also capable of accommodating relatively small amounts of ferric iron; dendrites (small branching crystals) of magnetite or chromite found oriented with respect to some crystallographic direction within such olivines may be attributed to exsolution. The presence of relatively large amounts of ferric oxide in the analyses of olivines, however, clearly indicates either an advanced state of oxidation or the mechanical inclusion of co-precipitating magnetite upon crystallization from the magma.

In addition to the forsterite-fayalite series, other complete solid-solution series exist among the various olivine minerals. Fayalite is soluble in all proportions with ash-gray tephroite (from Greek *tephros*, "ashen"), pure manganese silicate (Mn_2SiO_4); the intermediate in the series is knebelite ($FeMnSiO_4$). Tephroite and knebelite come from manganese and iron ore deposits, from metamorphosed manganese-rich sedimentary rocks, and from slags.

CRYSTAL STRUCTURE

All olivines crystallize in the orthorhombic crystal system. Olivine is classified as a nesosilicate which has isolated SiO_4 tetrahedrons bound to each other only by ionic bonds from interstitial cations. The structure of olivine can be viewed as a layered closest-packed oxygen network, with silicon

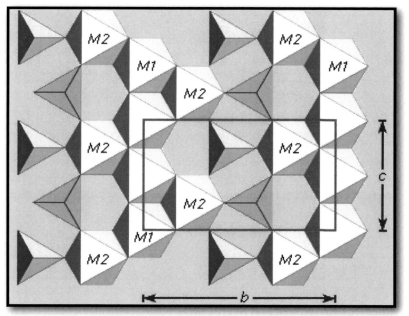

Portion of the idealized structure of olivine projected perpendicular to the a axis showing the positions of the M1 and M2 octahedral sites. Copyright Encyclopædia Britannica, Inc.; rendering for this edition by Rosen Educational Services

ions occupying some of the tetrahedral voids and the calcium, ferrous iron, and magnesium cations occupying some of the octahedral voids. The layers consist of octahedrons cross-linked by independent SiO_4 tetrahedrons. There are two symmetrically nonequivalent octahedral sites, *M1* and *M2*. In magnesium-iron olivines there is no *M1* or *M2* site preference for magnesium or ferric iron. However, in calcic olivines like monticellite, calcium preferentially enters the *M2* site and magnesium occupies the *M1* site.

PHYSICAL PROPERTIES

There are at least two cleavages—i.e., the tendency to split along preferred crystallographic directions (perpendicular to the *a* and *b* axes in this case)—both of which are better-developed in the iron-rich varieties. Forsterite contained in certain ultramafic rocks may show a banded structure when observed in thin sections with a polarizing microscope; in some dunites (a variety of rock consisting nearly entirely of olivine), for example, olivine is preferentially oriented so that the cleavage plane perpendicular to the b axis is parallel to the microscopic laminated structure of the rock. Individual grains of olivine within such rocks typically appear as oriented bands with angles of up to 10° between them. Such banding, which is undoubtedly the product of incipient mechanical deformation, also can be observed within the olivine nodules of some basalts.

To the unaided eye, pure forsterite appears colourless, but, as the content of ferrous oxide increases, specimens show yellow-green, dark green, and eventually brown to black tints. In thin sections under the microscope, however, even pure fayalite appears pale yellow. Pure tephroite is gray, and monticellite also appears gray or colourless.

Some variations of optical properties observed in natural olivine crystals probably result from small but varying replacements of magnesium and iron by calcium and manganese and of silicon by titanium, chromium, and ferric iron.

CRYSTAL HABIT AND FORM

The magnesium-iron olivines occur most commonly as compact or granular masses. Except for the well-shaped phenocrysts (single crystals) of such olivines found embedded in the fine-grained matrices (groundmass) of basalts, distinctly developed crystals are relatively rare. The phenocrysts in basalts are characterized by six- or eight-sided cross sections. With fayalite the morphology is often simple. Monticellite and tephroite commonly show prominent pyramidal faces. Twinning is rare. When twinning does occur, trillings (the intergrowth of three grains) may be produced, and, in monticellite, six-pointed star shapes are reported from the Highwood Mountains in Montana, U.S.

ORIGIN AND OCCURRENCE

Olivines appear in several different types of rocks. They are most prevalent in igneous rocks, but they also occur in metamorphic rocks, meteorites, and in certain ore and limestone deposits. Olivines are vulnerable to weatherings.

IGNEOUS ROCKS

Olivines are found most commonly in mafic and ultra-mafic igneous rocks such as peridotites, dunites, gabbros, and basalts. Forsteritic olivines, which have 88 to 92 percent forsterite, are the dominant phase of dunites and are common in peridotites. Gabbros and basalts typically contain forsteritic to intermediate-composition olivine ranging from 50 to 80 percent forsterite. Olivine is typically associated with calcic plagioclase, magnesium-rich pyroxenes, and iron-titanium oxides such as magnetite and ilmenite. This mineralogical association is diagnostic of the relatively high temperatures of crystallization of mafic rock types. Forsterite and protoenstatite crystallize together from about 1,550 °C to roughly 1,300 °C (about 2,820 to 2,370 °F) and are among the first minerals to crystallize from a mafic melt. Magnesium-rich olivine is unstable in a high-silica environment and is never found in equilibrium with quartz. The chemical reaction that precludes the stable coexistence of forsterite and quartz due to the formation of the orthopyroxene enstatite in the presence of excess silica is

$$Mg_2SiO_4 + SiO_2 \longrightarrow Mg_2Si_2O_6.$$
forsterite   quartz   enstatite

Fayalite (Fa), however, can coexist in equilibrium with quartz in iron-rich granites and rhyolites.

Olivines richer in iron than Fa_{50} are less common; they do occur in the iron-enriched layers of some intrusive rocks, however. Fayalite itself occurs in small amounts in some silicic volcanic rocks, both as a primary mineral and in the lithophysae and vugs (bubblelike hollows) of rhyolites and obsidians (volcanic glass). It also occurs in acidic plutonic rocks such as granites in association with iron-enriched amphiboles and pyroxenes.

METAMORPHIC ROCKS

Olivines also occur in metamorphic environments. Both forsterite and monticellite typically develop in the zones in which igneous intrusions make contact with dolomites. Forsterite tends to develop at lower temperatures than monticellite as the process of decarbonation in the contact zone progresses. Fayalitic olivines develop within metamorphosed iron-rich sediments. In the quaternary (i.e., four-component) system Fe_2O_3-FeO-SiO_2-H_2O, fayalite is associated with the minerals greenalite (iron-serpentine), minnesotaite (iron-talc), and grunerite (iron-amphibole) in various metamorphic stages. In chemically more complex environments, which, in addition to the above components, also involve lime (CaO) and alumina (Al_2O_3), fayalite may be associated with hedenbergite, orthopyroxene, grunerite, and almandine (iron-garnet).

METEORITES AND THE EARTH'S MANTLE

In meteorites, the olivine is usually a forsteritic variety containing only Fa_{15} to Fa_{30}. In the Nakhla (Egypt) meteorite (an achondrite meteorite), the olivine is more ferrous, however, containing as much as Fa_{65}. In the chondrites (stony meteorites), the olivine is commonly incorporated in the distinctive spheroidal bodies referred to as chondrules, which range up to 1 mm (0.04 inch) in diameter.

Because the rocks of the upper mantle directly below the Mohorovičić discontinuity (Moho) are believed to consist of peridotite and garnetiferous peridotite that contain olivines as their most abundant minerals, it is important to establish their behaviour when subjected to high pressures. Study of the olivine-like compound magnesium germanate, Mg_2GeO_4, showed that it has polymorphs that have both olivine and spinel structure. In the spinel structure, the oxygen atoms are arranged in cubic closest packing (in which the position of every third layer repeats that of the initial layer) instead of hexagonal closest packing (in which the position of every second layer repeats that of the initial layer) of the olivine structure. The spinel form of Mg_2GeO_4 was found to have a density exceeding that of the olivine form by 9 percent. In 1936 it was suggested that at high pressures Mg_2SiO_4 might also transform to a spinel structure; this suggestion was adopted in 1937 as a basis for explaining the so-called 20° discontinuity, an observed seismic discontinuity in the mantle at a depth of about 400 km (about 250 miles).

In 1966 it was shown that each of the three synthetic olivines—Fe_2SiO_4, Ni_2SiO_4, and CO_2SiO_4—could be transformed directly to a spinel structure at a temperature of 700° C (about 1,300 °F) and at pressures below 70 kilobars (1,000,000 pounds per square inch). These spinel structures were denser by approximately 10 percent than the corresponding olivine structures. In 1968 a series of synthetic magnesium and iron olivines was subjected to a range of pressures between 50 and 200 kilobars (725,000 and 2,900,000 pounds per square inch) at a temperature of 1,000 °C (about 1,830 °F). In the composition range Fe_2SiO_4 to $(Mg_{0.8}Fe_{0.2})_2SiO_4$, these olivines were transformed completely to their spinel polymorphs, which are isometric crystals, with an accompanying increase in density of 10 percent. In the composition range $(Mg_{0.8}Fe_{0.2})_2SiO_4$ to Mg_2SiO_4, however, the olivines were transformed to another orthorhombic structure (called β-orthosilicate) at a pressure of about 130 kilobars (about 1,900,000 pounds per square inch) and a temperature of 1,000 °C (about 1,830 °F). This β-phase polymorph, with a density only 8 percent greater than that of the corresponding olivine structure, is believed to be the stable phase in the field of its synthesis. The change in the crystalline structure of olivine to its spinel polymorph, accompanied by a change in the structure of magnesium-iron pyroxenes to a new garnetlike structure at depths of 350 to 450 km (about 220 to 280 miles) in the mantle, is believed to be responsible for the observed abrupt change in the velocity of seismic waves at these depths.

The spinel polymorph of olivine has been recorded in the Tenham (Queensland, Australia) chondrite as pseudomorphs after olivine. Portions of some large grains of olivine immediately adjacent to black, shock-generated veins are recognized as transforms to the spinel phase; the associated plagioclase feldspar was converted to maskelynite. The composition of the spinel phase in the meteorite has been analyzed by means of an electron probe and found to be $(Mg_{0.75}Fe_{0.25})_2SiO_4$; in thin sections it appears blue-gray to violet-blue. It has been named ringwoodite after Alfred E. Ringwood, an Australian earth scientist who synthesized spinel phases with compositions and properties close to those of the mineral found in the meteorite. More recently, ringwoodite also has been found in the Coorara (Western Australia) meteorite in association with a garnet phase. The β-phase polymorph has not yet been observed in shocked meteorites—i.e., those that have undergone impact shock—but it is highly probable that it, too, exists in relative abundance within the Earth's mantle.

OTHER OCCURRENCES

Knebelite olivines are restricted to iron-manganese ore deposits, to their associated skarn (lime-bearing silicate rocks) zones, and to metamorphosed manganiferous sediments. At Franklin, N.J., U.S., tephroite and glaucochroite occur in the same deposit as roepperite, a knebelite containing 10.7 percent by weight of zinc oxide (ZnO).

Monticellite occurs in some alkali peridotites and within limestones near their contact with peridotites. Pure kirschsteinite is known only from slags and has not yet been observed as part of a natural mineral assemblage. The most plausible natural environments for kirschsteinite are altered limestones; it is possible the mineral has remained unrecognized in such rocks because its optical properties (the chief means of identification) are similar to those of the much more common magnesium-iron olivines. A kirschsteinite containing 31 percent by weight of other olivines, particularly monticellite, has been reported from a nepheline-melilite in Nord-Kivu province, Congo (Kinshasa).

Glaucochroite, pure calcium and manganese silicate ($CaMnSiO_4$), is rare, reported only from a deposit in Franklin, N.J., where it occurs with tephroite. The limited availability of manganese in parent magmas is thought to account for the rarity of minerals intermediate in the solid-solution series between the calcium-rich olivines monticellite, glaucochroite, and kirschsteinite.

ALTERATION PRODUCTS AND WEATHERING

Olivines gelatinize in even weak acids and offer little resistance to attack by weathering agents and hot mineralizing (hydrothermal) solutions. The forsteritic olivines are altered principally through leaching, which results in the removal of magnesium and the addition of water and some iron. The chemical reactions are usually complex and involve hydration, oxidation, and carbonation. The fayalitic olivines are altered principally through oxidation and the removal of silica. The usual product of alteration is the mineral serpentine, which may occur as a pseudomorph (a form with the outward appearance of the original mineral but that has been completely replaced by another mineral). Serpentine, which is the most common alteration product of olivine in ultramafic rocks, often is accompanied by magnesite.

The mechanical weathering of olivine-rich rocks leads to the release of olivine particles that, in the absence of much chemical weathering, may accumulate to produce green or greenish black sands. Conspicuous examples of such sands occur on the beaches of the islands of Oahu and Hawaii, particularly at Diamond Head (Oahu) and South Point (Hawaii). Alluvial sands rich in olivine are also known from Navajo county of Arizona and from New Mexico in the United States; these sands provide the clear olivine (peridot) used in jewelry.

PYROXENES

Pyroxenes make up a group of important rock-forming silicate minerals of variable composition, among which calcium-, magnesium-, and iron-rich varieties predominate.

They are the most significant and abundant group of rock-forming ferromagnesian silicates. They are found in almost every variety of igneous rock and also occur in rocks of widely different compositions formed under conditions of regional and contact metamorphism. The name *pyroxene* is derived from the Greek pyro, meaning "fire," and xenos, meaning "stranger," and was given by Haüy to the greenish crystals found in many lavas which he considered to have been accidentally included there.

Pyroxenes crystallize in both the orthorhombic and monoclinic crystal systems. Typically pyroxenes occur as stubby prismatic crystals. They are chemically analogous to the amphiboles except that, as discussed above, hydroxyls are absent in the pyroxene structure. They are similar in colour, lustre, and hardness to the amphiboles but have slightly higher densities owing to the absence of hydroxyls. Pyroxenes have two distinctive planes of cleavage with intersecting angles of about 87° and 93°. Perpendicular to their cleavage planes, pyroxenes have nearly square cross sections, which, together with the cleavage directions, are diagnostic properties.

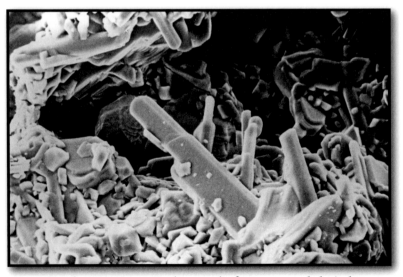

A scanning-electron-microscope photograph of pyroxene and plagioclase crystals (the long and the short crystals, respectively) that grew in a cavity in a fragment of Moon rock gathered during the Apollo 14 mission. NASA

CHEMICAL COMPOSITION

The chemical composition of minerals of the pyroxene group can be expressed by the general formula XYZ_2O_6, in which X= Na^+, Ca^{2+}, Mn^{2+}, Fe^{2+}, Mg^{2+}, Li^+; Y= Mn^{2+}, Fe^{2+}, Mg^{2+}, Fe^{3+}, Al^{3+}, Cr^{3+}, Ti^{4+}; and Z= Si^{4+}, Al^{3+}. The range of possible chemical substitutions in pyroxene is constrained by the sizes of the available sites in the structure and the charge of the substituting cations. The Xcation sites in general are larger than the Ycation sites. Extensive atomic substitution occurs between the ideal end-member compositions. Most pyroxenes have only limited substitution of aluminum for silicon in the Z(tetrahedral) site. When a substituting ion differs in charge, electrical neutrality is maintained by coupled substitutions. For example, the pair consisting of Na^+ and Al^{3+} substitutes for 2 Mg^{2+}. There are five major chemical subdivisions of pyroxenes.

The most common pyroxenes can be represented as part of the chemical system $CaSiO_3$ (wollastonite, a pyroxenoid), $MgSiO_3$ (enstatite), and $FeSiO_3$ (ferrosilite). Since no true pyroxenes exist with calcium contents greater than that of the diopside-hedenbergite join, the part of this system below this join is known as the pyroxene quadrilateral. Ferrous iron and magnesium substitute freely since they have similar ionic sizes and identical charges. Complete substitution exists between enstatite ($Mg_2Si_2O_6$) and ferrosilite ($Fe_2Si_2O_6$), and complete solid solution of iron for magnesium exists between diopside ($CaMgSi_2O_6$) and hedenbergite ($CaFeSi_2O_6$). Augite, subcalcic augite, and pigeonite lie within the interior of the pyroxene quadrilateral. Compositionally, augite is related to members of the diopside-hedenbergite series with limited substitution of Na^+ for Ca^{2+}, Al^{3+} for Mg^{2+} and Fe^{2+}, and Al^{3+} for Si^{4+} in the Z(tetrahedral) site. Augites with substantial aluminum or sodium cannot be strictly represented in the quadrilateral plane. Monoclinic pigeonite encompasses a field of magnesium-iron solid solution with a slightly higher calcium content than the orthorhombic enstatite-orthoferrosilite series.

Coupled substitutions involving Na^+, Li^+, or Al^{3+} for Mg^{2+} in the enstatite structure yield pyroxenes that lie outside the quadrilateral compositional field. The coupled substitution of Na^+ and Al^{3+} for 2 Mg^{2+} in enstatite produces the pyroxene jadeite. The coupled substitution of Na^+ and Fe^{3+} for 2 Mg^{2+} produces the pyroxene aegirine (acmite). Substitution of Li^+ and Al^{3+} for 2 Mg^{2+} yields spodumene. The substitution of Al^{3+} for Mg^{2+} and Al^{3+} for Si^{4+} yields the ideal tschermakite component $MgAlSiAlO_6$.

Other less common pyroxenes with compositions outside the pyroxene quadrilateral include johannsenite [$CaMnSi_2O_6$], and kosmochlor (ureyite) [$NaCrSi_2O_6$]. Johannsenite involves the substitution of manganese for iron in hedenbergite. Kosmochlor has chromium (Cr) in place of iron or aluminum in a sodic pyroxene.

The nature of aluminum substitution in pyroxenes varies significantly from one pyroxene to another. In the magnesium-iron pyroxene group, aluminum is usually present in only small amounts. In both jadeite and spodumene, which contain essential aluminum in the Y site, the substitution of silicon by aluminum in the Z tetrahedral site is almost negligible. In augite there can be extensive substitution of aluminum for tetrahedral silicon.

At high temperatures, pyroxenes have more extensive fields of solid solution than they do at lower ones. Consequently, as temperatures decrease, the pyroxene adjusts its composition in the solid state by exsolving a separate phase in the form of lamellae within the host pyroxene grain. The lamellae are exsolved along specific crystallographic directions, producing oriented intergrowths with parallel and herringbone texture. There are five principal combinations of exsolution pairs: (1) augite with enstatite lamellae, (2) augite with pigeonite lamellae, (3) augite with both pigeonite and enstatite lamellae, (4) pigeonite with augite lamellae, and (5) enstatite with augite lamellae.

The pyroxenes differ compositionally from the amphiboles in two major respects. Pyroxenes contain no essential water in the form of hydroxyls in their structure, whereas amphiboles are considered to be hydrous silicates. The second key chemical difference between the two is the presence of the Asite in amphiboles which contains the large alkali elements, typically sodium and at times potassium; the pyroxenes do not have an equivalent site that can accommodate potassium. Hydroxyl groups in the amphibole structure decrease their thermal stability relative to the more refractory pyroxenes. At high temperatures amphiboles decompose to anhydrous minerals.

ORTHOPYROXENES

Orthopyroxenes are common silicate minerals within the pyroxene family that typically occur as fibrous or lamellar (thin-plated) green masses in igneous and metamorphic rocks and in meteorites. These minerals differ in the ratio of magnesium to iron in the crystal structure; their composition ranges from pure magnesium silicate ($MgSiO_3$) to pure ferrous iron silicate ($FeSiO_3$). The series

Orthopyroxene from Labrador. Courtesy of the Field Museum of Natural History, Chicago; photograph, John H. Gerard—EB Inc.

includes: enstatite, which contains an iron (Fe) content of 0 to 50 percent, and ferrosilite, which contains an iron content of 50 to 100 percent.

All except the theoretical end-member ferrosilite occur naturally. The magnesium-rich varieties commonly occur in ultramafic igneous rocks, the iron-rich varieties in metamorphosed iron-rich sediments. Orthopyroxenes are essential constituents of norite; they also are characteristic of charnockite and granulite. Aside from olivine, magnesium-rich (less than 30 percent iron) orthopyroxene is the commonest silicate in meteorites; it is a major constituent of most chondrites and an important component of mesosiderites and calcium-poor achondrites.

The orthopyroxene series crystallizes in the orthorhombic system (three crystallographic axes unequal in length and at right angles to each other). An analogue crystallizing in the monoclinic system (three crystallographic axes unequal in length with one oblique intersection), the clinoenstatite–clinoferrosilite series is found largely in meteorites (achondrites, chondrites, and mesosiderites).

CRYSTAL STRUCTURE

The pyroxene group includes minerals that form in both the orthorhombic and monoclinic crystal systems. Orthorhombic pyroxenes are referred to as orthopyroxenes, and monoclinic pyroxenes are called clinopyroxenes. The essential feature of all pyroxene structures is the linkage of the silicon-oxygen (SiO_4) tetrahedrons by sharing two of the four corners to form continuous chains. The chains, which extend indefinitely parallel to the crystallographic axis, have the composition of $(SiO_3)n$. A repeat distance of approximately 5.3 Å along the length of the chain defines the caxis of the unit cell. The SiO_3 chains are bonded to a layer of octahedrally coordinated cation bands which also extend parallel to the caxis. The octahedral layer contains two distinct

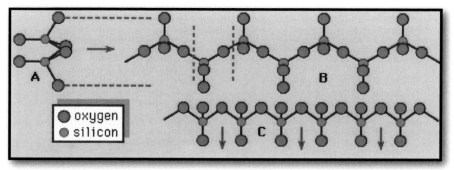

Single pyroxene chain, (SiO₃)n, in three projections: (A) along the c axis direction, (B) on (100), a plane that intersects the a axis and is parallel to the b and c axes, and (C) along the b axis direction. Copyright Encyclopædia Britannica, Inc.; rendering for this edition by Rosen Educational Services

cation sites called $M1$ and $M2$. The size and charge of the cations that occupy the $M2$ site chiefly determine the structural type of a pyroxene. Large, singly or doubly charged cations give rise to a diopside (monoclinic) structure, whereas small, singly or doubly charged cations result in an enstatite (orthorhombic) structure.

In most pyroxenes the chains are not exactly straight, but are rotated or kinked so that more than one type of chain is possible. The diopside, jadeite, augite, protoenstatite, and spodumene structures consist of only one chain type. Pigeonite, clinoenstatite, and omphacite have two symmetrically distinct types of tetrahedral chains. Orthopyroxenes also have two distinct types of tetrahedral chains and an octahedral stacking sequence that leads to a doubling of the a axis.

Jadeite is a representative pyroxene structure with tetrahedral and octahedral chains. The octahedral strips consist of $M1$ and $M2$ octahedrons sandwiched between two oppositely pointing tetrahedral chains. The $M1$ sites are occupied by smaller cations such as magnesium, iron, aluminum, and manganese, which are coordinated to six oxygen atoms to form a regular octahedron. In monoclinic pyroxenes, the $M2$ site is a large irregular polyhedron occupied by the larger calcium and sodium cations which are in eightfold coordination. In the low-calcium orthorhombic pyroxenes, $M2$ contains magnesium and iron, and the polyhedron takes on a more regular octahedral shape. The $M1$ cation strip is bonded to oxygen atoms of two oppositely pointing tetrahedral chains. Together, these form a tetrahedral-octahedral-tetrahedral (t-o-t) strip.

Pyroxenes in the quadrilateral with compositions near the diopside-hedenbergite join exist only in the monoclinic form. Those with compositions near the enstatite-orthoferrosilite join containing less than about 5 percent $CaSiO_3$ can be subdivided into two structural types, clinopyroxene or orthopyroxene. Those with approximately 5–20 percent $CaSiO_3$ are monoclinic at high temperatures (pigeonite) and invert to an orthorhombic structure at low temperatures (enstatite). Those with less than 50 percent $FeSiO_3$ can exist as clinoenstatite (monoclinic) or enstatite (orthorhombic) polymorphic structures. Those with more than 50 percent $FeSiO_3$ are

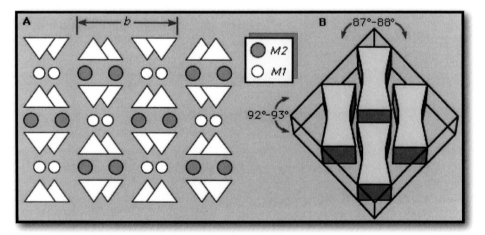

(A) Schematic projection of the monoclinic pyroxene structure perpendicular to the c axis. (B) Control of cleavage angles by the I beams in the pyroxene structure. Copyright Encyclopædia Britannica, Inc.; rendering for this edition by Rosen Educational Services

clinoferrosilite (monoclinic) or ferrosilite (orthorhombic) polymorphic structures. Pyroxenes outside the quadrilateral all have monoclinic pyroxene structures similar to that of diopside.

The inversion of high-temperature structures to low-temperature structures is often accompanied by the exsolution of lamellae of either a separate calcium-rich or magnesium-iron-rich phase. For example, as high-temperature monoclinic pigeonite slowly cools, it exsolves calcium ions to form augite lamellae and inverts to the orthorhombic enstatite structure. Consequently, the presence of the exsolution lamellae is evidence of a previous monoclinic structure.

PHYSICAL PROPERTIES

Within hand specimens, pyroxene can generally be identified by the following characteristics: two directions of cleavage intersecting at roughly right angles (approximately 87° and 93°), stubby prismatic crystal habit with nearly square cross sections perpendicular to cleavage directions, and a Mohs hardness between 5 and 7. Specific gravity values of the pyroxenes range from about 3.0 to 4.0. Unlike amphiboles, pyroxenes do not yield water when heated in a closed tube. Characteristically,

A micrograph of a twinned crystal of inverted pigeonite from a gabbro. Courtesy of G. Malcolm Brown

A micrograph showing a sample of inverted pigeonite from a slowly cooled gabbro. The augite lamellae here are relatively wide, separated from the enstatite host (magnified about 70.4×). Courtesy of G. Malcolm Brown

pyroxenes are dark green to black in colour, but they can range from dark green to apple-green and from lilac to colourless, depending on the chemical composition. Diopside ranges from white to light green, darkening in colour as the iron content increases. Hedenbergite and augite are typically black. Pigeonite is greenish brown to black. Jadeite is white to apple-green to emerald-green or mottled white and green. Aegirine (acmite) forms long, slender prismatic crystals that are brown to green in colour. Enstatite is yellowish or greenish brown and sometimes has a submetallic bronzelike lustre. Iron-rich ferrosilite orthopyroxenes range from brown to black. Spodumene is colourless, white, gray, pink, yellow, or green. The two gem varieties are a clear lilac-coloured type called kunzite, while the clear emerald-green type is known as hiddenite.

In thin sections, monoclinic pyroxenes are distinguished by two directions of cleavage at approximately 87° and 93°, eight-sided basal cross sections, and light brown or green colour. Orthorhombic pyroxenes differ from monoclinic pyroxenes in that they have parallel extinction.

Microscopically, many igneous pyroxenes show exsolution textures of thin lamellae of one pyroxene in a host of a different composition. The lamellae occur as oriented

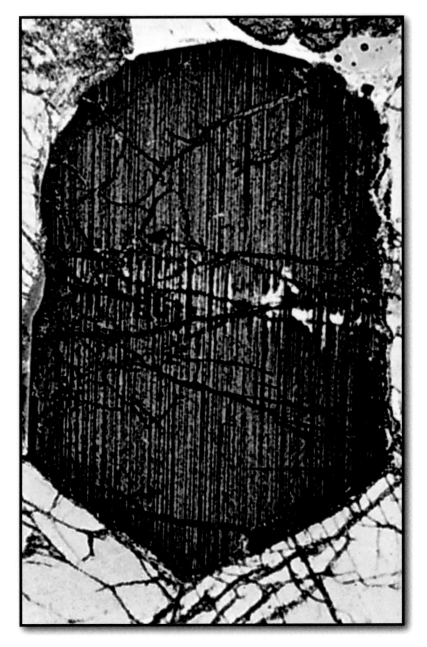

A micrograph of an enstatite crystal taken from an ultramatic rock. The thin lamellae of a calcium-rich species, probably pigeonite, have separated from the bronzite; the gray coloration of the host rock betrays its very low calcium content (magnified about 40×). Courtesy of G. Malcolm Brown

intergrowths that display parallel and herringbone textures. These lamellae result from the exsolution of a separate pyroxene phase from a host grain due to subsolidus re-equilibration (that occurs while the mineral is in the solid state) during slow cooling.

ORIGIN AND OCCURRENCE

Minerals in the pyroxene group are abundant in both igneous and metamorphic rocks. Their susceptibility to both chemical and mechanical weathering makes them a rare constituent of sedimentary rocks. Pyroxenes are classified as ferromagnesian minerals in allusion to their high content of magnesium and iron. Their conditions of formation are almost exclusively restricted to environments of high temperature, high pressure, or both. Characteristically the more common pyroxenes are found in mafic and ultramafic igneous rocks where they are associated with olivine and calcium-rich plagioclase and in high-grade metamorphic rocks such as granulites and eclogites. Enstatite, clinoenstatite, and kosmochlor occur in meteorites.

IGNEOUS ROCKS

Magnesium-rich orthopyroxenes and calcium-rich clinopyroxenes are important constituents of basalts, gabbros, peridotites, and norites. They are the major minerals in pyroxenites. Magnesium-rich orthopyroxenes occur in the earlier-formed rocks of layered ultramafic complexes.

Uninverted pigeonites (monoclinic) are common as phenocrysts in high-temperature, rapidly cooled lavas and in some intrusives such as diabases. In slowly cooled mafic intrusive rocks, pigeonite inverts to an orthorhombic pyroxene and undergoes exsolution.

Augite is the most common pyroxene and is found primarily in mafic igneous rocks. It occurs in basalts, gabbros, andesites, diorites, and peridotites. The augites in layered ultramafic intrusions show compositional trends of increasing iron and decreasing magnesium contents with fractionation. Augite is also known to occur in lunar basalts. Although more common in metamorphic rocks, diopside is found in some mafic and ultramafic rocks.

Aegirine (acmite) and aegirine-augite occur most commonly as products of the late crystallization of alkaline magmas. They are found in alkalic rocks such as nepheline syenites and phonolites, wherein they are associated with orthoclase, feldspathoids, augite, and sodium-rich amphiboles.

Spodumene is found almost exclusively in lithium-rich granite pegmatites. Some of the world's largest known crystals are spodumene. Single crystals of spodumene exceeding 13 metres (43 feet) in length were mined for their lithium content in the Black Hills of South Dakota, U.S. Spodumene is typically associated with microcline, albite, quartz, muscovite, lepidolite, beryl, and tourmaline.

METAMORPHIC ROCKS

Iron-rich orthopyroxenes are found in metamorphosed iron formations in association with the amphibole grunerite. At higher grades of regional metamorphism, the amphibole anthophyllite breaks down to form magnesium-iron orthopyroxenes. The orthopyroxene enstatite occurs in high-temperature and high-pressure granulite facies rocks such as quartz-rich, garnet-bearing granulites.

Diopside results from the thermal metamorphism of siliceous limestones or dolomites according to the following decarbonation reaction:

$$CaMg(CO_3)_2 + 2SiO_2 \longrightarrow CaMgSi_2O_6 + 2CO_2.$$

dolomite   quartz   diopside   carbon dioxide

In calc-silicate skarns produced by contact metamorphism, diopside is associated with wollastonite, vesuvianite, grossular, and tremolite. Diopside also forms under conditions of regional metamorphism by the breakdown of tremolite. Hedenbergite is a product of thermal metamorphism of iron-rich sediments where its formation is probably due to the breakdown of actinolite with increasing temperature. Augite can be found in quartz-free, aluminum-rich skarns associated with spinel, calcite, vesuvianite, garnet, clintonite, and diopside. Johannsenite is associated with rhodonite, bustamite, sphalerite, chalcopyrite, galena, pyrite, and magnetite in metasomatized limestones adjacent to igneous intrusions.

Aegirine (acmite) is associated with glaucophane or riebeckite in some metamorphic rocks. Jadeite is found only in metamorphic rocks. It either occurs as monomineralic veins or is associated with albite, glaucophane, aragonite, lawsonite, and quartz in high-pressure, low-temperature metamorphic rocks of blueschist facies. In some localities, jadeite is associated with serpentine in glaucophane-bearing metamorphic rocks.

Omphacite is restricted in occurrence to the high-pressure and high-temperature rocks called eclogites. Eclogites represent the most deep-seated conditions of metamorphism and are characterized by an assemblage of omphacite and magnesium-rich pyrope garnet. Omphacite-bearing eclogite nodules are associated with peridotites in the kimberlite pipes of South Africa. It can also be found in subduction zones that have been exhumed.

ZEOLITES

Zeolites belong to a family of hydrated aluminosilicate minerals that contain alkali and alkaline-earth metals. The zeolites are noted for their lability toward ion-exchange and reversible dehydration. They have a framework structure that encloses interconnected cavities occupied by large metal cations (positively charged ions) and water molecules.

The essential structural feature of a zeolite is a three-dimensional tetrahedral framework in which each oxygen atom is shared by two tetrahedra. If all tetrahedra contained silicon the framework would be neutral; substitution of aluminum for silicon creates a charge imbalance and requires other metal ions to be present in relatively large cavities of the framework. In naturally occurring zeolites these metal ions are typically mono- or di-valent ions such as sodium, potassium, magnesium, calcium, and barium. Zeolites are similar to feldspar minerals except that cavities are larger in zeolites and water is generally present. Structurally, zeolites are classified by the types of structural units that compose the framework, such as rings or polyhedra types. The cavities formed by the framework units have diameters ranging from about 2 to 8 angstroms, which permits relatively easy movement of ions between cavities.

This ease of movement of ions and water within the framework allows reversible dehydration and cation exchange, properties which vary considerably with chemical and structural differences. Dehydration character varies with the way water is bound in the structure. For those zeolites in which water is tightly bound, dehydration occurs at relatively high temperatures; by contrast, in certain zeolites with large cavities, some of the water can be released at low temperatures. The rate of ion exchange depends on the size and connections between cavities. Some ions are excluded because of specific structural properties.

Zeolite properties are exploited through commercial production of zeolites with particular structural and chemical features. Some commercial uses include separation of hydrocarbons, such as in petroleum refining;

drying of gases and liquids; and pollution control by selective molecular adsorption.

Natural zeolites occur in mafic volcanic rocks as cavity fillings, probably as a result of deposition by fluids or vapours. In sedimentary rocks zeolites occur as alteration products of volcanic glass and serve as cementing material in detrital rocks; they also are found in chemical sedimentary rocks of marine origin. Extensive deposits of zeolites occur in all oceans. Metamorphic rocks contain a sequence of zeolite minerals useful for assigning relative metamorphic grade; these minerals form at the expense of feldspars and volcanic glass.

CHAPTER 5
MICAS AND CLAY MINERALS

Micas and clay minerals are two additional groups of common silicates. Micas are hydrous potassium, aluminum silicate minerals. They are a type of phyllo-silicate that exhibits a two-dimensional sheet or layer structure. Among the principal rock-forming minerals, micas are found in all three major rock varieties—igneous, sedimentary, and metamorphic. Clay minerals also possess a layered (sheetlike) structure. They are hydrous aluminum silicates with a very small particle size. They may contain significant amounts of iron, alkali metals, or alkaline earths.

MICAS

Of the 28 known species of the mica group, only 6 are common rock-forming minerals. Muscovite, the common light-coloured mica, and biotite, which is typically black or nearly so, are the most abundant. Phlogopite, typically brown, and paragonite, which is macroscopically indis-tinguishable from muscovite, also are fairly common. Lepidolite, generally pinkish to lilac in colour, occurs in lithium-bearing pegmatites. Glauconite, a green species that does not have the same general macroscopic charac-teristics as the other micas, occurs sporadically in many marine sedimentary sequences. All of these micas except glauconite exhibit easily observable perfect cleavage into flexible sheets. Glauconite, which most often occurs as pelletlike grains, has no apparent cleavage.

The names of the rock-forming micas constitute a good example of the diverse bases used in naming minerals: Biotite was named for a person—Jean-Baptiste Biot, a 19th-century French physicist who studied the optical properties of micas; muscovite was named, albeit indirectly, for a place—it was originally called "Muscovy glass" because it came from the Muscovy province of Russia; glauconite, although typically green, was named for the Greek word for "blue;" lepidolite, from the Greek word meaning "scale," was based on the appearance of the mineral's cleavage plates; phlogopite, from the Greek word for "firelike," was chosen because of the reddish glow (colour and lustre) of some specimens; paragonite, from the Greek "to mislead," was so named because it was originally mistaken for another mineral, talc.

MUSCOVITE

Muscovite, which is also called common mica, potash mica, or isinglass, is an abundant silicate mineral that contains potassium and aluminum. Muscovite is the most common member of the mica group. Because of its perfect cleavage, it can occur in thin, transparent, but durable sheets. Sheets of muscovite were used in Russia for windowpanes and became known as Muscovy glass (isinglass), hence its common name. Muscovite typically occurs in metamorphic rocks, particularly gneisses and schists, where it forms crystals and plates. It also occurs in granites, in fine-grained sediments, and in some highly siliceous rocks. Large crystals of muscovite are often found in veins and pegmatites. One crystal mined near Nellore, India, measured 3 metres (10 feet) in diameter and 5 metres (15 feet) in length and weighed 85 tons.

Muscovite is usually colourless but may be light gray, brown, pale green, or rose-red in colour. The crystals are tabular with a hexagonal or pseudo-hexagonal outline; they are commonly lamellar and occur in aggregates. Muscovite is economically important because its low iron content makes it a good electrical and thermal insulator. Fine-grained muscovite is called sericite, or white mica.

CHEMICAL COMPOSITION

The general formula for minerals of the mica group is $XY_{2-3}Z_4O_{10}(OH, F)_2$ with X = K, Na, Ba, Ca, Cs, (H_3O), (NH_4); Y = Al, Mg, Fe^{2+}, Li, Cr, Mn, V, Zn; and Z = Si, Al, Fe^{3+}, Be, Ti.

Few natural micas have end-member compositions. For example, most muscovites contain sodium substituting for some potassium, and diverse varieties have chromium or vanadium or a combination of both replacing part of the aluminum; furthermore, the Si:Al ratio may range from the indicated 3:1 up to about 7:1. Similar variations in composition are known for the other micas. Thus, as in some of the other groups of minerals (e.g., the garnets), different individual pieces of naturally occurring mica specimens consist of different proportions of ideal end-member compositions. There are, however, no complete series of solid solutions between any dioctahedral mica and any trioctahedral mica.

CRYSTAL STRUCTURE

Micas have sheet structures whose basic units consist of two polymerized sheets of silica (SiO_4) tetrahedrons. Two such sheets are juxtaposed with the vertices of their tetrahedrons pointing toward each other; the sheets are cross-linked with cations—for example, aluminum in muscovite—and hydroxyl pairs complete the coordination of these cations. Thus, the cross-linked double layer is bound firmly, has the bases of silica tetrahedrons on both of its outer sides, and has a negative charge. The charge is balanced by singly charged large cations—for example, potassium in muscovite—that join the cross-linked double layers to form the complete structure. The differences among mica species depend upon differences in the X and Y cations.

Although the micas are generally considered to be monoclinic (pseudohexagonal), there also are hexagonal, orthorhombic, and triclinic forms generally referred to as polytypes. The polytypes are based on the sequences and number of layers of the basic structure in the unit cell and the symmetry thus produced. Most biotites are 1M and most muscovites are 2M; however, more than one polytype is commonly present in individual specimens. This feature cannot, however, be determined macroscopically; polytypes are distinguished by relatively sophisticated techniques such as those employing X-rays.

The micas other than glauconite tend to crystallize as short pseudohexagonal prisms. The side faces of these prisms are typically rough, some appearing striated and dull, whereas the flat ends tend to be smooth and shiny. The end faces are parallel to the perfect cleavage that characterizes the group.

PHYSICAL PROPERTIES

The rock-forming micas (other than glauconite) can be divided into two groups: those that are light-coloured (muscovite, paragonite, and lepidolite) and those that are dark-coloured (biotite and phlogopite). Most of the properties of the mica group of minerals, other than those of glauconite, can be described together; here they are described as pertaining simply to micas, meaning the micas other than glauconite. Properties of the latter are described separately later in the discussion.

The perfect cleavage into thin elastic sheets is probably the most widely recognized characteristic of the micas. The cleavage is a manifestation of the sheet structure described above. (The elasticity of the thin sheets distinguishes the micas from similarly appearing thin sheets of chlorite and talc.) The rock-forming micas exhibit certain characteristic colours. Muscovites range from colourless, greenish to blue-green to emerald-green, pinkish, and brownish to cinnamon-tan. Paragonites are colourless to white; biotites may be black, brown, red to red-brown, greenish brown, and blue-green. Phlogopites resemble biotites but are honey brown. Lepidolites are nearly colourless, pink, lavender, or tan. Biotites and phlogopites also exhibit the property termed pleochroism (or, more properly for these minerals, dichroism): When viewed along different crystallographic directions, especially using transmitted polarized light, they exhibit different colours or different absorption of light or both.

The lustre of the micas is usually described as splendent, but some cleavage faces appear pearly. The minutely crystalline variety consisting of muscovite or paragonite (or both), generally referred to as sericite, is silky.

Mohs hardness of the micas is approximately 2½ on cleavage flakes and 4 across cleavage. Consequently, micas can be scratched in either direction with a knife blade or geologic pick. Hardness is used to distinguish micas from chloritoid, which also occurs rather commonly as platy masses in some metamorphic rocks; chloritoid, with a Mohs hardness of 6½, cannot be scratched with a knife blade or geologic pick.

Specific gravity for the micas varies with composition. The overall range is from 2.76 for muscovite to 3.2 for iron-rich biotite.

Glauconite occurs most commonly as earthy to dull, subtranslucent, green to nearly black granules generally referred to as pellets. It is attacked readily by hydrochloric acid. The colour and occurrence of this mineral in sediments and sedimentary rocks formed from those sediments generally are sufficient for identification.

ORIGIN AND OCCURRENCE

Micas may originate as the result of diverse processes under several different conditions. Their occurrences, listed below, include crystallization from consolidating magmas, deposition by fluids derived from or directly associated with magmatic activities, deposition by fluids circulating during both contact and regional metamorphism, and formation as the result of alteration processes—perhaps even those caused by weathering—that involve minerals such as feldspars. The stability ranges of micas have been investigated in the laboratory, and in some associations their presence (as opposed to absence) or some aspect of their chemical composition may serve as geothermometers or geobarometers.

Distinct crystals of the micas occur in a few rocks—e.g., in certain igneous rocks and in pegmatites. Micas occuring as large crystals are often called books; these may measure up to several metres across. In most rocks, micas occur as irregular tabular masses or thin plates (flakes), which in some instances appear bent. Although some mica grains are extremely small, all except those constituting sericitic masses have characteristic shiny cleavage surfaces.

Glauconite is formed in marine environments. It can be found on seafloors where clastic sedimentation, which results from the relocation of minerals and organic matter to sites other than their places of origin, is lacking or nearly so. Although some glauconite has been interpreted to have been formed from preexisting layered silicates (e.g., detrital biotite), most of it appears to have crystallized from aluminosilicate gels—perhaps under the influence of biochemical activities that produce reducing environments.

The common rock-forming micas are distributed widely. The more important occurrences follow: Biotite occurs in many igneous rocks (e.g., granites and granodiorites), is common in many pegmatite masses, and constitutes one of the chief components of many metamorphic rocks (e.g., gneisses, schists, and hornfelses). It alters rather easily during chemical weathering and thus is rare in sediments and sedimentary rocks. One stage in the weathering of biotite has resulted in some confusion. During chemical weathering, biotite tends to lose its elasticity and become decolorized to silvery gray flakes. In a fairly common intermediate stage, weathered biotite is golden yellow, has a bronzy lustre, and may be mistaken by inexperienced observers as flakes of gold.

Phlogopite is rare in igneous rocks; it does, however, occur in some ultramafic (silica-poor) rocks. For example, it occurs in some peridotites, especially those called kimberlites, which are the rocks in which diamonds occur. Phlogopite also is a rare constituent of some magnesium-rich pegmatites. Its most common occurrence, however, is in impure limestones that have undergone contact metasomatism, a process through which the chemical composition of rocks is changed.

Muscovite is particularly common in metamorphic gneisses, schists, and phyllites. In fine-grained foliated rocks, such as phyllites, the muscovite occurs as microscopic grains (sericite) that give these rocks their silky lustres. It also occurs in some granitic rocks and is common in complex granitic pegmatites and within miarolitic druses, which are late-magmatic, crystal-lined cavities in igneous rocks. Much of the muscovite in igneous rocks is thought to have been formed late during, or immediately after, consolidation of the parent magma. Muscovite is relatively resistant to weathering and thus occurs in many soils developed over muscovite-bearing rocks and also in the clastic sediments and sedimentary rocks derived from them.

Paragonite is known definitely to occur in only a few gneisses, schists, and phyllites, in which it appears to play essentially the same role as muscovite. It may, however, be much more common than generally thought. Until fairly recently nearly all light-coloured micas in rocks were automatically called muscovite without checking their potassium:sodium ratios, so some paragonites may have been incorrectly identified as muscovites. Its weathering is essentially the same as that of muscovite.

Lepidolite occurs almost exclusively in complex lithium-bearing pegmatites but has also been recorded as a component of a few granites.

Glauconite, as noted above, is forming in some present-day marine environments. It also is a relatively common constituent of sedimentary rocks, the precursor sediments of which were apparently deposited on the deeper parts of ancient continental shelves. The name *greensand* is widely applied to glauconite-rich sediments. Most glauconite occurs as granules, which are frequently referred to as pellets. It also exists as pigment, typically as films that coat such diverse substrates as fossils, fecal pellets, and clastic fragments.

USES

Because of their perfect cleavage, flexibility and elasticity, infusibility, low thermal and electrical conductivity, and high dielectric strength, muscovite and phlogopite have found widespread application. Most "sheet mica" with these compositions has been used as electrical condensers, as insulation sheets between commutator segments, or in heating elements. Sheets of muscovite of precise thicknesses are utilized in optical instruments. Ground mica is used in many ways such as a dusting medium to prevent, for example, asphalt tiles from sticking to each other and also as a filler, absorbent, and lubricant. It is also used in the manufacture of wallpaper to give it a shiny lustre. Lepidolite has been mined as an ore of lithium, with rubidium generally recovered as a by-product. It is used in the manufacture of heat-resistant glass. Glauconite-rich greensands have found use within the United States as fertilizer—e.g., on the coastal plain of New Jersey—and some glauconite has been employed as a water softener because it has a high base-exchange capacity and tends to regenerate rather rapidly.

CLAY MINERALS

The term clay is generally applied to (1) a natural material with plastic properties, (2) particles of very fine size, customarily those defined as particles smaller than two micrometres (7.9 × 10^{-5} inch), and (3) very fine mineral fragments or particles composed mostly of hydrous-layer silicates of aluminum, though occasionally containing magnesium and iron. Although, in a broader sense, clay minerals can include virtually any mineral of the above-cited particle size, the definition adapted here is restricted to represent hydrous-layer silicates and some related short-range ordered aluminosilicates, both of which occur either exclusively or frequently in very fine-size grades.

The development of X-ray diffraction techniques in the 1920s and the subsequent improvement of microscopic and thermal procedures enabled investigators to establish that clays are composed of a few groups of crystalline minerals. The introduction of electron microscopic methods proved very useful in determining the characteristic shape and size of clay minerals. More recent analytical techniques such as infrared spectroscopy, neutron diffraction analysis, Mössbauer spectroscopy, and nuclear magnetic resonance spectroscopy have helped advance scientific knowledge of the crystal chemistry of these minerals.

Clay minerals are composed essentially of silica, alumina or magnesia or both, and water, but iron substitutes for aluminum and magnesium in varying degrees, and appreciable quantities of potassium, sodium, and calcium are frequently present as well. Some clay minerals may be expressed using ideal chemical formulas as the following: $2SiO_2 \cdot Al_2O_3 \cdot 2H_2O$ (kaolinite), $4SiO_2 \cdot Al_2O_3 \cdot H_2O$ (pyrophyllite), $4SiO_2 \cdot 3MgO \cdot H_2O$ (talc), and $3SiO_2 \cdot Al_2O_3 \cdot 5FeO \cdot 4H_2O$ (chamosite). The SiO_2 ratio in a formula is the key factor determining clay mineral types. These minerals can be classified on the basis of variations of chemical composition and atomic structure into nine groups: (1) kaolin-serpentine (kaolinite, halloysite, lizardite, chrysotile), (2) pyrophyllite-talc, (3) mica (illite, glauconite, celadonite), (4) vermiculite, (5) smectite (montmorillonite, nontronite, saponite), (6) chlorite (sudoite, clinochlore, chamosite), (7) sepiolite-palygorskite, (8) interstratified clay minerals (e.g., rectorite, corrensite, tosudite), and (9) allophane-imogolite. Information and structural diagrams for these groups are given below.

Kaolinite is derived from the commonly used name *kaolin*, which is a corruption of the Chinese Gaoling (Pinyin; Wade-Giles: Kao-ling) meaning "high ridge," the name of a hill near Ching-te-chen where the occurrence of the mineral is known as early as the 2nd century BCE. Montmorillonite and nontronite are named after the localities Montmorillon and Nontron, respectively, in France, where these minerals were first reported. Celadonite is from the French *céladon* (meaning grayish yellow-green) in allusion to its colour. Because sepiolite is a light and porous material, its name is based on the Greek word for cuttlefish, the bone of which is similar in nature. The name saponite is derived from the Latin *sapon* (meaning soap), owing to its appearance and cleaning ability. Vermiculite is from the Latin *vermiculari* ("to breed worms"), because of its physical characteristic of exfoliation upon heating, which causes the mineral to exhibit a spectacular volume change from small grains to long wormlike threads. Baileychlore, brindleyite, corrensite, sudoite, and tosudite are examples of clay minerals that were named after distinguished clay mineralogists— Sturges W. Bailey, George W. Brindley, Carl W. Correns, and Toshio Sudō, respectively.

STRUCTURE

The structure of clay minerals has been determined largely by X-ray diffraction methods. The essential features of

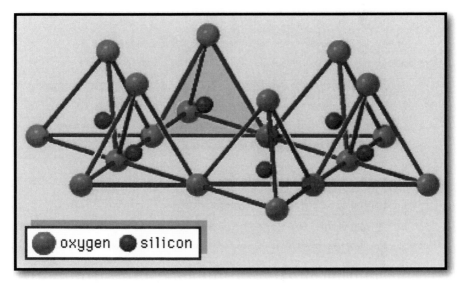

Single silica tetrahedron (shaded) and the sheet structure of silica tetrahedrons arranged in a hexagonal network. Copyright Encyclopædia Britannica, Inc.; rendering for this edition by Rosen Educational Services

hydrous-layer silicates were revealed by various scientists including Charles Mauguin, Linus C. Pauling, W.W. Jackson, J. West, and John W. Gruner through the late 1920s to mid-1930s. These features are continuous two-dimensional tetrahedral sheets of composition Si_2O_5, with SiO_4 tetrahedrons linked by the sharing of three corners of each tetrahedron to form a hexagonal mesh pattern. Frequently, silicon atoms of the tetrahedrons are partially substituted for by aluminum and, to a lesser extent, ferric iron. The apical oxygen at the fourth corner of the tetrahedrons, which is usually directed normal to the sheet, forms part of an adjacent octahedral sheet in which octahedrons are linked by sharing edges. The junction plane between tetrahedral and octahedral sheets consists of the shared apical oxygen atoms of the tetrahedrons and unshared hydroxyls that lie at the centre of each hexagonal ring of tetrahedrons and at the

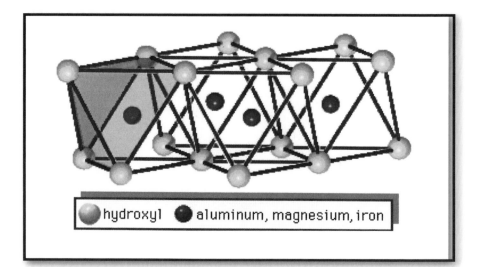

Single octahedron (shaded) and the sheet structure of octahedral units. Copyright Encyclopædia Britannica, Inc.; rendering for this edition by Rosen Educational Services

same level as the shared apical oxygen atoms. Common cations that coordinate the octahedral sheets are Al, Mg, Fe^{3+}, and Fe^{2+}; but occasionally Li, V, Cr, Mn, Ni, Cu, and Zn substitute in considerable amounts. If divalent cations (M^{2+}) are in the octahedral sheets, the composition is $M^{2+}{}_3$ $(OH)_2O_4$ and all the octahedrons are occupied. If there are trivalent cations (M^{3+}), the composition is $M^{3+}{}_2$ $(OH)_2O_4$ and two-thirds of the octahedrons are occupied, with the absence of the third octahedron. The former type of octahedral sheet is called trioctahedral, and the latter dioctahedral. If all the anion groups are hydroxyl ions in the compositions of octahedral sheets, the resulting sheets may be expressed by $M^{2+}(OH)_2$ and $M^{3+}(OH)_3$, respectively. Such sheets, called hydroxide sheets, occur singly, alternating with silicate layers in some clay minerals. Brucite, $Mg(OH)_2$, and gibbsite,

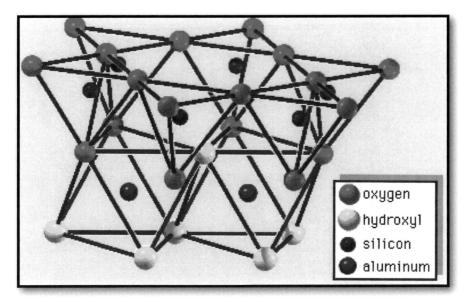

Structure of 1:1 layer silicate (kaolinite) illustrating the connection between tetrahedral and octahedral sheets. Copyright Encyclopædia Britannica, Inc.; rendering for this edition by Rosen Educational Services

Al(OH)$_3$, are typical examples of minerals having similar structures. There are two major types for the structural "backbones" of clay minerals called silicate layers. The unit silicate layer formed by aligning one octahedral sheet to one tetrahedral sheet is referred to as a 1:1 silicate layer, and the exposed surface of the octahedral sheet consists of hydroxyls. In another type, the unit silicate layer consists of one octahedral sheet sandwiched by two tetrahedral sheets that are oriented in opposite directions and is termed a 2:1 silicate layer. These structural features, however, are limited to idealized geometric arrangements.

Real structures of clay minerals contain substantial crystal strains and distortions, which produce irregularities such as deformed octahedrons and tetrahedrons rather than polyhedrons with equilateral triangle faces, ditrigonal symmetry modified from the ideal hexagonal

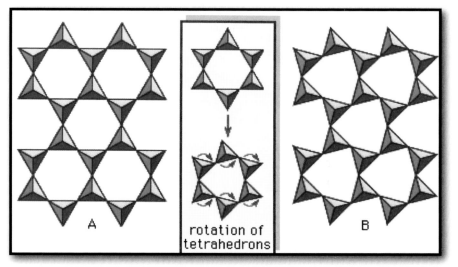

(A) Ideal hexagonal tetrahedral sheet. (B) Contracted sheet of ditrigonal symmetry owing to the reduction of mesh size of the tetrahedral sheet by rotation of the tetrahedrons. Copyright Encyclopædia Britannica, Inc.; rendering for this edition by Rosen Educational Services

surface symmetry, and puckered surfaces instead of the flat planes made up by the basal oxygen atoms of the tetrahedral sheet. One of the major causes of such distortions is dimensional "misfits" between the tetrahedral and octahedral sheets. If the tetrahedral sheet contains only silicon in the cationic site and has an ideal hexagonal symmetry, the longer unit dimension within the basal plane is 9.15 Å, which lies between the corresponding dimensions 8.6 Å of gibbsite and 9.4 Å of brucite. To fit the tetrahedral sheet into the dimension of the octahedral sheet, alternate SiO_4 tetrahedrons rotate (up to a theoretical maximum of 30°) in opposite directions to distort the ideal hexagonal array into a doubly triangular (ditrigonal) array. By this distortion mechanism, tetrahedral and octahedral sheets of a wide range of compositions resulting from ionic substitutions can link together and maintain silicate layers. Among ionic substitutions, those between ions of distinctly different sizes most significantly affect geometric configurations of silicate layers.

Another significant feature of layer silicates, owing to their similarity in sheet structures and hexagonal or near-hexagonal symmetry, is that the structures allow various ways to stack up atomic planes, sheets, and layers, which may be explained by crystallographic operations such as translation or shifting and rotation, thereby distinguishing them from polymorphs (e.g., diamond-graphite and calcite-aragonite). The former involves one-dimensional variations, but the latter generally three-dimensional ones. The variety of structures resulting from different stacking sequences of a fixed chemical composition are termed polytypes. If such a variety is caused by ionic substitutions that are minor but consistent, they are called polytypoids.

CLAY

Soil particles with diameters less than 0.005 mm (0.0002 inch) make up clay. Clay also refers to a rock that is composed essentially of clay particles. Rock in this sense includes soils, ceramic clays, clay shales, mudstones, glacial clays (including great volumes of detrital and transported clays), and deep-sea clays (red clay, blue clay, and blue mud). These are all characterized by the presence of one or more clay minerals, together with varying amounts of organic and detrital materials, among which quartz is predominant. Clay materials are plastic when wet, and coherent when dry. Most clays are the result of weathering.

No other earth material has so wide an importance or such extended uses as do the clays. They are used in a wide variety of industries. As soils, they provide the environment for almost all plant growth and hence for nearly all life on the Earth's surface. They provide porosity, aeration, and water retention and are a reservoir of potassium oxide, calcium oxide, and even nitrogen.

The use of clay in pottery making antedates recorded human history, and pottery remains provide a record of past civilizations. As building materials, bricks (baked and as adobe) have been used in construction since earliest time. Impure clays may be used to make bricks, tile, and the cruder types of pottery, while kaolin (*q.v.*), or china clay, is required for the finer grades of ceramic materials. Another major use of kaolin is as paper coating and filler; it gives the paper a gloss and increases the opacity. Refractory materials, including fire brick, chemical ware, and melting pots for glass, also make use of kaolin together with other materials that increase resistance to heat. Certain clays known as fuller's earth have long been used in wool scouring. In rubber compounding, the addition of clay increases resistance to wear and helps eliminate molding troubles.

Clay materials have a wide variety of uses in engineering. Earth dams are made impermeable to water by adding suitable clay materials to porous soil; water loss in canals may be reduced by adding clay. The essential raw materials of portland cement are limestone and clays, commonly impure. After acid treatment, clays have been used as water softeners; the clay removes calcium and magnesium from the solution and substitutes sodium. A major use of clay is as drilling mud—i.e., heavy suspension consisting of chemical additives and weighting materials, along with clays, employed in rotary drilling.

KAOLIN-SERPENTINE GROUP

Minerals of this groups are 1:1 layer silicates. Their basic unit of structure consists of tetrahedral and octahedral sheets in which the anions at the exposed surface of the octahedral sheet are hydroxyls. The general structural formula may be expressed by $Y_{2-3}Z_2O_5(OH)_4$, where Y are cations in the octahedral sheet such as Al^{3+} and Fe^{3+} for dioctahedral species and Mg^{2+}, Fe^{2+}, Mn^{2+}, and Ni^{2+} for trioctahedral species, and Z are cations in the tetrahedral sheet, largely Si and, to a lesser extent, Al and Fe^{3+}. A typical dioctahedral species of this group is kaolinite, with an ideal structural formula of $Al_2Si_2O_5(OH)_4$. Kaolinite is electrostatically neutral and has triclinic symmetry. Oxygen atoms and hydroxyl ions between the layers are paired with hydrogen bonding. Because of this weak bonding, random displacements between the layers are quite common and result in kaolinite minerals of lower crystallinity than that of the triclinic kaolinite. Dickite and nacrite are polytypic varieties of kaolinite. Both of them consist of a double 1:1 layer and have monoclinic symmetry, but they distinguish themselves by different stacking sequences of the two 1:1 silicate layers.

Halloysite also has a composition close to that of kaolinite and is characterized by its tubular nature in contrast to the platy nature of kaolinite particles. Although tubular forms are the most common, other morphological varieties are also known: prismatic, rolled, pseudospherical, and platy forms. The structure of halloysite is believed to be similar to that of kaolinite, but no precise structure has been revealed yet. Halloysite has a hydrated form with a composition of $Al_2Si_2O_5(OH)_4 \cdot 2H_2O$. This hydrated form irreversibly changes to a dehydrated variety at relatively low temperatures (60 °C [140 °F]) or upon being exposed to conditions of low relative humidity. The dehydrated form has a basal spacing about the thickness of a kaolinite layer (approximately 7.2 Å), and the hydrated form has a basal spacing of about 10.1 Å. The difference of 2.9 Å is approximately the thickness of a sheet of water one molecule thick. Consequently, the layers of halloysite in the hydrated form are separated by monomolecular water layers that are lost during dehydration.

In trioctahedral magnesium species, chrysotile, antigorite, and lizardite are commonly known; the formula of these three clay minerals is $Mg_3Si_2O_5(OH)_4$. Chrysotile crystals have a cylindrical roll morphology, while antigorite crystals exhibit an alternating wave structure. These morphological characteristics may be attributed to the degree of fit between the lateral dimensions of the tetrahedral and octahedral sheets. On the other hand, lizardite crystals are platy and often have a small amount of substitution of aluminum or ferric iron for both silicon and magnesium. This substitution appears to be the main reason for the platy nature of lizardite. Planar polytypes of the trioctahedral species are far more complicated than those of dioctahedral ones, owing to the fact that the trioctahedral silicate layer has a higher symmetry because all octahedral cationic sites are occupied. In addition, recent detailed structural investigations have shown that there are considerable numbers of hydrous-layer silicates whose structures are periodically perturbed by inversion or revision of SiO_4 tetrahedrons. Modulated structures therefore produce two characteristic linkage configurations: strips and islands. Antigorite is an example of the strip configuration in the modulated 1:1 layer silicates. Greenalite, a species rich in ferrous iron, also has a modulated layer structure containing an island configuration.

PYROPHYLLITE-TALC GROUP

Minerals of this group have the simplest form of the 2:1 layer with a unit thickness of approximately 9.2 to 9.6 Å—i.e., the structure consists of an octahedral sheet sandwiched by two tetrahedral sheets. Pyrophyllite and talc represent the dioctahedral and trioctahedral members, respectively, of the group. In the ideal case, the structural formula is expressed by $Al_2Si_4O_{10}(OH)_2$ for pyrophyllite and by $Mg_3Si_4O_{10}(OH)_2$ for talc. Therefore, the 2:1 layers of these minerals are electrostatically neutral and are held together with van der Waals bonding. One-layer triclinic and two-layer monoclinic forms are known for polytypes of pyrophyllite and talc. The ferric iron analogue of pyrophyllite is called ferripyrophyllite.

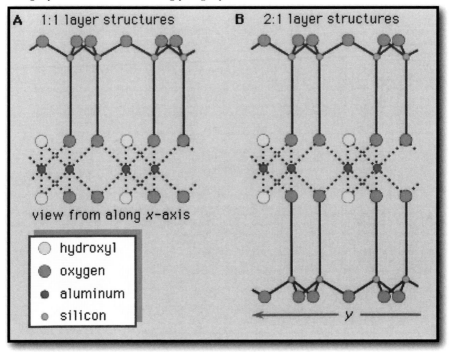

Schematic presentation of (A) 1:1 layer structures and (B) 2:1 layer structures. Copyright Encyclopædia Britannica, Inc.; rendering for this edition by Rosen Educational Services

MICA MINERAL GROUP

Mica minerals have a basic structural unit of the 2:1 layer type like pyrophyllite and talc, but some of the silicon atoms (ideally one-fourth) are always replaced by those of aluminum. This results in a charge deficiency that is balanced by potassium ions between the unit layers. The sheet thickness (basal spacing or dimension along the direction normal to the basal plane) is fixed at about 10 Å. Typical examples are muscovite, $KAl_2(Si_3Al)O_{10}(OH)_2$, for dioctahedral species, and phlogopite, $KMg_3(Si_3Al)O_{10}(OH)_2$, and biotite, $K(Mg, Fe)_3(Si_3Al)O_{10}(OH)_2$, for trioctahedral species. (Formulas rendered may vary slightly due to possible substitution within certain structural sites.) Various polytypes of the micas are known to occur. Among them, one-layer monoclinic (1M), two-layer monoclinic (2M, including $2M_1$ and $2M_2$), and three-layer trigonal (3T) polytypes are most common. The majority of clay-size micas are dioctahedral aluminous species; those similar to muscovite are called illite and generally occur in sediments. The illites are different from muscovite in that the amount of substitution of aluminum for silicon is less; sometimes only one-sixth of the silicon ions are replaced. This reduces a net unbalanced-charge deficiency from 1 to about 0.65 per unit chemical formula. As a result, the illites have a lower potassium content than the muscovites. To some extent, octahedral aluminum ions are replaced by magnesium (Mg^{2+}) and iron ions (Fe^{2+}, Fe^{3+}). In the illites, stacking disorders of the layers are common, but their polytypes are often unidentifiable.

Celadonite and glauconite are ferric iron-rich species of dioctahedral micas. The ideal composition of celadonite may be expressed by $K(Mg, Fe^{3+})(Si_{4-x}Alx)O_{10}(OH)_2$, where $x = 0-0.2$. Glauconite is a dioctahedral mica species with tetrahedral Al substitution greater than 0.2 and octahedral Fe^{3+} or R^{3+} (total trivalent cations) greater than 1.2. Unlike illite, a layer charge deficiency of celadonite and glauconite arises largely from the unbalanced charge due to ionic substitution in the octahedral sheets.

VERMICULITE

The vermiculite unit structure consists of sheets of trioctahedral mica or talc separated by layers of water molecules; these layers occupy a space about two water molecules thick (approximately 4.8 Å). Substitutions of aluminum cations (Al^{3+}) for silicon cations (Si^{4+}) constitute the chief imbalance, but the net charge deficiency may be partially balanced by other substitutions within the mica layer; there is always a residual net charge deficiency commonly in the range from 0.6 to 0.8 per $O_{10}(OH)_2$. This charge deficiency is satisfied with interlayer cations that are closely associated with the water molecules between the mica layers. In the natural mineral, the balancing cation is magnesium (Mg^{2+}). The interlayer cation, however, is readily replaced by other inorganic and organic cations. A number of water molecules are related to the hydration state of cations located at the interlayer sites. Therefore, the basal spacing of vermiculite changes from about 10.5 to 15.7 Å, depending on relative humidity and the kind of interlayer cation. Heating vermiculite to temperatures (depending on its crystal size) as high as 500 °C (about 930 °F) drives the water out from between the mica layers, but the mineral quickly rehydrates at room temperature to maintain its normal basal spacing of approximately 14 to 15 Å if potassium or ammonium ions are not present in the interlayer sites. It has been reported that some dioctahedral analogues of vermiculite occur in soils.

SMECTITE

The structural units of smectite can be derived from the structures of pyrophyllite and talc. Unlike pyrophyllite and talc, the 2:1 silicate layers of smectite have a slight negative charge owing to ionic substitutions in the octahedral and tetrahedral sheets. The net charge deficiency is normally smaller than that of vermiculite—from 0.2 to 0.6 per $O_{10}(OH)_2$—and is balanced by the interlayer cations as in vermiculite. This weak bond offers excellent cleavage between the layers. The distinguishing feature of the smectite structure is that water and other polar molecules (in the form of certain organic substances) can, by entering between the unit layers, cause the structure to expand in the direction normal to the basal plane. Thus this dimension may vary from about 9.6 Å, when there are no polar molecules between the unit layers, to nearly complete separation of the individual layers.

The structural formula of smectites of the dioctahedral aluminous species may be represented by $(Al_{2-y}Mg^{2+}{}_y)(Si_{4-x}Al_x)O_{10}(OH)_2M^+{}_{x+y} \cdot nH_2O$, where M^+ is the interlayer exchangeable cation expressed as a monovalent cation and where x and y are the amounts of tetrahedral and octahedral substitutions, respectively ($0.2 \leq x + y \leq 0.6$). The smectites with $y > x$ are called montmorillonite and those with $x > y$ are known as beidellite. In the latter type of smectites, those in which ferric iron is a dominant cation in the octahedral sheet instead of aluminum and magnesium, are called nontronite. Although less frequent, chromium (Cr^{3+}) and vanadium (V^{3+}) also are found as dominant cations in the octahedral sheets of the beidellite structure, and chromium species are called volkonskoite. The ideal structural formula of trioctahedral ferromagnesian

DIFFERENTIAL THERMAL ANALYSIS (DTA)

In analytical chemistry, DTA is a technique for identifying and quantitatively analyzing the chemical composition of substances by observing the thermal behaviour of a sample as it is heated. The technique is based on the fact that as a substance is heated, it undergoes reactions and phase changes that involve absorption or emission of heat. In DTA the temperature of the test material is measured relative to that of an adjacent inert material. A thermocouple imbedded in the test piece and another in the inert material are connected so that any differential temperatures generated during the heating cycle are graphically recorded as a series of peaks on a moving chart. The amount of heat involved and temperature at which these changes take place are characteristic of individual elements or compounds; identification of a substance, therefore, is accomplished by comparing DTA curves obtained from the unknown with those of known elements or compounds. Moreover, the amount of a substance present in a composite sample will be related to the area under the peaks in the graph, and this amount can be determined by comparing the area of a characteristic peak with areas from a series of standard samples analyzed under identical conditions. The DTA technique is widely used for identifying minerals and mineral mixtures.

smectites, the series saponite through iron saponite, is given by $(Mg, Fe^{2+})_3(Si_{4-x}Al_x)O_{10}(OH)_2M^+{}/{x} \cdot nH_2O$. The tetrahedral substitution is responsible for the net charge deficiency in the smectite minerals of this series. Besides magnesium and ferrous iron, zinc, cobalt, and manganese are known to be dominant cations in the octahedral sheet. Zinc dominant species are called sauconite. There are other types of trioctahedral smectites in which the net charge deficiency arises largely from the imbalanced charge due to ionic substitution or a small number of cation vacancies in the octahedral sheets or both conditions. Ideally x is zero, but most often it is less than 0.15. Thus, the octahedral composition varies to maintain similar amounts of the net charge deficiency as those of other smectites. Typical examples are $(Mg_{3-y}\square_y)$ and $(Mg_{3-y}Li_y)$ for stevensite and hectorite, respectively. [The $\square$ denotes a vacant site in the structure. $(Mg_{3-y}\square_y)$ indicates, therefore, that y sites out of three are vacant.]

CHLORITE

The structure of the chlorite minerals consists of alternate micalike layers and brucitelike hydroxide sheets about 14 Å thick. Structural formulas of most trioctahedral chlorites may be expressed by four end-member compositions:

- $(Mg_5Al)(Si_3Al)O_{10}(OH)_8$: (clinochlore)
- $(Fe_5^{2+}Al)(Si_3Al)O_{10}(OH)_8$: (chamosite)
- $(Mn_5Al)(Si_3Al)O_{10}(OH)_8$: (pennantite)
- $(Ni_5Al)(Si_3Al)O_{10}(OH)_8$: (nimite)

The unbalanced charge of the micalike layer is compensated by an excess charge of the hydroxide sheet that is caused by the substitution of trivalent cations (Al^{3+}, Fe^{3+}, etc.) for divalent cations (Mg^{2+}, Fe^{2+}, etc.). Chlorites with a muscovite-like silicate layer and an aluminum hydroxide sheet are called donbassite and have the ideal formula of $Al_{4.33}(Si_3Al)O_{10}(OH)_8$ as an end-member for the dioctahedral chlorite. In many cases, the octahedral aluminum ions are partially replaced by magnesium, as in magnesium-rich aluminum dioctahedral chlorites called sudoite. Cookeite is another type of dioctahedral chlorite, in which lithium substitutes for aluminum in the octahedral sheets.

Chlorite structures are relatively thermally stable compared to kaolinite, vermiculite, and smectite minerals and are thus resistant to high temperatures. Because of this, after heat treatment at 500–700 °C (930–1,300 °F), the presence of a characteristic X-ray diffraction peak at 14 Å is widely used to identify chlorite minerals.

INTERSTRATIFIED CLAY MINERALS

Many clay materials are mixtures of more than one clay mineral. One such mixture involves the interstratification of the layer clay minerals where the individual component layers of two or more kinds are stacked in various ways to make up a new structure different from those of its constituents. These interstratified structures result from the strong similarity that exists between the layers of the different clay minerals, all of which are composed of tetrahedral and octahedral sheets of hexagonal arrays of atoms, and from the distinct difference in the heights (thicknesses) of clay mineral layers.

The most striking examples of interstratified structures are those having a regular *ABAB*...-type structure, where *A* and *B* represent two component layers. There are several minerals that are known to have structures of this type—i.e., rectorite (dioctahedral mica/montmorillonite), tosudite (dioctahedral chlorite/smectite), corrensite (trioctahedral vermiculite/chlorite), hydrobiotite (trioctahedral mica/vermiculite), aliettite (talc/saponite), and kulkeite (talc/chlorite). Other than the *ABAB*...type with equal numbers of the two component layers in a structure, many modes of layer-stacking sequences ranging from nearly regular to completely random are possible. The following interstratifications of two components are found in these modes in addition to those given above: illite/smectite, glauconite/smectite, dioctahedral mica/chlorite, dioctahedral mica/vermiculite, and kaolinite/smectite.

As the mixing ratio (proportion of the numbers of layers) for the two component layers varies, the number of possible layer-stacking modes increases greatly.

For interstratified structures of three component layers, structures consisting of illite/chlorite/smectite and illite/vermiculite/smectite have been reported. Because certain interstratified structures are known to be stable under relatively limited conditions, their occurrence may be used as a geothermometer or other geoindicator.

SEPIOLITE AND PALYGORSKITE

Sepiolite and palygorskite are papyrus-like or fibrous hydrated magnesium silicate minerals and are included in the phyllosilicate group because they contain a continuous two-dimensional tetrahedral sheet of composition Si_2O_5. They differ, however, from the other layer silicates because they lack continuous octahedral sheets. The structures of sepiolite and palygorskite are alike and can be regarded as consisting of narrow strips or ribbons of 2:1 layers that are linked stepwise at the corners. One ribbon is linked to the next by inversion of the direction of the apical oxygen atoms of SiO_4 tetrahedrons; in other words, an elongated rectangular box consisting of continuous 2:1 layers is attached to the nearest boxes at their elongated corner edges. Therefore, channels or tunnels due to the absence of the silicate layers occur on the elongated sides of the boxes. The elongation of the structural element is related to the fibrous morphology of the minerals and is parallel to the a axis. Since the octahedral sheet is discontinuous, some octahedral magnesium ions are exposed at the edges and hold bound water molecules (OH_2). In addition to the bound water, variable amounts of zeolitic (i.e., free) water (H_2O) are contained in the rectangular channels. The major difference between the structures of sepiolite and palygorskite is the width of the ribbons, which is greater in sepiolite than in palygorskite. The width determines the number of octahedral cation positions per formula unit. Thus, sepiolite and palygorskite have the ideal compositions $Mg_8Si_{12}O_{30}(OH)_4(OH_2)_4(H_2O)_8$ and $(Mg, Al, \square)_5Si_8O_{20}(OH)_2(OH_2)_4(H_2O)_4$, respectively.

IMOGOLITE AND ALLOPHANE

Imogolite is an aluminosilicate with an approximate composition of $SiO_2 \cdot Al_2O_3 \cdot 2.5H_2O$. This mineral was discovered in 1962 in a soil derived from glassy volcanic ash known as "imogo." Electron-optical observations indicate that imogolite has a unique morphological feature of smooth and curved threadlike tubes varying in diameter from 10 to 30 nanometres (3.9×10^{-7} to 1.2×10^{-6} inches) and extending several micrometres in length. The structure of imogolite is cylindrical and consists of a modified gibbsite sheet in which the hydroxyls of one side of a gibbsite octahedral sheet lose protons and bond to silicon atoms that are located at vacant octahedral cation sites of gibbsite. Thus, three oxygen atoms and one hydroxyl as the fourth anion around one silicon atom make up an isolated SiO_4 tetrahedron as in orthosilicates, and such tetrahedrons make a planar array on the side of a gibbsite sheet. Because silicon-oxygen bonds are shorter than aluminum-oxygen bonds, this effect causes that sheet to curve. As a result, the curved sheet ideally forms a tubelike structure with inner and outer diameters of about 6.4 Å and 21.4 Å, respectively, and with all hydroxyls exposed at the surface. The number of modified gibbsite units therefore determines the diameter of the threadlike tubes.

Allophane can be regarded as a group of naturally occurring hydrous aluminosilicate minerals that are not totally amorphous but are short-range (partially) ordered. Allophane structures are characterized by the dominance of Si-O-Al bonds—i.e., the majority of aluminum atoms are tetrahedrally coordinated. Unlike imogolite, the morphology of allophane varies from fine, rounded particles through ring-shaped particles to irregular aggregates. There is a good indication that the ring-shaped particles may be hollow spherules or polyhedrons. Sizes of the small individual allophane particles are on the order of 30–50 Å in diameter. In spite of their indefinable structure, their chemical compositions surprisingly fall in a relatively narrow range, as the SiO_2:Al_2O_3 ratios are mostly between 1.0 and 2.0. In general, the SiO_2:Al_2O_3 ratio of allophane is higher than that of imogolite.

CHEMICAL AND PHYSICAL PROPERTIES

Clay minerals possess a number of interesting properties. In addition to their relatively small size, they exchange ions from external sources and adhere to and hold water. They often serve as catalysts and oil attractors. Naturally, the extent to which a clay mineral can engage in these chemical reactions depends upon its type.

ION EXCHANGE

Depending on deficiency in the positive or negative charge balance (locally or overall) of mineral structures, clay minerals are able to adsorb certain cations and anions and retain them around the outside of the structural unit in an exchangeable state, generally without affecting the basic silicate structure. These adsorbed ions are easily exchanged by other ions. The exchange reaction differs from simple sorption because it has a quantitative relationship between reacting ions.

Exchange capacities vary with particle size, perfection of crystallinity, and nature of the adsorbed ion; hence, a range of values exists for a given mineral rather than a single specific capacity. With certain clay minerals—such

as imogolite, allophane, and to some extent kaolinite—
that have hydroxyls at the surfaces of their structures,
exchange capacities also vary with the pH (index of acidity
or alkalinity) of the medium, which greatly affects dissociation of the hydroxyls.

Under a given set of conditions, the various cations are
not equally replaceable and do not have the same replacing power. Calcium, for example, will replace sodium
more easily than sodium will replace calcium. Sizes of
potassium and ammonium ions are similar, and the ions
are fitted in the hexagonal cavities of the silicate layer.
Vermiculite and vermiculitic minerals preferably and irreversibly adsorb these cations and fix them between the
layers. Heavy metal ions such as copper, zinc, and lead are
strongly attracted to the negatively charged sites on the
surfaces of the 1:1 layer minerals, allophane and imogolite,
which are caused by the dissociation of surface hydroxyls
of these minerals.

The ion-exchange properties of the clay minerals are
extremely important because they determine the physical
characteristics and economic use of the minerals.

CLAY-WATER RELATIONS

Clay materials contain water in several forms. The water
may be held in pores and may be removed by drying
under ambient conditions. Water also may be adsorbed
on the surface of clay mineral structures and in smectites, vermiculites, hydrated halloysite, sepiolite, and
palygorskite; this water may occur in interlayer positions
or within structural channels. Finally, the clay mineral
structures contain hydroxyls that are lost as water at elevated temperatures.

The water adsorbed between layers or in structural
channels may further be divided into zeolitic and bound
waters. The latter is bound to exchangeable cations

CATION-EXCHANGE CAPACITIES AND SPECIFIC SURFACE AREAS OF CLAY MINERALS		
MINERAL	CATION-EXCHANGE CAPACITY AT pH 7 (MILLIEQUIVALENTS PER 100 GRAMS)	SPECIFIC SURFACE AREA (SQUARE METRE PER GRAM)
kaolinite	3–15	5–40
halloysite (hydrated)	40–50	1,100*
illite	10–40	10–100
chlorite	10–40	10–55
vermiculite	100–150	760*
smectite	80–120	40–800
palygorskite-sepiolite	3–20	40–180
allophane	30–135	2,200*
imogolite	20–30	1,540*

*Upper limit of estimated values.

or directly to the clay mineral surfaces. Both forms of water may be removed by heating to temperatures on the order of 100–200 °C (about 200–400 °F) and in most cases, except for hydrated halloysite, are regained readily at ordinary temperatures. It is generally agreed that the bound water has a structure other than that of liquid water; its structure is most likely that of ice. As the thickness of the adsorbed water increases outward from the surface and extends beyond the bound water, the nature of the water changes either abruptly or gradually to that of liquid water. Ions and molecules adsorbed on the clay mineral surface exert a major influence on the thickness of the adsorbed water layers and on the nature of this water. The nonliquid water may extend out from the clay mineral surfaces as much as 60–100 Å.

Hydroxyl ions are driven off by heating clay minerals to temperatures of 400–700 °C (about 750–1,300 °F). The rate of loss of the hydroxyls and the energy required for their removal are specific properties characteristic of the various clay minerals. This dehydroxylation process results in the oxidation of Fe^{2+} to Fe^{3+} in ferrous-iron-bearing clay minerals.

The water-retention capacity of clay minerals is generally proportional to their surface area. As the water content increases, clays become plastic and then change to a near-liquid state. The amounts of water required for the two states are defined by the plastic and liquid limits, which vary with the kind of exchangeable cations and the salt concentration in the adsorbed water. The plasticity index (PI), the difference between the two limits, gives a measure for the rheological (flowage) properties of clays. A good example is a comparison of the PI of montmorillonite with that of allophane or palygorskite. The former is considerably greater than either of the latter, indicating that montmorillonite has a prominent plastic nature. Such rheological properties of clay minerals have great impact on building foundations, highway construction, chemical engineering, and soil structure in agricultural practices.

INTERACTIONS WITH INORGANIC AND ORGANIC COMPOUNDS

Smectite, vermiculite, and other expansible clay minerals can accommodate relatively large, inorganic cations between the layers. Because of this multivalency, the interlayer space is only partially occupied by such inorganic cations that are distributed in the space like islands. Hydroxy polymers of aluminum, iron, chromium, zinc, and titanium are known examples of the interlayering materials. Most of these are thermally stable and hold as pillars to allow a porous structure in the interlayer space. The resulting complexes, often called pillared clays, exhibit attractive properties as catalysts—namely, large surface area, high porosity, regulated pore size, and high solid acidity.

Cationic organic molecules, such as certain aliphatic and aromatic amines, pyridines, and methylene blue, may replace inorganic exchangeable cations present in the interlayer of expansible minerals. Polar organic molecules may replace adsorbed water on external surfaces and in interlayer positions. Ethylene glycol and glycerol are known to form stable specific complexes with smectites and vermiculites. The formation of such complexes is frequently utilized for identifying these minerals. As organic molecules coat the surface of a clay mineral, the surface of its constituent particles changes from hydrophilic to hydrophobic, thereby losing its tendency to bind water. Consequently, the affinity of the material for oil increases, so that it can react with additional organic molecules. As a result, the surface of such clay materials can accumulate organic materials. Some of the clay minerals can serve as catalysts for reactions in which one organic substance is transformed to another on the mineral's surface. Some of these organic reactions develop particular colours that may be of diagnostic value in identifying specific clay minerals. Organically clad clay minerals are used extensively in paints, inks, and plastics.

PHYSICAL PROPERTIES

Clay mineral particles are commonly too small for measuring precise optical properties. Reported refractive indices of clay minerals generally fall within a relatively narrow range from 1.47 to 1.68. In general, iron-rich mineral species show high refractive indices, whereas the water-rich porous species have lower ones. Specific gravities of most clay minerals are within the range from 2 to 3.3. Their hardness generally falls below 2½, except for antigorite, whose hardness is reported to be 2½–3½.

SIZE AND SHAPE

These two properties of clay minerals have been determined by electron micrographs. Well-crystallized kaolinite occurs as well-formed, six-sided flakes, frequently with a prominent elongation in one direction. Halloysite commonly occurs as tubular units with an outside diameter ranging from 0.04 to 0.15 micrometre (1.58×10^{-6} to 6×10^{-6} inch).

Electron micrographs of smectite often show broad undulating mosaic sheets. In some cases the flake-shaped units are discernible, but frequently they are too small or too thin to be seen individually without special attention.

Illite occurs in poorly defined flakes commonly grouped together in irregular aggregates. Although their sizes vary more widely, vermiculite, chlorite, pyrophyllite, talc, and serpentine minerals except for chrysotile are similar in character to the illites. Chrysotile occurs in slender tube-shaped fibres having an outer diameter of 100–300 Å. Their lengths commonly reach several micrometres. Electron micrographs show that palygorskite occurs as elongated laths, singly or in bundles. Frequently the individual laths are many micrometres in length and 50 to 100 Å in width. Sepiolite occurs in similar lath-shaped units. As mentioned above, allophane occurs in very small spherical particles (30–50 Å in diameter), individually or in aggregated forms, whereas imogolite occurs in long (several micrometres in length) threadlike tubes.

High-Temperature Reactions

When heated at temperatures beyond dehydroxylation, the clay mineral structure may be destroyed or simply modified, depending on the composition and structure of the substance. In the presence of fluxes, such as iron or potassium, fusion may rapidly follow dehydroxylation. In the absence of such components, particularly for aluminous dioctahedral minerals, a succession of new phases may be formed at increasing temperatures prior to fusion. Information concerning high-temperature reactions is important for ceramic science and industry.

Solubility

The solubility of the clay minerals in acids varies with the nature of the acid and its concentration, the acid-to-clay ratio, the temperature, the duration of treatment, and the chemical composition of the clay mineral attacked. In general, ferromagnesian clay minerals are more soluble in acids than their aluminian counterparts. Incongruent dissolutions may result from reactions in a low-acid-concentration medium where the acid first attacks the adsorbed or interlayer cations and then the components of the octahedral sheet of the clay mineral structure. When an acid of higher concentration is used, such stepwise reactions may not be recognizable, and the dissolution appears to be congruent. One of the important factors controlling the rate of dissolution is the concentration in the aquatic medium of the elements extracted from the clay mineral. Higher concentration of an element in the solution hinders to a greater degree the extractions of the element.

In alkaline solutions, a cation-exchange reaction first takes place, and then the silica part of the structure is attacked. The reaction depends on the same variables as those stated for acid reactions.

OCCURRENCE

Clay minerals appear frequently in soils. They are also significant parts of recent sediments, but their abundance declines in soils dating to the Mesozoic and Paleozoic eras (542 million to 65.5 million years ago). Clay minerals also serve as indicators of diagenesis (the sum of all chemical processes occurring between the deposition of a layer of sediment and its lithification), and most clay minerals can be associated with hydrothermal deposits.

SOILS

All types of clay minerals have been reported in soils. Allophane, imogolite, hydrated halloysite, and halloysite are dominant components in ando soils, which are the soils developed on volcanic ash. Smectite is usually the sole dominant component in vertisols, which are clayey soils. Smectite and illite, with occasional small amounts of kaolinite, occur in mollisols, which are prairie chernozem soils. Illite, vermiculite, smectite, chlorite, and interstratified clay minerals are found in podzolic soils. Sepiolite and palygorskite have been reported in some aridisols (desert soils), and kaolinite is the dominant component in oxisols (lateritic soils). Clay minerals other than those mentioned above usually occur in various soils as minor components inherited from the parent materials of those soils.

Soils composed of illite and chlorite are better suited for agricultural use than kaolinitic soils because of their relatively high ion-exchange properties and hence their capacity to hold plant nutrients. Moderate amounts of smectite, allophane, and imogolite in soils are advantageous for the same reason, but when present in large amounts these clay minerals are detrimental because they are impervious and have too great a water-holding capacity.

RECENT SEDIMENTS

Sediment accumulating under nonmarine conditions may have any clay mineral composition. In the Mississippi River system, for example, smectite, illite, and kaolinite are the major components in the upper Mississippi and Arkansas rivers, whereas chlorite, kaolinite, and illite are the major components in the Ohio and Tennessee rivers. Hence, in the sediments at the Gulf of Mexico, as a weighted average, smectite, illite, and kaolinite are found to be the major components in the clay mineral composition. Although kaolinite, illite, chlorite, and smectite are the principal clay mineral components of deep-sea sediments, their compositions vary from place to place. In general, illite is the dominant clay mineral in the North Atlantic Ocean (greater than 50 percent), while smectite is the major component in the South Pacific and Indian oceans. In some limited regions, these compositions are significantly altered by other factors such as airborne effects, in which sediments are transported by winds and deposited when the carrying force subsides. The high kaolinite concentration off the west coast of Africa near the Equator reflects this effect.

Under highly saline conditions in desert areas, as in soils, palygorskite and sepiolite also form in lakes and estuaries (perimarine environments).

ANCIENT SEDIMENTS

Analyses of numerous ancient sediments in many parts of the world indicate that smectite is much less abundant in sediments formed prior to the Mesozoic Era (from 251 million to 65.5 million years ago) with the exception of those of the Permian Period (from 299 million to 251 million years ago) and the Carboniferous Period (359.2 million to 299 million years ago), in which it is relatively abundant.

The available data also suggest that kaolinite is less abundant in very ancient sediments than in those deposited after the Devonian Period (416 million to 359.2 million years ago). Stated another way, the very old argillaceous (clay-rich) sediments called physilites are composed largely of illite and chlorite. Palygorskite and sepiolite have not been reported in sediments older than early Cenozoic age — i.e., those more than about 65.5 million years old.

Kaolinite and illite have been reported in various coals. Bentonite generally is defined as a clay composed largely of smectite that occurs in sediments of pyroclastic materials as the result of devitrification of volcanic ash in situ.

SEDIMENTS AFFECTED BY DIAGENESIS

As temperature and pressure increase with the progression of diagenesis, clay minerals in sediments under these circumstances change to those stable under given conditions. Therefore, certain sensitive clay minerals may serve as indicators for various stages of diagenesis. Typical examples are the crystallinity of illite, the polytypes of illite and chlorite, and the conversion of smectite to illite. Data indicate that smectite was transformed into illite through interstratified illite-smectite mineral phases as diagenetic processes advanced. Much detailed work has been devoted to the study of the conversion of smectite to illite in lower Cenozoic-Mesozoic sediments because such conversion appears to be closely related to oil-producing processes.

HYDROTHERMAL DEPOSITS

All the clay minerals, except palygorskite and sepiolite, have been found as alteration products associated with hot springs and geysers and as aureoles around metalliferous deposits. In many cases, there is a zonal arrangement of the clay minerals around the source of the alteration, a process which involves changes in the composition of rocks caused by hydrothermal solutions. The zonal arrangement varies with the type of parent rock and the nature of the hydrothermal solution. An extended kaolinite zone occurs around the tin-tungsten mine in Cornwall-Devon, Eng. Mica (sericite), chlorite, tosudite, smectite, and mica-smectite interstratifications are contained in an extensive clay zone formed in a close association with kuroko (black ore) deposits. Smectites are known to occur as alteration products of tuff and rhyolite. Pottery stones consisting of kaolinite, illite, and pyrophyllite occur as alteration products of acidic volcanic rocks, shales, and mudstone.

ORIGIN

All the clay minerals, with the possible exception of halloysite, have been synthesized from mixtures of oxides or hydroxides and water at moderately low temperatures and pressures. Kaolinite tends to form in alumina-silica systems without alkalies or alkaline earths. Illite is formed when potassium is added to such systems; and either smectite or chlorite results upon the addition of magnesium, depending on its concentration. The clay minerals can be synthesized at ordinary temperatures and pressures if the reactants are mixed together very slowly and in greatly diluted form.

Clay minerals of certain types also have been synthesized by introducing partial structural changes to clay minerals through the use of chemical treatments. Vermiculite can be formed by a prolonged reaction in which the potassium of mica is exchanged with any hydrated alkali or alkaline earth cation. Chloritic minerals can be synthesized by precipitating hydroxide sheets between the layers of vermiculite or montmorillonite. The reverse reactions of these changes are also known. A mechanism of mineral formation involving a change from one mineral to another is called transformation and can be distinguished from neoformation, which implies a mechanism for the formation of minerals from solution.

In nature both mineral formation mechanisms, neoformation and transformation, are induced by weathering and hydrothermal and diagenetic actions.

The formation of the clay minerals by weathering processes is determined by the nature of the parent rock, climate, topography, vegetation, and the time period during which these factors operated. Climate, topography, and vegetation influence weathering processes by their control of the character and direction of movement of water through the weathering zone.

In the development of clay minerals by natural hydrothermal processes, the presence of alkalies and alkaline earths influences the resulting products in the same manner as shown by synthesis experiments. Near-neutral hydrothermal solutions bring about rock alteration, including the formation of illite, chlorite, and smectite, whereas acid hydrothermal solutions result in the formation of kaolinite.

INDUSTRIAL USES

Clays are perhaps the oldest materials from which humans have manufactured various artifacts. The making of fired bricks possibly started some 5,000 years ago and was most likely humankind's second earliest industry after agriculture. The use of clays (probably smectite) as soaps and absorbents was reported in *Natural History* by the Roman author Pliny the Elder (*c.* 77 CE).

Clays composed of kaolinite are required for the manufacture of porcelain, whiteware, and refractories. Talc, pyrophyllite, feldspar, and quartz are often used in whiteware bodies, along with kaolinite clay, to develop desirable shrinkage and burning properties. Clays composed of a mixture of clay minerals, in which illite is most abundant, are used in the manufacture of brick, tile, stoneware, and glazed products. In addition to its use in the ceramic industry, kaolinite is utilized as an extender in aqueous-based paints and as a filler in natural and synthetic polymers.

Smectitic clays (bentonite) are employed primarily in the preparation of muds for drilling oil wells. This type of clay, which swells to several times its original volume in water, provides colloidal and wall-building properties. Palygorskite and sepiolite clays also are used because of their resistance to flocculation under high salinity conditions. Certain clay minerals, notably palygorskite, sepiolite, and some smectites, possess substantial ability to remove coloured bodies from oil. These so-called fuller's earths are used in processing many mineral and vegetable oils. Because of their large absorbing capacity, fuller's earths are also used commercially for preparing animal litter trays and oil and grease absorbents. Acid treatment of some smectite clays increases their decolorizing ability. Much gasoline is manufactured by using catalysts prepared from a smectite, kaolinite, or halloysite type of clay mineral.

Tons of kaolinite clays are used as paper fillers and paper coating pigments. Palygorskite-sepiolite minerals and acid-treated smectites are used in the preparation of no-carbon-required paper because of the colour they develop during reactions with certain colourless organic compounds.

Clays have a tremendous number of miscellaneous uses, and for each application a distinct type with particular properties is important. Recently, clays have become important for various aspects of environmental science and remediation. Dense smectite clays can be compacted as bentonite blocks to serve as effective barriers to isolate radioactive wastes. Various clays may absorb various pollutants including organic compounds (such as atrazine, trifluraline, parathion, and malathion) and inorganic trace metals (such as copper, zinc, cadmium, and mercury) from soils and groundwater. Clay is also used as an effective barrier in landfills and mine tailing ponds to prevent contaminants from entering the local groundwater system. For the most part, clays are not a health hazard except possibly palygorskites, which may damage respiratory health. As research continues, clay minerals are playing an increasing role in solving modern environmental problems.

CHAPTER 6
SILICA MINERALS

Silica minerals make up a group composed of any of the forms of silicon dioxide (SiO_2), including quartz, tridymite, cristobalite, coesite, stishovite, lechatelierite, and chalcedony. They make up approximately 12 percent of the Earth's crust and are second only to the feldspars in mineral abundance. Free silica occurs in many crystalline forms with a composition very close to that of silicon dioxide, 46.75 percent by weight being silicon and 53.25 percent oxygen.

PHYSICAL AND CHEMICAL PROPERTIES

The crystallographic structures of the silica minerals, except stishovite, are three-dimensional arrays of linked tetrahedrons, each consisting of a silicon atom coordinated by four oxygen atoms. The tetrahedrons are usually quite regular, and the silicon-oxygen bond distances are 1.61 ± 0.02 Å. Principal differences are related to the geometry of the tetrahedral linkages, which may cause small distortions within the silica tetrahedrons. High pressure forces silicon atoms to coordinate with six oxygen atoms, producing nearly regular octahedrons in the stishovite structure.

The silica minerals when pure are colourless and transparent and have a vitreous lustre. They are nonconductors of electricity and are diamagnetic. All are hard and strong and fail by brittle fracture under an imposed stress.

SOME PHYSICAL PROPERTIES OF SILICA MINERALS

PHASE	SYMMETRY	SPECIFIC GRAVITY	HARDNESS
* quartz *(alpha-quartz)	*hexagonal *trigonal *trapezohedral	2.651	7
*high quartz *(beta-quartz)	*hexagonal *hexagonal *trapezohedral	2.53 at 600 degrees Celsius (1112 °F)	7
low tridymite	monoclinic?	2.26	7
high tridymite	orthorhombic	2.20 at 200 degrees Celsius (392 °F)	7?
low cristobalite	tetragonal	2.32	6–7
high cristobalite	isometric	2.20 at 500 degrees Celsius (932 °F)	6–7
keatite	tetragonal	2.50	?
coesite	monoclinic	2.93	7.5
stishovite	tetragonal	4.28	?
vitreous silica	amorphous	2.203	6
opal	*poorly *crystalline or *amorphous	1.99–2.05	5 1/2–6 1/2

There is a linear relationship between the specific gravity values and the arithmetic mean of the indices of refraction (measures of the velocity of light that is transmitted in different crystallographic directions) for silica minerals composed of linked tetrahedrons.

This relationship does not extend to stishovite because it is not made up of silica tetrahedrons. The specific gravities of silica minerals are less than those of most of the dark-coloured silicate minerals associated with them in nature; in general, the lighter-coloured rocks have lower specific gravity for this reason. Silica minerals are insoluble to sparingly soluble in strong acids except hydrofluoric acid, in which there is a correlation between specific gravity and solubility.

ORIGIN AND OCCURRENCE

Silicon and oxygen are the two most abundant elements in the Earth's crust, in which they largely occur in combination with other elements as silicate minerals. Free silica (SiO_2) appears as a mineral in crystallizing magma only when the relative abundance of SiO_2 exceeds that of all other cations available to form silicates. Silica minerals thus occur only in magmas containing more than about 47 percent by weight of SiO_2 and are incompatible with minerals with low cation:silica ratios — such as olivine, nepheline, or leucite. Basaltic and alkalic igneous magmas therefore can crystallize only minor amounts of silica minerals, and sometimes none are produced. The gas released from such rocks can dissolve the silica components, however, and later precipitate silica minerals upon cooling. The amount of silica minerals crystallized from magma increases with increasing silica content of magma, reaching 40 percent in some granites and rhyolites.

SOLUBILITY OF SILICA MINERALS

The solubility of silica minerals in natural solutions and gases is of great importance. The solubility of all silica minerals increases regularly with increasing temperature and pressure except in the region of 340–550 °C (645–1,020 °F) and 0–600 bars (0–8,700 pounds per square inch), where retrograde solubility occurs because of changes in the physical state of water. The solubility of silica increases in the presence of anions such as OH⁻ and CO_3^{2-}, which form chemical complexes with it.

Quartz is the least soluble of the forms of silica at room temperature. In pure water its solubility at 25 °C (77 °F) is about 6 parts per million, that of vitreous silica being at least 10 times greater. Typical temperate-climate river water contains 14 parts per million of silica, and enormous tonnages of silica are carried away in solution annually from weathering rocks and soils. The amount so removed may be equivalent to that transported mechanically in many climates. Silica dissolved in moving groundwater may partially fill hollow spheroids and precipitate crystals to form geodes, or it may cement loose sand grains together to form concretions and nodules or even entire sedimentary beds into sandstone, which, when all pore space is eliminated by selective solution and nearby deposition during metamorphism, form tough, pore-free quartzite.

Gases or solutions escaping from cooling igneous rocks or deep fractures commonly are saturated with silica and other compounds that, as they cool, precipitate quartz along their channelways to form veins. It may be fine-grained (as chalcedony), massive granular, or in coarse crystals as large as tens of tons. Most natural colourless quartz crystals, "rock crystal," were formed in this way.

The emergence of heated silica-bearing solutions onto the surface results in rapid cooling and the loss of complexing anions. Rapid precipitation of fine-grained silica results in formation of siliceous sinter or geyserite, as at

Mammoth Hot Springs in Yellowstone National Park in the western United States.

Quartz is mechanically resistant and relatively inert chemically during rock weathering in temperate and cold climates. Thus, it becomes enriched in river, lake, and beach sediments, which commonly contain more than one-half quartz by weight. Some strata consist almost entirely of quartz over large lateral distances and tens or hundreds of metres in thickness. Known as glass sands, these strata are important economic sources of silica for glass and chemical industries. Quartz-bearing strata are abundant in metamorphic terrains. The reincorporation of free silica into complex silicates and the solution and redeposition of silica into veins is characteristic of such terrains.

THE SILICA PHASE DIAGRAM

In diagrams of pressure-temperature fields of stability of silica minerals, stability fields are not shown for keatite, melanophlogite, opal, or the low forms of tridymite and cristobalite because they have not been demonstrated. Quartz is the stable phase of silica under the physical conditions that prevail over most of the Earth's crust. Coesite occurs at depths of about 100 km (60 miles) in the Earth's mantle. Stishovite would require even greater depths of burial, and no rocks that occur on the terrestrial surface have been buried so deeply. Stishovite is reported only in a few localities that were subjected to very high pressures from meteorite impact events.

USES

Quartz is the only natural silica mineral used in significant quantities; millions of tons are consumed annually by many industries. The sand that is an essential ingredient of concrete and mortar is largely quartz, as are the sandstone and quartzite used as building stones. Crushed sandstone and quartzite are used for road and railway construction, roofing granules, and riprap—erosion-control linings of river channels. Quartz is hard (7 on the Mohs scale) and resists fracture because it lacks easy cleavage. These properties, combined with its ready availability, lead to its use as a sandpaper abrasive and in sandblasting; for polishing and cutting glass, stone, and metal; and for providing traction on stairs, streets, and rails. Large amounts of relatively pure quartz are used in refractory products, such as insulation and firebricks, foundry molds, and electrical insulators, because of the combination of its high melting temperatures, low coefficients of expansion, inertness of the high-temperature forms of silica, and low costs.

Relatively pure quartz is required in large tonnages as an ingredient for glass and porcelain manufacture. High purity quartz is fused to make premium grades of chemical and optical glass for which one or more of its desirable properties of low thermal expansion, high-shape stability, elasticity, low solubility, and transparency to various kinds of light can justify the greatly increased costs involved. Fibres of vitreous silica are essential for precision instruments, such as balances, galvanometers, and gravimeters. Tons of quartz of various qualities are used as raw materials for processes in which silica is not the final product. These include the production of water glass, or sodium silicate, various sols—very fine dispersions of solids in liquids—that are used as hydrophobic (water-repelling) coatings, organic silicates and silicones, silicon carbide, silicon metal, smelting flux, and alloying in metallurgy.

Quartz and its varieties have been used since antiquity as semiprecious gems, ornamental stones, and collector's items. Precious opal, a hydrous form of silica, has been a gemstone since Roman times.

INDIVIDUAL SILICA MINERALS

Quartz is by far the most commonly occurring form. Tridymite, cristobalite, and the hydrous silica mineral opal are uncommon, and vitreous (glassy) silica, coesite, and stishovite have been reported from only a few localities. Several other forms have been produced in the laboratory but have not been found in nature. Keatite is one example of a silica mineral that has been produced synthetically.

QUARTZ

Quartz occurs in many varieties in almost all types of igneous, sedimentary, and metamorphic rocks. It has also been found in meteorites and in some lunar rocks. Quartz is a widely distributed mineral that occurs in many varieties. It consists primarily of silica, or silicon dioxide (SiO_2). Minor impurities such as lithium, sodium, potassium, and titanium may be present. Quartz has attracted attention from the earliest times; water-clear crystals were known to the ancient Greeks as *krystallos*—hence the name *crystal*, or more commonly *rock crystal*, applied to this variety. The name *quartz* is an old German word of uncertain origin first used by Georgius Agricola in 1530.

Quartz is the second most abundant mineral in the Earth's crust after feldspar. It occurs in nearly all acid igneous, metamorphic, and sedimentary rocks. It is an essential mineral in such silica-rich felsic rocks as granites, granodiorites, and rhyolites. It is highly resistant to weathering and tends to concentrate in sandstones and other detrital rocks. Secondary quartz serves as a cement in sedimentary rocks of this kind, forming overgrowths on detrital grains. Microcrystalline varieties of silica known as chert, flint, agate, and jasper consist of a fine network of quartz. Metamorphism of quartz-bearing igneous and sedimentary rocks typically increases the amount of quartz and its grain size.

Quartz crystals lack a centre of symmetry or planes of symmetry and have one crystallographic axis (c) perpendicular to three polar axes (a) that are 120° apart. One end of a polar axis is different from its other end; when mechanical stress is applied on such an axis, opposite electrical charges develop on each end. This leads to important applications in electronics as a frequency control and in pressure gauges and other devices. The lack of symmetry planes parallel to the vertical axis allows quartz crystals to occur as two types: left-handed or right-handed (enantiomorphism). Left-handed quartz is less than 1 percent more abundant than right-handed quartz. The structural tetrahedrons spiral upward through the crystal in the sense of the handedness parallel to the c axis. Similarly, if polarized light is transmitted by a quartz crystal along the c-axis direction, the plane is rotated in the direction of the handedness by tens of degrees per millimetre, the amount depending on the wavelength of the light. This property is used in optical instruments such as monochromators.

Quartz is piezoelectric: a crystal develops positive and negative charges on alternate prism edges when it is subjected to pressure or tension. The charges are proportional to the change in pressure. Because of its piezoelectric property, a quartz plate can be used as a pressure gauge, as in depth-sounding apparatus.

Just as compression and tension produce opposite charges, the converse effect is that alternating opposite charges will cause alternating expansion and contraction. A section cut from a quartz crystal with definite orientation and dimensions has a natural frequency of this expansion and contraction (i.e., vibration) that is very high, measured in millions of vibrations per second. Properly cut plates of quartz are used for frequency control in radios, televisions, and other electronic communications equipment and for crystal-controlled clocks and watches.

Quartz shows less range in chemical composition than do most other minerals, but it commonly contains tens to hundreds of parts per million of aluminum atoms substituting for silicon atoms, with charge balance maintained by the incorporation of small atoms, such as hydrogen, lithium, or sodium. Titanium, magnesium, or iron atoms substituting for silicon atoms also have been reported, but anionic substitution (i.e., substitution for the negative ion, oxygen) is limited because the linkage of the tetrahedrons is disrupted.

Quartz exists in two forms: (1) alpha-, or low, quartz, which is stable up to 573° C (1,063° F), and (2) beta-, or high, quartz, stable above 573° C. The two are closely related, with only small movements of their constituent atoms during the alpha-beta transition. The structure of beta-quartz is hexagonal, with either a left- or right-handed symmetry group equally populated in crystals. The structure of alpha-quartz is trigonal, again with either a right- or left-handed symmetry group. At the transition temperature the tetrahedral framework of beta-quartz twists, resulting in the symmetry of alpha-quartz; atoms

Quartz agates from Mexico. Courtesy of Joseph and Helen Guetterman collection;photograph, John H. Gerard—EB Inc.

move from special space group positions to more general positions. At temperatures above 867° C (1,593° F), beta-quartz changes into tridymite, but the transformation is very slow because bond breaking takes place to form a more open structure. At very high pressures alpha-quartz transforms into coesite and, at still higher pressures, stishovite. Such phases have been observed in impact craters.

Quartz may contain inclusions of other minerals, such as rutile (rutilated quartz), tourmaline, asbestiform amphiboles, or platy minerals, such as mica, iron oxides, or chlorite (aventurine).

Coloured varieties of quartz are numerous and have many causes. Most colours result from mechanically incorporated admixtures within fine-crystallized or granular quartz, but some coarse-crystallized varieties,

Rose quartz. B.M. Shaub

such as amethyst (violet), citrine (yellow), milky quartz, smoky quartz or morion (black), or rose quartz, may be coloured by ions other than silicon and oxygen that occur within the crystal structure. Small fractions of 1 percent by weight of iron, aluminum, manganese, titanium, hydrogen, and small alkali atoms, such as lithium and sodium, have been shown to be the cause of different colours. Heat treatment or various irradiation treatments under oxidizing or reducing atmospheres are used to change one coloured variety to another. Citrine is commonly produced by heat-treating amethyst at 250–400 °C (482–752 °F), for example.

Quartz has great economic importance. Many varieties are gemstones, including amethyst, citrine, smoky quartz, and rose quartz. Sandstone, composed mainly of quartz, is an important building stone. Large amounts of quartz sand (also known as silica sand) are used in the manufacture of glass and ceramics and for foundry molds in metal casting. Crushed quartz is used as an abrasive in sandpaper, silica sand is employed in sandblasting, and sandstone is still used whole to make whetstones, millstones, and grindstones. Silica glass (also called fused quartz) is used in optics to transmit ultraviolet light. Tubing and various vessels of fused quartz have important laboratory applications, and quartz fibres are employed in extremely sensitive weighing devices.

SARD AND SARDONYX

Sard and sardonyx are translucent, light- to dark-brown varieties of the silica mineral chalcedony, historically two of the most widely used semiprecious stones. Sard and its close relative carnelian have been used in engraved jewelry for centuries. Sard (from Sardis, the ancient capital of Lydia) was originally called sardion, which included both sard and carnelian until the Middle Ages. Except for crystal, it is the oldest known name for a silica mineral. One locality famous as a source of sard is Ratnapura, Sri Lanka. Bands of sard and white chalcedony are called sardonyx, which at one time was more precious than gold, silver, or sapphire. Sardonyx is widely used in cameos and intaglios. Its properties are those of quartz.

CHALCEDONY

Chalcedony is a white, buff, or light tan, finely crystallized or fibrous quartz that forms rounded crusts, rinds, or stalactites (mineral deposits suspended from the roofs of caverns) in volcanic and sedimentary rocks as a precipitate from moving solutions. If chalcedony is conspicuously colour-banded, it may be called agate; onyx is agate with alternate bands of white and black or dark brown. Some concentrically banded "eye" agate nodules contain cores of coarsely crystalline quartz, and other agates are mottled or variegated in colour. Arborescent or dendritic (branching) dark-coloured patterns set in a lighter field are called moss agate or Mocha stone. Translucent red chalcedony is called carnelian, and translucent brown shades are referred to as sard; both are pigmented by admixed iron oxides.

Chrysoprase, plasma, and prase are names for green varieties of chalcedony coloured by admixed green minerals, such as chlorite, fibrous amphiboles, or hydrous nickel silicates. Bloodstone and heliotrope are green chalcedony with red spots.

JASPER, CHERT, AND FLINT

Jasper is opaque red, brown, or yellow quartz that is pigmented by admixed iron oxides. Chert and flint are finely crystallized varieties of gray to black quartz that occur as nodules or bands in sedimentary rocks.

JASPER

Jasper is an opaque, fine-grained or dense variety of the silica mineral chert that exhibits various colours. Chiefly brick red to brownish red, it owes its colour to admixed hematite; but when it occurs with clay admixed, the colour is a yellowish white or gray, or with goethite a brown or yellow. Jasper, long used for jewelry and ornamentation, has a dull lustre but takes a fine polish, and its hardness and other physical properties are those of quartz.

The name jasper is from the Greek *iaspis,* of Semitic origin; in ancient writings the term was chiefly applied to translucent and brightly coloured stones, particularly chalcedony, but also was applied to the opaque jasper. Medicinal values were long attributed to jasper, including a belief that wearing it strengthened the stomach.

Jasper is common and widely distributed, occurring chiefly as veinlets, concretions, and replacements in sedimentary and metamorphic rocks, as in the Urals, North Africa, Sicily, Germany, and elsewhere. Some varieties are colour-banded, and beautiful examples of jasperized fossil wood are found in Arizona, U.S. Jasper is also common as detrital pebbles.

For thousands of years, black jasper (and also black slate) was used to test gold-silver alloys for their gold content. Rubbing the alloys on the stone, called a touchstone, produces a streak the colour of which determines the gold content within one part in one hundred.

CHERT AND FLINT

 Chert and flint are varieties of very fine-grained quartz. Several varieties are included under the general term chert: jasper, chalcedony, agate, flint, porcelanite, and novaculite.

Flint is gray to black and nearly opaque (translucent brown in thin splinters) because of included carbonaceous matter. Opaque, dull, whitish to pale-brown or gray specimens are simply called chert; the light colour and opacity are caused by abundant, extremely minute inclusions of water or air. The physical properties are those of quartz.

Chert and flint provided the main source of tools and weapons for Stone Age man. The uniform fine grain, brittleness, and conchoidal fracture made it relatively easy to shape arrowheads by flaking off chips, and the edges produced were quite sharp. Quarrying and manufacture of flint weapons were among humankind's earliest business ventures, and it is sometimes possible to trace ancient trade routes by knowing where a particular type of flint was obtained. From the 17th through the early 19th century, flints again found extensive military use in flintlock rifles. Crushed flint is still used as the abrasive agent on sandpapers for the finishing of wood and leather. In addition, flint pebbles are used in mills that grind raw materials for the ceramic and paint industries; the use of flint pebbles instead of steel balls as a grinding agent is desirable in order to avoid contaminating the product with iron. Considerable amounts of chert are also used in road construction and as concrete aggregate. Some chert takes an excellent polish and serves as semiprecious jewelry.

Chert and flint occur as individual nodules or layers of nodules in limestone or dolomite; they are common in rocks of all ages (notably in the Cretaceous chalk of England). Hard and chemically resistant, the nodules become concentrated in residual soils as the surrounding carbonate rock weathers away. In places, chert forms massive beds several hundred metres thick with a lateral extent of hundreds of kilometres. Chert also occurs as a fine powder disseminated throughout carbonate rock; it impregnates shale and, rarely, forms cement in sandstone. It also develops in the vicinity of some metalliferous veins, precipitated by hot ore-depositing (hydrothermal) solutions. Erosion of chert beds or chert-bearing limestone produces chert pebbles, which are abundant in river and beach gravel.

Most chert and flint has formed by replacement of the enclosing carbonate sediment after burial beneath the seafloor. This replacement origin (similar to the petrification of wood) is substantiated by preservation in chert of the minute textural details of the enclosing carbonate rocks.

Bedded chert, also referred to as ribbon chert, is made up of layers of chert interbedded with thin layers of shale. Many bedded cherts are made up of the remains of siliceous organisms such as diatoms, radiolarians, or sponge spicules.

HIGH QUARTZ (β-QUARTZ)

High quartz, or β-quartz, is the more symmetrical form quartz takes at sufficiently high temperatures (about 573 °C [about 1,060 °F] at one atmosphere of pressure), but the relationship is pressure-sensitive. High quartz may be either left- or right-handed, and its c axis is one of sixfold symmetry rather than threefold; thus, many twin laws of ordinary quartz cannot occur. High quartz twins typically involve inclined sets of axes. High quartz can form directly from silicate magma or from high-temperature gases or solutions. It invariably undergoes the transition to ordinary quartz (low quartz) on cooling, and all ordinary quartz, when heated above the transition temperature, is transformed into high quartz. The transformation involves displacement of the linkage between the tetrahedrons; no bonds are broken.

TRIDYMITE

Tridymite may occur as a primary magmatic phase (i.e., as a direct result of crystallization from a silicate melt) in siliceous rocks but is most abundant in voids in volcanic rocks where it probably was deposited metastably from hydrous gases. Tridymite also forms in contact-metamorphosed rocks. It has been found in meteorites and is common in lunar basalts. It occurs in quantity in firebricks and other siliceous refractories. Natural tridymite has no specific commercial use.

CRISTOBALITE

Cristobalite is probably more abundant in nature than tridymite, although it seldom forms as distinctive crystals. The devitrification (transformation from the glassy to the crystalline state) of siliceous volcanic glasses yields abundant tiny crystallites of cristobalite, and the mineral is also deposited metastably from hot hydrous gases in cavities and cracks of many volcanic rocks. It has been found in lunar basalts and in meteorites and is common in silica refractories exposed to very high temperatures.

OPAL

Opal is poorly crystalline or amorphous hydrous silica that is compact and vitreous and most commonly translucent white to colourless. Precious opal reflects light with a play of brilliant colours across the visible spectrum, red being the most valued. Opal forms by precipitation from silica-bearing solutions near the Earth's surface. Electron microscopy has shown that many opals are composed of spheres of tens to a few thousand angstroms in size that are arranged in either hexagonal or cubic close packing. The spheres are composed of hydrous silica that may be either almost cristobalite-like, tridymite-like, mixtures of both, or random and nondiffracting. The specific gravity and refractive index are lower than those of pure silica minerals. The play of colours in precious opal arises from the diffraction of light from submicroscopic layers of regularly oriented silica spheres. When heated, opal may lose as much as 20 percent of its weight of water, fracture, and then crystallize to one of the silica minerals described above.

Opal usually contains 4 to 9 percent water, but lower and much higher values have been observed. The contents of alumina, ferric oxide, and alkalis are variable but may amount to several percent in light-coloured opals and more if pigmenting minerals are also present. Precious opal has been synthesized. Opaline silica is a friable hydrous silica found near hot springs and geysers.

VITREOUS SILICA

Vitreous silica, lechatelierite, is supercooled liquid silica. It has been observed in nature as the result of fusion of quartz by lightning strikes (fulgurites) or by shock associated with large meteorite impacts and may approach artificial, very pure silica glass in composition and physical properties.

MELANOPHLOGITE

Melanophlogite is a tetragonal or cubic silica mineral with a gas-hydrate structure containing many large voids. In nature these are filled with 6 to 12 percent by weight of compounds of hydrogen, carbon, and sulfur, which may be necessary for mineral growth. If these compounds are destroyed by heating, they do not cause the crystal to collapse, but the free carbon formed does darken it. Melanophlogite occurs with bitumen and forms at temperatures below 112 °C (about 234 °F). It has been found on native sulfur crystals in Sicily and Santa Clara county, Calif.

KEATITE

Keatite is a tetragonal form of silica known only from the laboratory, where it can be synthesized metastably in the presence of steam over a temperature range of 300 to 600 °C (about 570 to 1,100 °F) and a pressure range of 400 to 4,000 bars (standard atmospheric pressure at sea level is 1,013.3 millibars, or slightly more than 1 bar, which equals 760 mm of mercury). It has negative thermal expansion along the *a* axis and positive thermal expansion along the *c* axis, so that the overall expansion is very low or negative.

COESITE AND STISHOVITE

Coesite and stishovite are rare dense forms of silica. They are observed in nature only where quartz-bearing rocks have been severely shocked by a large meteorite impact, such as Meteor Crater in Arizona, U.S. Coesite is found in ultrahigh-pressure metamorphic rocks such as in Dora Maira, Italy, and the Dabie Mountains, China. Coesite is made up of tetrahedrons arranged like those in feldspars. Stishovite is the densest form of silica and consists of silicon that is octahedrally coordinated with oxygen. Both coesite and stishovite have been synthesized and found to be stable only at high pressures.

CHAPTER 7

CARBONATES AND OTHER MINERALS

Any member of a family of minerals that contain the carbonate ion, CO_3^{2-}, as the basic structural and compositional unit is referred to as a carbonate mineral. The carbonates are among the most widely distributed minerals in the Earth's crust.

The crystal structure of many carbonate minerals reflects the trigonal symmetry of the carbonate ion, which is composed of a carbon atom centrally located in an equilateral triangle of oxygen atoms. This anion group usually occurs in combination with calcium, sodium, uranium, iron, aluminum, manganese, barium, zinc, copper, lead, or the rare-earth elements. The carbonates tend to be soft, soluble in hydrochloric acid, and have a marked anisotropy in many physical properties (e.g., high birefringence) as a result of the planar structure of the carbonate ion.

Most such rock-forming carbonates belong to one of two structure groups—either calcite or aragonite. The calcite structure is usually described with reference to the sodium chloride structure in which the sodium and chloride of halite are replaced by calcium atoms and CO_3 groups, respectively. The unit cell of halite is distorted by compression along a three-fold axis, resulting in a rhombohedral cell. In calcite all CO_3 groups are parallel and lie in horizontal layers; CO_3 groups in adjacent layers, however, point in opposite directions. The calcium atoms are bonded to six oxygen atoms, one each from three CO_3 groups in a layer above and three from CO_3 groups in a layer below. The structure of dolomite, $CaMg(CO_3)_2$, is similar to that of calcite, $CaCO_3$, except that there is regular alternation of calcium and magnesium, and a lower symmetry, though still rhombohedral, results. The second structure group, that of aragonite, is orthorhombic. Like the calcite structure, the cation in the aragonite structure is surrounded by six carbonate groups; the CO_3 groups, however, are rotated about an axis perpendicular to their plane and the cation is coordinated to nine oxygen atoms instead of six.

Carbonate minerals other than simple carbonates include hydrated carbonates, bicarbonates, and compound carbonates containing other anions in addition to carbonate. The first two groups include nahcolite, trona, natron, and shortite; they typically occur in sedimentary evaporite deposits and as low-temperature hydrothermal alteration products. The members of the third group generally contain rare-earth elements and almost always result from hydrothermal alteration at low temperatures. Examples of these carbonate minerals are bastnäsite, doverite, malachite, and azurite.

A number of other, smaller mineral groups are also included in this chapter. Many of these groups form bonds with oxygen in a manner similar to the silicates. Others, however, produce salts.

THE CARBONATES

There are approximately 80 known carbonate minerals, but most of them are rare. The commonest varieties, calcite, dolomite, and aragonite, are prominent constituents of certain rocks: calcite is the principal mineral of limestones and marbles; dolomite occurs as a replacement for calcite in limestones, and when this is extensive the rock is termed dolomite; and aragonite occurs in some recent sediments and in the shells of organisms that have calcareous skeletons. Other relatively common carbonate minerals serve as metal ores: siderite, for iron; rhodochrosite, for manganese; strontianite, for strontium; smithsonite, for zinc; witherite, for barium; and cerussite, for lead. Aragonite, calcite, and dolomite are described in greater detail below.

ARAGONITE

Aragonite is a widespread mineral, the stable form of calcium carbonate ($CaCO_3$) at high pressures. It may be distinguished from calcite, the commoner form of calcium carbonate, by its greater hardness and specific gravity. Aragonite is always found in deposits formed at low temperatures near the surface of the Earth, as in caves as stalactites, in the oxidized zone of ore minerals (with lead substituting for calcium), in serpentine and other basic rocks, in sediments, and in iron-ore deposits. Aragonite is the mineral normally found in pearls. It is polymorphous (same chemical formula but different crystal structure) with calcite and vaterite, and, with geologic time, probably inverts to calcite even under normal conditions.

Aragonite is an important element in the shells and tests of many marine invertebrates. These animals can secrete the mineral from waters that would ordinarily yield only calcite; they do so by physiological mechanisms that are not fully understood.

CALCITE

Calcite is the most common form of natural calcium carbonate ($CaCO_3$), a widely distributed mineral known for the beautiful development and great variety of its crystals. It is polymorphous (same chemical formula but different crystal structure) with the minerals aragonite and vaterite and with several forms that apparently exist only under rather extreme experimental conditions.

The carbonate minerals calcite, aragonite, and dolomite have been calculated to make up approximately 15 percent of the Earth's sediments and sedimentary rocks and about 2 percent of the terrestrial crust. A large percentage of the calcite, the most abundant of these carbonate minerals, occurs in limestones, which constitute noteworthy proportions of many sequences of marine sediments. Calcite is also the chief component of marls, travertines, calcite veins, most speleothems (cave deposits), many marbles and carbonatites, and some ore-bearing veins.

Calcite is the stable form of $CaCO_3$ at most temperatures and pressures. The orthorhombic polymorph of $CaCO_3$, aragonite, though frequently deposited in nature, is metastable at room temperature and pressure and readily inverts to calcite; the inversion has been shown experimentally to be spontaneous when aragonite is heated to 400 °C (about 750 °F) in dry air and at lower temperatures when it is in contact with water. Hexagonal vaterite, the other natural polymorph of $CaCO_3$, is extremely rare and has been shown in the laboratory to transform into calcite or aragonite or both penecontemporaneously with its formation—i.e., it appears to be metastable under essentially all known natural conditions.

CHEMICAL COMPOSITION

Some natural calcites are essentially pure $CaCO_3$; others contain noteworthy percentages of other cations (e.g., Mg, Mn, Fe, boron [B], bromine [Br], Sr, and/or Y), substituting for some of their calcium. In general, however, only minor substitution occurs. Only manganese and magnesium are known to substitute extensively for the calcium: manganocalcite and calcian rhodochrosite (i.e., calcium-bearing $MnCO_3$) have been identified, and solid solution has been shown to be possible from pure $CaCO_3$ to 40 percent $MnCO_3$ and from pure $MnCO_3$ to about 25 percent $CaCO_3$. Metastable magnesian calcites containing from approximately 5 to 18 percent $MgCO_3$ occur rather widely as biogenic skeletal material and as cement in some modern marine sediments. Magnesian calcites at the lower end of this range of $MgCO_3$ contents constitute some marine oöids and calcareous tufas.

Between 60 and 70 elements have been recorded in minor or trace amounts in limestone analyses. Some of these elements may occur as substitutions within calcite; others seem more likely to represent minor constituents, such as clay minerals, within the analyzed rocks.

The chemical composition of calcite is responsible for the test that is widely used to identify it, especially in the field. This test is based on the fact that calcite reacts with dilute hydrochloric acid (HCl), and the reaction is manifested by vigorous effervescence. (The dilution of the HCl usually used is about 90:10 [water:concentrated HCl].) The reactions involved are

$$CaCO_3 + 2HCl \longrightarrow CaCl_2 + H_2CO_3$$
and
$$H_2CO_3 \longrightarrow H_2O + CO_2.$$

The effervescence is due to the spontaneous breakdown of the carbonic acid (H_2CO_3) to produce carbon dioxide gas, CO_2.

CRYSTAL STRUCTURE

The structure of calcite—one of the first mineral structures to be determined by X-ray methods—has been described on three different bases. The two most

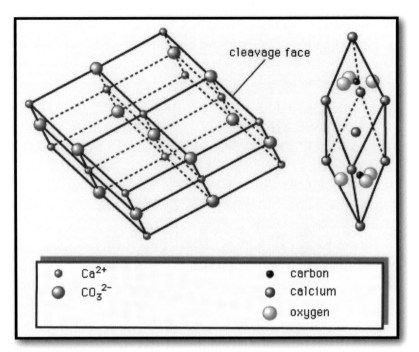

The crystal structure of calcite. This schematic diagram shows both (left) the true unit cell (the acute rhombohedron, which contains 2[CaCo₃]) and (right) an alternative cell based on the cleavage rhombohedron. Copyright Encyclopædia Britannica, Inc.; rendering for this edition by Rosen Educational Services

frequently used bases are the true rhombohedral unit cell, which is the acute rhombohedron, and the cleavage rhombohedron setup. The true unit cell includes 2 $CaCO_3$ with calcium ions at the corners of the rhombohedrons and CO_3 groups, each of which consists of a carbon ion at the centre of a planar group of oxygen atoms whose centres define an equilateral triangle. The configuration can be considered another way: the structure consists of alternating sheets of hexagonally arranged calcium ions and CO_3 complex anions. This array is in the hexagonal (trigonal) crystal system. The threefold symmetry is quite obvious in both crystals and cleavage rhombohedrons. The crystals occur most commonly in cavities in rocks—e.g., in vugs

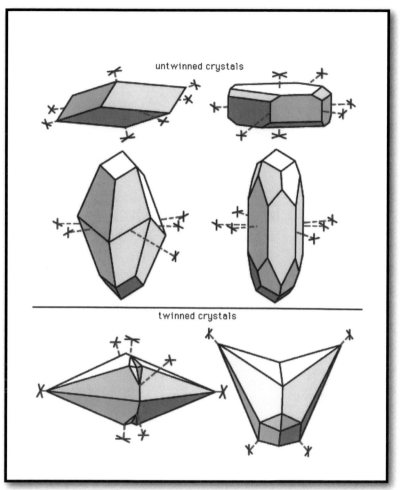

Calcite crystals. Some of the many fairly common crystal habits represented by natural calcite crystals are illustrated here. Copyright Encyclopædia Britannica, Inc.; rendering for this edition by Rosen Educational Services

(including druses), in vesicles in igneous rocks, and lining partially filled fissures. More than 300 forms of calcite have been recognized.

PHYSICAL PROPERTIES

Calcite is colourless or white when pure but may be of almost any colour—reddish, pink, yellow, greenish, bluish, lavender, black, or brown—owing to the presence of diverse impurities. It may be transparent, translucent, or opaque. Its lustre ranges from vitreous to dull; many crystals, especially the colourless ones, are vitreous, whereas granular masses, especially those that are fine-grained, tend to be dull. Calcite is number 3 on the Mohs hardness scale; thus, it can be scratched readily by a knife blade or geologic pick. It has a specific gravity of 2.71. Three perfect cleavages give calcite its six-sided polyhedrons with diamond-shaped faces; the angles defining the faces are 78° and 102°. The three important crystal habits (distinctive shapes of the mineral) of calcite are: (1) prismatic (both short and long), (2) rhombohedral, and (3) scalenohedral. Twinning is very common and may be of secondary origin in crystalline limestones. Some calcites fluoresce under ultraviolet light; some are also triboluminescent (luminescent when scratched). When light passes through some minerals, it is split into two rays that travel at different speeds and in different directions. This phenomenon is known as birefringence. The difference between the velocities is especially notable in calcite, and consequently crystals of a colourless variety—sometimes called Iceland spar—exhibit double refraction that can be observed with the naked eye.

The previously described fact that calcite effervesces vigorously with dilute hydrochloric (muriatic) acid distinguishes calcite from dolomite, which it tends to resemble in both appearance and occurrence. (Dolomite effervesces only when powdered and with only a slow, smoldering action.)

In rocks made up predominantly of calcite, the mineral is typically granular, with grains ranging from those discernible only under a microscope to those that are a few millimetres in greatest dimension. The colour of most of these rocks is gray or tan, but some calcite marbles are white and a few are multicoloured.

ORIGIN AND OCCURRENCE

A large percentage of the calcite in rocks was deposited in sedimentary environments; consequently, calcite is a constituent of several diverse sediments, sedimentary rocks, and their metamorphosed products. A minor amount of the Earth's calcite is of magmatic (i.e., igneous) origin; it is the chief constituent of the rare rock called carbonatite. Calcite also occurs widely in veins: some of the veins are wholly or largely calcite; others contain valuable ore minerals and are usually described as ore veins, even though calcite is the predominant constituent.

The sedimentary rocks composed largely of calcite include limestones of chemical and biochemical origin and also limestones usually referred to as clastic because they consist of transported fragments of previously deposited, typically biogenetic materials. Travertine (also known as tufa), chalk, and micrite, respectively, are examples of these kinds of limestones.

Many limestones have gained their mineralogical makeups and textures during diagenesis. Aragonite, the orthorhombic polymorph of $CaCO_3$, was deposited and subsequently transformed into the calcite of some limestones; magnesian calcites that constitute some organic skeletal parts and cements of marine sediments were the precursors of the calcite of many other limestones. During diagenesis, most of the magnesian calcites were transformed into stable assemblages of rather pure calcite, often along with scattered grains of dolomite.

When sedimentary and diagenetic limestones undergo metamorphism, the calcite is frequently recrystallized and tends to become coarsely crystalline. The resulting rocks are calcite marbles. Some calcite marbles, however, appear to have had dolostone rather than limestone precursors; i.e., the dolostone underwent dedolomitization during metamorphism. The calcite grains in some marbles have cleavage planes that are curved; this is usually interpreted to reflect recrystallization during deformation or plastic flowage associated with dynamic metamorphism.

The calcite of carbonatites is generally thought to have formed from dense H_2O-CO_2 fluids that in many ways are more like the volatile-rich fluids from which pegmatites are believed to have been deposited than the more "normal" magmas from which igneous rocks such as granites and basalt have consolidated. These rocks closely resemble marbles, and some masses of both marble and carbonatite were originally misidentified, one as the other. In most cases, the identities of the accessory minerals serve as ready criteria for differentiating between an igneous and metamorphic origin.

Calcite is deposited by solutions, either ordinary groundwater solutions or hydrothermal solutions associated with magmatic activities. Such calcite constitutes the cement for many clastic sediments—e.g., some sandstones—and also the calcite or aragonite of speleothems and of both calcite and calcitic ore-bearing veins.

Calcite breaks down in most areas where chemical weathering takes place. It is dissolved and its products are carried in surface-water and groundwater solutions. The excavation of caves is a subsurface manifestation of these processes, just as their subsequent filling-in with speleothems is a manifestation of one of the modes whereby calcite is deposited. As might be suspected, most karst topography, which is characterized by sinkholes and underground drainage, occurs in areas underlain by limestone.

USES

Calcite has many uses. Since ancient times, limestone has been burned to quicklime (CaO), slaked to hydrated lime [Ca(OH)$_2$], and mixed with sand to make mortar. Limestone is one of the ingredients used in the manufacture of portland cement and is often employed as a flux in metallurgical processes, such as the smelting of iron ores. Crushed limestone is utilized widely as riprap, as aggregate for both concrete and asphalt mixes, as agricultural lime, and as an inert ingredient of medicines. Marble is used for statuary and carvings, and as polished slabs it is a popular facing stone. The term *marble* is used differently in the marketplace than in geology; in the marketplace, it is applied to any coarse-grained carbonate rock that will take a good polish rather than to metamorphic carbonate-rich rocks exclusively. Some coarsely crystalline diagenetic limestones are among the most widely used commercial "marbles." Travertine and onyx marble (banded calcite) are also popular facing stones, usually for interior use. Iceland spar has been employed for optical purposes for nearly two centuries. These uses constitute only a few of the many applications of calcite.

DOLOMITE

Dolomite is a type of limestone, the carbonate fraction of which is dominated by the mineral dolomite, calcium magnesium carbonate [CaMg(CO$_3$)$_2$].

Along with calcite and aragonite, dolomite makes up approximately 2 percent of the Earth's crust. The bulk of the dolomite constitutes dolostone formations that occur as thick units of great areal extent in many sequences of chiefly marine strata. (The rock dolostone is referred to by only the mineral name—i.e., dolomite—by many geologists.) The Dolomite Alps of northern Italy are a well-known example. Other relatively common occurrences of the mineral dolomite are in dolomite marble and dolomite-rich veins. It also occurs in the rare igneous rock known as dolomite carbonatite.

From the standpoint of its origin, the dolomite of dolostones is one of the most interesting of all the major rock-forming minerals. As discussed below, a large percentage of the dolomite in thick marine dolostone units is thought by many geologists and geochemists to have been formed by replacement of $CaCO_3$ sediment rather than by direct precipitation.

CHEMICAL COMPOSITION

Ferrous iron commonly substitutes for some of the magnesium in dolomite, and a complete series very likely extends between dolomite and ankerite [~$CaFe(CO_3)_2$]. Manganese also substitutes for magnesium, but typically only to the extent of a few percent and in most cases only along with iron. Other cations known to substitute—albeit in only relatively minor amounts—within the dolomite structure are barium and lead for calcium and zinc and cobalt for magnesium.

Nearly all the natural elements have been recorded as present in at least trace quantities in dolostones. It is, however, unclear which ones actually occur in the dolomite; some of them may occur within other mineral constituents of the analyzed rocks. Indeed, only a few of these elements—e.g., strontium, rubidium, boron, and uranium (U)—are known definitely to occur within the dolomite structure.

Dolomite effervesces with dilute hydrochloric acid, but slowly rather than vigorously as calcite does; in general, it appears to smolder slowly, and in some cases it does so only after the rock has been powdered or the acid warmed, or both. This difference in the character of the effervescence serves as the test usually used to distinguish dolomite from calcite in the field. In the laboratory, staining techniques, also based on chemical properties or typical compositions, may be used to distinguish between these minerals. The stains generally employed are especially valuable for investigating rocks made up of alternate lamellae of dolostone and limestone composition.

CRYSTAL STRUCTURE

In a somewhat simplified way, the dolomite structure can be described as resembling the calcite structure but with magnesium ions substituted for calcium ions in every other cation layer. Thus, the dolomite structure can be viewed as ideally comprising a calcium layer, a CO_3 layer, a magnesium layer, another CO_3 layer, and so forth. However, as described for the potassium feldspars, dolomites—unlike calcites—may also exhibit order-disorder relationships. This results because the purity of some of the cation layers may be less than ideal—i.e., some of the "calcium layers" may contain magnesium, and some of the "magnesium layers" may contain some calcium. The term *protodolomite* is frequently applied to Holocene dolomites (those formed during approximately the last 11,700 years) that have less than ideal dolomite structures. Most dolomites of ancient dolostones, however, appear to be well ordered. Modifications that may reflect diverse calcium-versus-magnesium layering aberrations are treated extensively in professional literature.

PHYSICAL PROPERTIES

Dolomite crystals are colourless, white, buff-coloured, pinkish, or bluish. Granular dolomite in rocks tends to be light to dark gray, tan, or white. Dolomite crystals range from transparent to translucent, but dolomite grains in rocks are typically translucent or nearly opaque. The lustre ranges from subvitreous to dull. Dolomite, like calcite, cleaves into six-sided polyhedrons with diamond-shaped

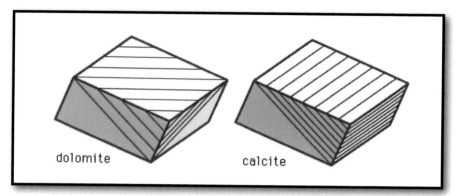

Relations between lamellar twinning and cleavage planes in dolomite and calcite. This difference can be discerned best when thin sections of the minerals are viewed under a microscope. Copyright Encyclopædia Britannica, Inc.; rendering for this edition by Rosen Educational Services

faces. Relations between lamellar twinning and cleavage planes of dolomite, however, differ from those of calcite, and this difference may be used to distinguish the two minerals in coarse-grained rocks such as marbles. Dolomite has a Mohs hardness of 3½ to 4 and a specific gravity of 2.85 ± 0.01. Some dolomites are triboluminescent.

The dolomite of most dolostones is granular, with the individual grains ranging in size from microscopic up to a few millimetres across. Most dolomite marbles are coarsely granular with individual grains ranging between 2 and 6 mm (0.079 and 0.24 inch) in greatest dimension. Vein dolomite grains may be up to several centimetres across. Saddle-shaped groups of dolomite crystals, most of which occur on fracture surfaces, measure from 0.5 to 2 cm (0.20 to 0.79 inch) across.

ORIGIN AND OCCURRENCE

Dolomite occurs widely as the major constituent of dolostones and dolomite marbles. As mentioned above, the origin of dolomite-rich rocks in marine sequences remains an unresolved problem of petrogenesis.

Dolomite—actually protodolomite—is known to have formed fairly recently in restricted environments such as on supratidal flats that occur in the Bahamas and Florida Keys. Also, no dolomite has been synthesized in an environment comparable to natural conditions. Thus, the explanation for the formation of dolomite in these marine units remains in question. It is now thought that dolostones may be of various origins. Indeed, several different models have been suggested for dolomite formation, each based on diverse considerations, combined with empirical and/or experimental data.

Except for models invoking formation of dolomite by direct precipitation, a process thought by most geologists to apply to only a small percentage of all dolostones, each model is based on the assumption that the dolomite of dolostones has been formed by conversion of $CaCO_3$ sediment or sedimentary rocks to dolostone. Thus, the models have been formulated to account for this conversion, which is known as dolomitization.

The most widely discussed models for dolomitization, either partial or complete, involve four chief variables: time, location with respect to the sediment-seawater interface, composition and derivation of the solutions involved, and fluxing mechanisms. The time ranges from dolomitization that occurs penecontemporaneously with deposition to that which takes place subsequent to relatively deep burial of the precursor sediments. The location ranges from at or very near the sediment-seawater interface to well beneath some overlying sediments that were deposited at a later time. The solutions supply the magnesium needed and must have the appropriate pH and concentrations of other necessary ions; these solutions are generally considered to be seawater (either "normal" seawater or brines concentrated by evaporation), connate water, meteoric water, or some combination of these waters. (Connate refers to water that becomes enclosed within sediments upon their deposition; meteoric water is derived from the atmosphere as rain or snow, which often occurs in pore spaces within rocks.) Another important variable is the presence of dissolved sulfate (SO_4^{-2}) ions, as this retards the dolomitization process. The fluxing mechanisms are generally attributed to density differences of the solutions involved and the permeability characteristics available for percolation through the precursor sediment. In addition, the presence of a geothermal heat source in a basin may enhance both fluid flux and the rate of dolomitization. There also are additional direct and indirect controls—e.g., climate, biochemical processes, and $HDO:H_2O$ and/or $D_2O:H_2O$ ratios in the water. (The symbol D represents deuterium, the hydrogen isotope with a nucleus containing one neutron in addition to the single proton of the ordinary hydrogen nucleus.) Bacteria may also play a role in the formation of dolomite. In any case, it has been shown that some dolostones have gained their current characteristics as a consequence of certain combinations of these conditions and processes.

Criteria involving factors such as the identity of associated rocks and the coarseness of the grains of dolostones have been suggested for use in attributing one versus the other hypothesized models to certain occurrences of dolostone. None, however, has been accepted as an absolute criterion by many carbonate petrologists.

The desire for an understanding of dolomitization of sedimentary strata has been based on economic as well as scientific interests. In many places, dolomitization has led to increases in permeability and porosity and thus increased the potential of such rock strata as good oil, gas, and groundwater reservoirs and, in some cases, even as hosts of certain kinds of ore deposits.

The other fairly common dolomite occurrences include the following: Dolostones have been metamorphosed to both dolomite and calcite marbles; dedolomitization processes account for the latter. Some dolomite marbles are nearly pure dolomite. Dolomite carbonatites are of the same general origin as calcite carbonatites. The dolomite present in dolomite veins has also been ascribed diverse origins; some appears to have been deposited by percolating connate or meteoric groundwater, and some seems more likely to have been deposited by hydrothermal solutions charged with magmatic volatiles.

USES

Dolomite is used as a source of magnesium metal and of magnesia (MgO), which is a constituent of refractory bricks. Dolostone is often used instead of limestone as an aggregate for both cement and bitumen mixes and also as a flux in blast furnaces. The use of dolostone as a flux has increased, especially since environmental contamination has become a widely heeded consideration, because the resulting slag can be employed for such things as lightweight aggregate, whereas that formed when limestone is used cannot. Such is the case because dolostone-based slag does not slake (disintegrate in water), but limestone-based slag does.

OTHER COMMON ROCK-FORMING MINERALS

A number of other important rock-forming minerals are listed below even though they do not make up large percentages of any common rocks. Each of these minerals is a major constituent of some sizable rock masses, occurs widely as an accessory mineral in many common rocks, or assumes both roles. Consequently, they warrant brief description here.

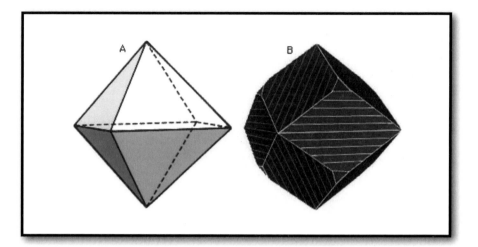

Typical crystal forms of magnetite. (left) *An octahedron and* (right) *an octahedron modified by dodecahedral faces.* Copyright Encyclopædia Britannica, Inc.; rendering for this edition by Rosen Educational Services

MAGNETITE AND CHROMITE

Magnetite (Fe_3O_4—that is, $Fe^{2+}Fe^{3+}{}_2O_4$) and chromite ($Fe^{2+}Cr_2O_4$) are both members of the spinel group. The spinels, comprising some 21 species (including the well-known gemstone balas ruby), are cubic (isometric) and commonly occur as octahedrons. Magnetite and chromite are opaque and dark gray to iron-black; magnetite is strongly magnetic. Magnetite and chromite are the major constituents of the rocks called magnetitite and chromitite, respectively. In addition, each is a common accessory mineral in one or more igneous rocks. Magnetite also occurs widely in several metamorphic and sedimentary rocks; one or both of these minerals occur in several placer deposits. Magnetite has been recovered as iron ore; chromite is the only important commercial mineral of chromium.

MAGNESITE

Magnesite from Okanogan, Wash.
B.M. Shaub

Magnesite, the mineral magnesium carbonate ($MgCO_3$), is a member of the calcite group of carbonate minerals that is a principal source of magnesium. The mineral has formed as an alteration product from magnesium-rich rocks or through the action of magnesium-containing solutions upon calcite. Notable deposits are those at Radenthein, Austria; the Liaotung Peninsula, Liaoning Province, China; and Clark County, Nev., U.S. Iron is usually present, and a complete chemical substitution series exists between magnesite and siderite in which iron replaces magnesium. Magnesite is used as a refractory material, a catalyst and filler in the production of synthetic rubber, and a material in the preparation of magnesium chemicals and fertilizers.

HALITE, GYPSUM, AND ANHYDRITE

Halite (NaCl), gypsum ($CaSO_4 \cdot 2H_2O$), and anhydrite ($CaSO_4$) are the major constituents of the sedimentary rocks rock salt, rock gypsum, and rock anhydrite, respectively. These rocks are usually referred to as evaporites. Halite, the mineral name for common salt, is cubic and is typically colourless or white but may be tinted various colours by impurities. It breaks into cubes because of its three perfect cleavages at right angles to each other and has a characteristic salty taste. Gypsum is monoclinic and commonly occurs as tabular crystals, either simple or twinned, and also forms coarse to fine granular masses. It is typically colourless or white but may be red, orange, brown, or black because of the presence of impurities,

Anhydrite from Lockport, N.Y. Courtesy of the Field Museum of Natural History, Chicago; photograph, John H. Gerard

and it cleaves into plates that may be bent but are not flexible. Gypsum is so soft (Mohs hardness of 2) that it can be scratched easily with one's fingernail. Anhydrite is orthorhombic and resembles granular dolomite in many rocks, but it does not react with dilute hydrochloric acid. When altered, anhydrite usually takes on a thin coating of white gypsum. Halite has been recovered from rock salt deposits for diverse uses for at least seven millennia. The major use of gypsum is for the manufacture of plaster of paris.

EPIDOTE

Epidote is the name given to both a group of minerals and a mineral species. Epidote, the species [Ca_2(Al,

$Fe)_3(SiO_4)_3(OH)$], crystallizes in the monoclinic system. Its presence in rocks is generally recognized on the basis of its yellowish to bilious-green colour. Macroscopically, it is usually distinguished from olivine, which it may closely resemble, on the basis of its association with quartz. Epidote commonly occurs in quartz-bearing metamorphic and igneous rocks, whereas olivine occurs only rarely in rocks that contain quartz. Epidote may be cut as a gem.

HEMATITE

Hematite (α-Fe_2O_3) is hexagonal. Although it is present as silvery-gray, highly lustrous platelike masses in some rocks, it is most widely encountered as the henna-red pigment of many diverse rocks—e.g., red sandstones and many other red beds. Some sedimentary rocks and their metamorphosed products contain such high percentages of hematite that they have been recovered as iron ore. Hematite may also be used as a polishing powder and as a paint pigment.

LIMONITE

Limonite is the catchall name widely applied to hydrous iron oxide minerals. Goethite [α-$Fe^{3+}O(OH)$], which is hexagonal, is the most common of these minerals; indeed, in nature most $FeO(OH)$ minerals ultimately become this α-phase. Goethite, much of which has the general colour of iron rust, occurs wherever chemical weathering affects rocks that contain one or more iron-bearing minerals. In some cases, only surficial stains have resulted; in others, masses large enough to constitute iron ore deposits have been formed. Goethite also is common in modern sediments; e.g., it is the typical iron mineral in marine ferromanganese nodules.

OTHER MINERAL GROUPS

Several mineral groups are distinct from the silicates, clays, and carbonates. All of these are relatively rare, occurring in limited amounts or across limited geographic areas. Some of the groups listed below, such as the borate and arsenate minerals, incorporate oxygen into their structures. Others, such as the phosphate and sulfate minerals, occur as inorganic salts of various acids.

BORATE MINERALS				
NAME	COLOUR	LUSTRE	Mohs HARD- NESS	SPECIFIC GRAVITY
boracite	colourless or white	vitreous	7–7½	2.9–3.0
borax	colourless to white; grayish, bluish, greenish	vitreous to resinous	2–2½	1.7
colemanite	colourless; white, yellowish, gray	brilliant vitreous to adamantine	4½	2.4
inyoite	colourless, becoming white and cloudy after partial dehydration	vitreous	2	1.7
kernite	colourless	vitreous	2½	1.9
ludwigite	dark green to coal black	silky	5	3.6 (lud) to 4.7 (paig)
priceite	white	earthy	3–3½	2.4
sussexite	white to straw-yellow	silky to dull or earthy	3–3½	2.6 (szai) to 3.3 (suss)

NAME	COLOUR	LUSTRE	MOHS HARDNESS	SPECIFIC GRAVITY
tincalconite	white (natural); colourless (artificial)	vitreous		1.9
ulexite	colourless; white	vitreous; silky or satiny	2½	2.0

BORATE MINERALS				
NAME	HABIT OR FORM	FRACTURE OR CLEAVAGE	REFRACTIVE INDICES	CRYSTAL SYSTEM
boracite	isolated, embedded, cubelike crystals	conchoidal to uneven fracture	alpha = 1.658–1.662 beta = 1.662–1.667 gamma = 1.668–1.673	orthorhombic (isometric above 265 degrees C [509 °F])
borax	short prismatic crystals	one perfect, one good cleavage	alpha = 1.445 beta = 1.469 gamma = 1.472	monoclinic
colemanite	short prismatic crystals; massive	one perfect, one distinct cleavage	alpha = 1.586 beta = 1.592 gamma = 1.614	monoclinic
inyoite	short prisms and coarse crystal aggregates; geodes; drusy crusts; granular massive	one good cleavage	alpha = 1.492–1.495 beta = 1.501–1.510 gamma = 1.516–1.520	monoclinic

NAME	HABIT OR FORM	FRAC-TURE OR CLEAVAGE	REFRAC-TIVE INDICES	CRYSTAL SYSTEM
kernite	very large crystals; fibrous, cleavable, irregular masses	two perfect cleavages	alpha = 1.454 beta = 1.472 gamma = 1.488	monoclinic
lud-wigite	fibrous masses; rosettes; sheaf-like aggregates	no observed cleavage	alpha = 1.83–1.85 beta = 1.83–1.85 gamma = 1.97–2.02	ortho-rhombic
priceite	soft and chalky to hard and tough nodules	earthy to conchoidal	alpha = 1.569–1.576 beta = 1.588–1.594 gamma = 1.590–1.597	triclinic(?)
sussexite	fibrous or felted masses or vein-lets; nodules		alpha = 1.575–1.670 beta = 1.646–1.728 gamma = 1.650–1.732	probably ortho-rhombic
tincal-conite	found in nature as a fine-grained powder; physi-cal properties are given for artificial pseu-docubic crystals	hackly fracture	omega = 1.461 epsilon = 1.474	hexagonal

NAME	HABIT OR FORM	FRAC-TURE OR CLEAVAGE	REFRAC-TIVE INDICES	CRYSTAL SYSTEM
ulexite	small nodular, rounded, or lenslike crystal aggregates; fibrous botryoi-dal crusts; rarely as single crystals	one perfect, one good cleavage	alpha = 1.491–1.496 beta = 1.504–1.506 gamma = 1.519–1.520	triclinic

Minerals formed from naturally occurring compounds of boron and oxygen are called borate minerals. Most borate minerals are rare, but some form large deposits that are mined commercially. Borate mineral structures incorporate either the BO_3 triangle or BO_4 tetrahedron in which oxygen or hydroxyl groups are located at the vertices of a triangle or at the corners of a tetrahedron with a central boron atom, respectively. Both types of units may occur in one structure. Vertices may share an oxygen atom to form extended boron–oxygen networks, or if bonded to another metal ion consist of a hydroxyl group. The size of the boron–oxygen complex in any one mineral generally decreases with an increase of the temperature and pressure at which the mineral forms.

Two geological settings are conducive for the formation of borate minerals. The first is commercially more valuable and consists of an environment where an impermeable basin received borate-bearing solutions that resulted from volcanic activity. Subsequent evaporation caused precipitation of hydrated alkali and alkaline-earth borate minerals. With increased depth of burial resulting from additional sedimentation, beds of compositionally stratified borates crystallized as a consequence of temperature and pressure gradients. Because evaporation must occur for precipitation of the borates, such basin deposits usually occur in desert regions, as for example the Kramer district of the Mojave Desert and Death Valley in California, where enormous beds of stratified kernite, borax, colemanite, and ulexite are recovered, primarily by stripping away the overburden and mining the borates by classical open-pit techniques. Other noteworthy evaporite deposits occur in the Inderborsky district of Kazakhstan and in Tuscany, Italy. The sequence of precipitating alkali borates can be duplicated in the laboratory because the temperatures and pressures of their formation are low and easily accessible. Solutions of the alkali borates and the addition of metal ions such as calcium and magnesium result in the precipitation of yet other borate compounds. Among the borates commonly found in evaporite deposits are borax, colemanite, inyoite, kernite, and tincalconite.

The second geologic setting for borate minerals is a metamorphic carbonate-rich environment, where they are formed as a result of alteration of the surrounding rocks by heat and pressure; similar borates also occur as nodules in some deeply buried sediments. These compounds were formed at relatively high temperatures and usually consist of densely packed BO_3 triangles associated with such small metal ions as magnesium, manganese, aluminum, or iron. The origin of these borates is not as obvious as that of the evaporite varieties. Some were produced by the reaction of boron-bearing vapour derived from hot intruding granites during metamorphism; others are the recrystallization products of evaporite borates. Numerous borosilicates (e.g., dumortierite and tourmaline) were formed under these conditions. Compounds of this type contain both BO_3 triangular units and SiO_4 tetrahedral units. Among the borate minerals associated with metamorphosed environments are boracite, ludwigite, sussexite, and kotoite.

ARSENATE MINERALS

An arsenate mineral is a compound of arsenic, oxygen, and various metals. Most arsenate minerals are rare, having crystallized under very restricted conditions. At the mineralogically famous Långban iron and manganese mines in central Sweden, more than 50 species of arsenate minerals have been described, many peculiar to the locality. Such compounds occur in open cavities and resulted from the reaction of arsenic acid (H_3AsO_4) upon pyrochroite [manganese hydroxide; $Mn(OH)_2$] at moderate to low temperature. Arsenates at other localities are often oxidation products of arsenide ores and are deposited at low temperatures in late-stage veins and open cavities.

Only a few arsenate minerals have economic importance. Because the transition metals (e.g., cobalt, copper, nickel) give brilliant colour to some of the arsenates, these can be used to advantage in prospecting; such arsenate oxidation products, or blooms, as erythrite (bright pink) and annabergite (green) are indicators of nickel and cobalt arsenide ores. Many of the nickel and cobalt deposits at Sudbury and Cobalt, Ont., were located in this manner.

The arsenate minerals, which are salts of arsenic acid, contain arsenate groups (AsO_4) in which four oxygen (O) atoms are arranged at the corners of a tetrahedron about a central arsenic (As) atom. Each arsenate tetrahedron has a net electric charge of -3, which is neutralized by large, positively charged metal ions (e.g., calcium, manganese, or ferrous iron) outside the tetrahedron. Unlike the similar silicate tetrahedra, which link to form chains, sheets, rings, or frameworks, arsenate tetrahedra are insular.

The crystal structure of the arsenate minerals is very similar to that of the phosphate and vanadate minerals; indeed, many arsenate minerals form solid solutions with both the phosphates and the vanadates.

HALIDE MINERALS

Halide minerals make up a group of naturally occurring inorganic compounds that are salts of the halogen acids (e.g., hydrochloric acid). Such compounds, with the notable exceptions of halite (rock salt), sylvite, and fluorite, are rare and of very local occurrence. Compositionally and structurally, three broad categories of halide minerals are recognized; these categories, which are also distinguishable in their modes of occurrence, include the simple halides, the halide complexes, and the oxyhydroxy-halides.

The simple halides are salts of the alkali, alkaline earth, and transition metals. Most are soluble in water; the transition-metal halides are unstable under exposure to air. Halite, sodium chloride ($NaCl$), is the most familiar example; it often occurs with other evaporite minerals in enormous beds resulting from the accumulation of brines and trapped oceanic water in impermeable basins and their evaporation. Minor amounts of sylvite, potassium chloride (KCl), also are present in such beds.

Fluorite, or calcium fluoride (CaF_2), another simple halide, is found in limestones that have been permeated by aqueous solutions containing the fluoride anion. Noteworthy deposits of fluorite occur in Mexico; Cumberland, Eng.; and Illinois, Missouri, Kentucky, and Colorado in the United States.

Other simple halides such as sal-ammoniac, ammonium chloride (NH_4Cl); lawrencite, ferrous chloride ($FeCl_2$); and molysite, ferric chloride ($FeCl_3$) occur in fumarolic vents and are highly unstable in air. A few hydrothermal vein minerals in silver deposits, such as chlorargyrite and calomel, serve as minor and occasional ores of silver and mercury, respectively. A few double salts (e.g., carnallite and tachyhydrite) included among the simple halides have formed under conditions similar to the formation of halite.

In the halide complexes, halide anions are tightly bound to a cation, usually aluminum; the resulting unit behaves as a single negative ion. The most common examples are the fluoroaluminates cryolite, cryolithionite, thomsenolite, and weberite. Enormous quantities of cryolite formerly were mined at Ivigtut, Greenland, to be used for flux in the recovery of aluminum from bauxite.

Most oxyhydroxy-halides are rare and highly insoluble compounds. Many have formed by the action of halide-bearing waters upon the oxidation products of previously existing sulfides; atacamite, matlockite, nadorite, and diaboleite are examples. A few compounds such as a fiedlerite, laurionite, and penfieldite have formed through the action of seawater upon ancient lead slags from the historic deposits at Laurium, Greece.

HALIDE MINERALS				
NAME	COLOUR	LUSTRE	MOHS HARD-NESS	SPECIFIC GRAVITY
atacamite	various bright green shades; dark emerald-green to blackish	adamantine	3–3½	3.8
calomel	colourless, white, grayish, yellowish, brown	adamantine	1½	7.15
carnallite	milk-white; sometimes reddish (from included hematite)	greasy, dull to shining	2½	1.6
cerargy-rite	colourless when pure and fresh; usually gray; becomes purple or violet-brown on exposure to light (cerargyrite)	hornlike	2½	5.6 (AgCl) to 6.5 (AgBr)

NAME	COLOUR	LUSTRE	MOHS HARD-NESS	SPECIFIC GRAVITY
cryolite	colourless to white, brownish, reddish, brick red	vitreous to greasy	2½	3.0
fluorite	variable	vitreous	4	3.2
halite	colourless when pure, often splotched blue or purple	vitreous	2	2.2
sal ammoniac	colourless, white, grayish, yellow	vitreous	1–2	1.5
sylvite	colourless, white, grayish, bluish, or red (from included hematite)	vitreous	2	2.0

HALIDE MINERALS

NAME	HABIT OR FORM	FRAC-TURE OR CLEAVAGE	REFRAC-TIVE INDICES	CRYSTAL SYSTEM
ataca-mite	brittle, transparent to translucent tabular to slender prismatic crystals	one perfect cleavage	alpha = 1.831 beta = 1.861 gamma = 1.880	ortho-rhombic
calomel	tabular crystals; drusy crusts; earthy masses	one good cleavage	omega = 1.956–1.991 epsilon = 2.601–2.713	tetragonal
carnall-ite	granular, massive	conchoidal fracture	alpha = 1.465–1.466 beta = 1.474–1.455 gamma = 1.444–1.446	ortho-rhombic

NAME	HABIT OR FORM	FRAC-TURE OR CLEAVAGE	REFRAC-TIVE INDICES	CRYSTAL SYSTEM
cerargy-rite	crusts; waxy coat-ings; hornlike masses	uneven to subcon-choidal fracture	$n =$ 2.071–2.253	isometric
cryolite	coarsely granular masses	no cleavage	alpha = 1.338 beta = 1.338 gamma = 1.339	mono-clinic
fluorite	brittle, transpar-ent or translucent cubes and two-cube penetration twins	perfect octahedral cleavage	$n =$ 1.432–1.437	isometric
halite	transparent cubic (often cavernous or stepped) crystals; granular masses	perfect cubic cleavage	$n = 1.544$	isometric
sal ammo-niac	skeletal aggregates	conchoidal fracture	$n = 1.639$	isometric
sylvite	transparent cubes or granular masses	perfect cubic cleavage	$n = 1.490$	isometric

NITRATE AND IODATE MINERALS

This small group of naturally occurring inorganic com-pounds is practically confined to the Atacama Desert of northern Chile; the principal locality is Antofagasta. These minerals occur under the loose soil as beds of gray-ish caliche (a hard cemented mixture of nitrates, sulfates, halides, and sand) 2–3 m (7–10 feet) thick. The much rarer iodate minerals occur sporadically, intermixed with the nitrates, and are distinguished from the former by their yellow colour. The caliche has accumulated as a result of drainage. Because most of these compounds are soluble and unstable, they are practically confined to arid regions and soils, which possess a paucity of microorganisms.

Before World War I, Chile possessed a near monopoly on nitrates, with as many as 100 plants in operation. The introduction of practical methods for the fixation of nitrogen early in the 20th century resulted in a decline of the marketing of natural nitrates.

The nitrate and iodate minerals are structurally related to the carbonate minerals. The most important nitrates are soda nitre, nitre (saltpetre), darapskite, and humberstonite. Among the iodates are lautarite and dietzeite.

OXIDE MINERALS

Any naturally occurring inorganic compound with a structure based on close-packed oxygen atoms in which smaller, positively charged metal or other ions occur in interstices is considered an oxide. Oxides are distinguished from other oxygen-bearing compounds such as the silicates, borates, and carbonates, which have a readily definable group containing oxygen atoms covalently bonded to an atom of another element.

The oxide minerals can be grouped as simple oxides and multiple oxides. Simple oxides are a combination of one metal or semimetal and oxygen, whereas multiple oxides have two nonequivalent metal sites. The oxide structures are usually based on cubic or hexagonal close-packing of oxygen atoms with the octahedral or tetrahedral sites (or both) occupied by metal ions; symmetry is typically isometric, hexagonal, tetragonal, or orthorhombic.

A sample of the oxide mineral cuprite from Morenci, Ariz. U.S. Geological Survey (Bureau of Mines, Mineral Specimens C\01786)

The simple oxides can be subdivided on the basis of the ratio of the numbers of atoms of metal (or other elements) and oxygen, giving general formulas of the A_xO_y type. In such formulas A represents a metal atom, and x and y represent integers. Chemical compositions then fall into categories such as those designated AO, A_2O, A_2O_3, AO_2. Specific simple oxide minerals include periclase (MgO), cuprite (Cu_2O), hematite (Fe_2O_3), and uraninite (UO_2).

Complex oxides show a more varied chemistry, often with extensive solid solution. Most common is the spinel group, with the general formula AB_2O_4, in which A and B are ions of different metals, the same metal with different oxidation states, or a combination of the two; A (with oxidation state +2), B (with oxidation state +3) is the commonest, as, for example, in spinel itself, $MgAl_2O_4$. Frequently occurring doubly charged ions include magnesium, iron, zinc, and manganese, while common triply charged ions are aluminum, iron, manganese, and chromium.

Oxide minerals occur as decomposition products of sulfide minerals, in pegmatites, early crystallizing minerals in ultrabasic rocks, and as accessory minerals in many igneous rocks.

OXIDE MINERALS				
NAME	COLOUR	LUSTRE	MOHS HARDNESS	SPECIFIC GRAVITY
anatase	brown to indigo blue and black; also variable	adamantine to metallic adamantine	5½–6	3.8–4.0
boehmite	white, when pure		3	3.0–3.1
brookite	various browns	metallic adamantine to submetallic	5½–6	4.1–4.2
brucite	white to pale green, gray, or blue	waxy to vitreous	2½	2.4
cassiterite	reddish or yellowish brown to brownish black	adamantine to metallic adamantine, usually splendent	6–7	7.0
chromite	black	metallic	5½	4.5–4.8
chryso-beryl	variable	vitreous	8½	3.6–3.8
columbite	iron black to brownish black; often with iridescent tarnish		6–6½	5.2 (columbite) to 8.0 (tantalite)

NAME	COLOUR	LUSTRE	MOHS HARDNESS	SPECIFIC GRAVITY
corundum	red (ruby); blue (sapphire); also variable	adamantine to vitreous	9 (a hardness standard)	4.0–4.1
cuprite	various shades of red	adamantine to earthy	3½–4	6.1
delafossite	black	metallic	5½	5.4–5.5
diaspore	white, grayish white, colourless; variable	brilliant vitreous	6½–7	3.2–3.5
euxenite	black	brilliant submetallic to greasy or vitreous	5½–6½	5.3–5.9
franklinite	brownish black to black	metallic to semimetallic	5½–6½	5.1–5.2
gibbsite	white; grayish, greenish, reddish white	vitreous	2½–3½	2.3–2.4
goethite	blackish brown (crystals); yellowish or reddish brown	adamantine-metallic	5–5½	3.3–4.3
hausmannite	brownish black	submetallic	5½	4.8
hematite	steel gray; dull to bright red	metallic or submetallic to dull	5–6	5.3
ilmenite	iron black	metallic to submetallic	5–6	4.7–4.8
lepidocrocite	ruby red to reddish brown	submetallic	5	4.0–4.1

NAME	COLOUR	LUSTRE	MOHS HARDNESS	SPECIFIC GRAVITY
litharge	red	greasy to dull	2	9.1–9.2
magnetite	black to brownish black	metallic to semimetallic	5½–6½	5.2
manganite	dark steel gray to iron black	submetallic	4	4.3–4.4
massicot	sulfur to orpiment yellow	greasy to dull	2	9.6
periclase	colourless to grayish; also green, yellow, or black	vitreous	5½–6	3.6–3.7
perovskite (often containing rare earths)	black; grayish or brownish black; reddish brown to yellow	adamantine to metallic	5½	4.0–4.3
psilomelane	iron black to dark steel gray	submetallic to dull	5–6	4.7
pyrochlore	brown to black (pyro); pale yellow to brown (micro)	vitreous or resinous	5–5½	4.2–6.4
pyrolusite	light steel gray to iron black	metallic	2–6	4.4–5.0
rutile	reddish brown to red; variable	metallic adamantine	6–6½	4.2–5.5
spinel	various	vitreous	7½–8	3.55
tenorite	steel or iron gray to black	metallic	3½	5.8–6.4

NAME	COLOUR	LUSTRE	MOHS HARDNESS	SPECIFIC GRAVITY
thorianite	dark gray to brownish black and bluish	hornlike to submetallic	6½	9.7–9.9
uraninite	steel to velvet black; grayish, greenish	submetallic to greasy or dull	5–6	6.5–8.5 (massive); 8.0–10.0 (crystals)

OXIDE MINERALS

NAME	HABIT	FRAC- TURE OR CLEAVAGE	REFRACTIVE INDICES OR POLISHED SECTION DATA	CRYSTAL SYSTEM
anatase	pyramidal or tabular crystals	two perfect cleavages	omega = 2.561 epsilon = 2.488 extremely variable	tetragonal
boehmite	disseminated or in pisolitic aggregates	one very good cleavage	alpha = 1.64–1.65 beta = 1.65–1.66 gamma = 1.65–1.67	ortho- rhombic
brookite	only as crys- tals, usually tabular	subcon- choidal to uneven fracture	alpha = 2.583 beta = 2.585 gamma = 2.700–2.741	ortho- rhombic
brucite	tabular crystals; platy aggre- gates; fibrous or foliated massive	one perfect cleavage	omega = 1.56–1.59 epsilon = 1.58–1.60	hexagonal

NAME	HABIT	FRAC-TURE OR CLEAVAGE	REFRACTIVE INDICES OR POLISHED SECTION DATA	CRYSTAL SYSTEM
cassiterite	repeatedly twinned crystals; crusts and concretions	one imperfect cleavage	omega = 1.984–2.048 epsilon = 2.082–2.140 light gray; strongly anisotropic	tetragonal
chromite	granular to compact massive	no cleavage; uneven fracture	n = 2.08–2.16 brownish gray-white; isotropic	isometric
chryso-beryl	tabular or prismatic, commonly twinned, crystals	one distinct cleavage	alpha = 1.746 beta = 1.748 gamma = 1.756	ortho-rhombic
columbite	prismatic crystals, often in large groups; massive	one distinct cleavage	brownish gray-white; weakly anisotropic	ortho-rhombic
corundum	pyramidal or barrel-shaped crystals; large blocks; rounded grains	no cleavage; uneven to conchoidal fracture	omega = 1.767–1.772 epsilon = 1.759–1.763	hexagonal

NAME	HABIT	FRAC-TURE OR CLEAVAGE	REFRACTIVE INDICES OR POLISHED SECTION DATA	CRYSTAL SYSTEM
cuprite	octahedral, cubic, or capillary crystals; granular or earthy massive	conchoidal to uneven fracture	n = 2.849 bluish white; anomalously anisotropic and plechroic	isometric
delafossite	tabular crystals; botryoidal crusts	one imperfect cleavage	rosy brown-white; strongly anisotropic; distinctly pleochroic	hexagonal
diaspore	thin, platy crystals; scaly massive; disseminated	one perfect cleavage, one less so	alpha = 1.682–1.706 beta = 1.705–1.725 gamma = 1.730–1.752	ortho-rhombic
euxenite	prismatic crystals; massive	conchoidal to subconchoidal fracture	n = 2.06–2.25	ortho-rhombic
franklinite	octahedral crystals; granular massive		n = about 2.36 white; isotropic	isometric
gibbsite	tabular crystals; crusts and coatings; compact earthy	one perfect cleavage	alpha = 1.56–1.58 beta = 1.56–1.58 gamma = 1.58–1.60	mono-clinic

NAME	HABIT	FRAC-TURE OR CLEAVAGE	REFRACTIVE INDICES OR POLISHED SECTION DATA	CRYSTAL SYSTEM
goethite	prismatic crystals; massive	one perfect cleavage, one less so	alpha = 2.260–2.275 beta = 2.393–2.409 gamma = 2.398–2.515 gray; strongly anisotropic	ortho-rhombic
hausman-nite	pseudo-octahedral crystals; granular massive	one nearly perfect cleavage	omega = 2.43–2.48 epsilon = 2.13–2.17 gray-white; distinctly anisotropic	tetragonal
hematite	tabular crys-tals; rosettes; columnar or fibrous mas-sive; earthy massive; reniform masses	no cleavage	omega = 2.90–3.22 epsilon = 2.69–2.94 anisotropic; weakly pleo-chroic; often shows lamellar twinning	hexagonal
ilmenite	thick, tabular crystals; compact massive; grains	no cleav-age; conchoidal fracture	n = about 2.7 grayish white; anisotropic	hexagonal

NAME	HABIT	FRAC-TURE OR CLEAVAGE	REFRACTIVE INDICES OR POLISHED SECTION DATA	CRYSTAL SYSTEM
lepido-crocite	flattened scales; isolated rounded crystals; massive	one perfect cleavage, one less so	alpha = 1.94 beta = 2.20 gamma = 2.51 gray-white; strongly aniso-tropic and pleochroic	ortho-rhombic
litharge	crusts; altera-tion product on massicot	one cleavage	omega = 2.665 epsilon = 2.535	tetragonal
magnetite	octahedral crystals; granular massive		n = 2.42 brownish gray; isotropic	isometric
manganite	prismatic crystals, often in bun-dles; fibrous massive	one very perfect cleavage, two less so	alpha = 2.25 beta = 2.25 gamma = 2.53 brownish gray-white; aniso-tropic; weakly pleochroic	mono-clinic
massicot	earthy or scaly massive	two cleavages	alpha = 2.51 beta = 2.61 gamma = 2.71	ortho-rhombic
periclase	irregular, rounded grains; octahedral crystals	one perfect cleavage	n = 1.730–1.746	isometric

NAME	HABIT	FRAC-TURE OR CLEAVAGE	REFRACTIVE INDICES OR POLISHED SECTION DATA	CRYSTAL SYSTEM
perovskite (often containing rare earths)	cubic crystals	uneven to subconchoidal fracture	n = 2.30–2.38 dark bluish gray	orthorhombic
psilomelane	massive; crusts; stalactites; earthy masses			orthorhombic
pyrochlore	octahedral crystals; irregular masses	subconchoidal to uneven fracture	n = 1.93–2.02	isometric
pyrolusite	columnar or fibrous massive; coatings and concretions	one perfect cleavage	cream-white; distinctly anisotropic; very weakly pleochroic	tetragonal
rutile	slender to capillary prismatic crystals; granular massive; as inclusions, often oriented	one distinct cleavage	omega = 2.556–2.651 epsilon = 2.829–2.895	tetragonal

NAME	HABIT	FRAC-TURE OR CLEAVAGE	REFRACTIVE INDICES OR POLISHED SECTION DATA	CRYSTAL SYSTEM
spinel	octahedral crystals; round or embed-ded grains; granular to compact massive		$n = 1.715-1.725$	isometric
tenorite	thin aggre-gates or laths; curved plates or scales; earthy masses	conchoidal fracture	light gray-white; strongly anisotropic; pleochroic	mono-clinic
thorianite	rounded cubic crystals	uneven to subcon-choidal fracture	n = about 2.2 (variable) isotropic	isometric
uraninite	crystals; massive; dendritic aggregates of crystals	uneven to conchoidal fracture	light brownish gray; isotropic	isometric

CHROMATE MINERALS

Chromate minerals make up a small group of rare inorganic compounds that have formed from the oxidation of copper-iron-lead sulfide ores containing minor amounts of chromium. A noteworthy occurrence is at Dundas, Tasm., known for its large, brilliant orange prismatic crystals of crocoite; of trivial economic importance, crocoite is one of the most highly prized of minerals among collectors and museums.

The basic structural unit of the chromate minerals is a tetrahedron formed from four oxygen atoms, each at one corner of a tetrahedron surrounding a central chromium atom; thus each CrO_4 tetrahedron has a net electric charge of -2, which is neutralized by metal ions outside the tetrahedron.

PHOSPHATE MINERALS

Phosphate minerals constitute a group of naturally occurring inorganic salts of phosphoric acid, $H_3(PO_4)$. More than 200 species of phosphate minerals are recognized, and structurally they all have isolated (PO_4) tetrahedral units. Phosphates can be grouped as: (1) primary phosphates that have crystallized from a liquid; (2) secondary phosphates formed by the alteration of primary phosphates; and (3) fine-grained rock phosphates formed at low temperatures from phosphorus-bearing organic material, primarily underwater.

Primary phosphates usually crystallize from aqueous fluids derived from the late stages of crystallization. Particularly common in granitic pegmatites are the primary phosphates apatite $[Ca_5(F,Cl,OH)(PO_4)_3]$, triphylite $[LiFePO_4]$, lithiophilite $[LiMnPO_4]$, and the rare-earth phosphates monazite $[(LaCe)(PO_4)]$ and xenotime $[Y(PO_4)]$. Primary phosphates commonly occur in ultramafic rocks (i.e., those very low in silica), including carbonatites and nepheline syenites. Metamorphic apatite occurs in calc-silicate rocks and impure limestones.

Secondary phosphates are extremely varied, forming at low temperatures, in the presence of water, and under variable oxidation states. Both di- and tri-valent oxidation states of iron and manganese are usually present, producing brilliant colours. Two common species are strengite $[Fe(PO_4)(H_2O)_2]$ and vivianite $[Fe_3(PO_4)_2(H_2O)_8]$.

PHOSPHATE MINERALS				
NAME	COLOUR	LUSTRE	MOHS' HARD-NESS	SPECIFIC GRAVITY
amblygo-nite	white to creamy white; slightly tinted	vitreous to greasy	5½–6	3.0–3.1
apatite				
carbonate-apatite	variable, greens predominating	vitreous	5	2.9–3.2
chlorapatite				
fluorapatite				
hydroxyl-apatite				
autunite	lemon yellow to sulfur yellow; greenish yellow to pale green	vitreous to pearly	2–2½	3.1–3.2
brushite	colourless to pale yellow	vitreous or pearly	2½	2.3
collophane (massive apatite)	grayish white; yellowish; brown	weakly vitre-ous to dull	3–4	2.5–2.9
lazulite	azure blue or sky blue; bluish white, bluish green; deep blue	vitreous	5½–6	3.1–3.4

NAME	COLOUR	LUSTRE	MOHS' HARD-NESS	SPECIFIC GRAVITY
monazite	yellowish brown or reddish brown to brown	usually resin-ous or waxy; sometimes vitreous or adamantine	5–5½	4.6–5.4; usually 5.0–5.2
pyromor-phite	olive green; yel-low; gray; brown to orange	resinous to subadaman-tine	3½–4	7.0
torbernite	various shades of green	vitreous to subadaman-tine	2–2½	3.2
triphylite	bluish or greenish gray (triphylite); clove brown, honey yellow, or salmon (lithiophilite)	vitreous to subresinous	4–5	3.3–3.6 not varying linearly with com-position
triplite	dark brown; flesh red; salmon pink	vitreous to resinous	5–5½	3.5–3.9
turquoise	blue to various shades of green; greenish to yel-lowish gray	waxy	5–6	2.6–2.8
variscite	yellowish green, pale to emerald green, bluish green or colour-less (variscite); peach-blossom red, carmine, violet (strengite)	vitreous to faintly waxy	3½–4½	2.2–2.5

NAME	COLOUR	LUSTRE	MOHS' HARD-NESS	SPECIFIC GRAVITY
vivianite	colourless when fresh, darkening to deep blue or bluish black	vitreous	1½–2	2.7
wavellite	greenish white; green to yellow	vitreous	3½–4	2.4
xenotime	yellowish brown to reddish brown; flesh red, grayish white, pale yellow, or greenish	vitreous	4–5	4.4–5.1

PHOSPHATE MINERALS

NAME	HABIT OR FORM	FRAC-TURE OR CLEAVAGE	REFRAC-TIVE INDICES	CRYSTAL SYSTEM
amblygo-nite	large, trans-lucent, cleavable masses; small transparent crystals	one perfect and one good cleavage	ambl mont alpha = 1.578–1.611 beta = 1.595–1.619 gamma = 1.598–1.633	triclinic
apatite				
carbonate-apatite	prismatic or thick tabu-lar crystals; coarse granular to compact mas-sive; nodular concretions	conchoidal to uneven fracture	n = 1.63–1.67	hexagonal

NAME	HABIT OR FORM	FRAC-TURE OR CLEAVAGE	REFRAC-TIVE INDICES	CRYSTAL SYSTEM
chlorapatite				
fluorapatite				
hydroxyl-apatite				
autunite	thin tabular crystals; flaky aggregates; crusts	one perfect, micalike cleavage	alpha = 1.553 beta = 1.575 gamma = 1.577	tetragonal
brushite	transpar-ent to translucent efflorescences or minute crystals	two perfect cleavages	alpha = 1.539 beta = 1.546 gamma = 1.551	mono-clinic
collophane (massive apatite)	crypto-crystalline massive; hornlike con-cretions and nodules		n = 1.59–1.61	
lazulite	crystals; compact masses; grains	two cleavages; uneven to splintery fracture	lazul scorz alpha = 1.604–1.639 beta = 1.626–1.670 gamma = 1.637–1.680	mono-clinic
monazite	translu-cent, small flattened crystals	one distinct cleavage	alpha = 1.79–1.80 beta = 1.79–1.80 gamma = 1.84–1.85	mono-clinic

NAME	HABIT OR FORM	FRAC-TURE OR CLEAVAGE	REFRAC-TIVE INDICES	CRYSTAL SYSTEM
pyromor-phite	barrel-shaped prisms; globular, kidney-shaped, or grape-like masses	uneven to subcon-choidal fracture	epsilon = 2.030–2.031 omega = 2.041–2.144	hexagonal
torbernite	tabular crys-tals; micalike masses	one per-fect, platy cleavage	epsilon = 1.582 omega = 1.592	tetragonal
triphylite	transpar-ent to translucent cleavable or compact massive	one perfect cleavage	triph lith alpha = 1.694–1.669 beta = 1.695–1.673 gamma = 1.700–1.682	ortho-rhombic
triplite	massive	one good cleavage	alpha = 1.643–1.696 beta = 1.647–1.704 gamma = 1.668–1.713	mono-clinic
turquoise	opaque, dense, cryp-tocrystalline to fine granu-lar massive	one perfect and one good cleavage	alpha = 1.61 beta = 1.62 gamma = 1.65	triclinic

NAME	HABIT OR FORM	FRAC-TURE OR CLEAVAGE	REFRAC-TIVE INDICES	CRYSTAL SYSTEM
variscite	fine-grained, round or grapelike aggregates, nodules, veins, or crusts	one good cleavage	varis stren alpha = 1.563–1.707 beta = 1.588–1.719 gamma = 1.594–1.741	ortho-rhombic
vivianite	rounded prismatic crystals; kidney-shaped, tubelike, or globu-lar masses; concretions	one perfect cleavage	alpha = 1.579–1.616 beta = 1.602–1.656 gamma = 1.629–1.675	mono-clinic
wavellite	translucent, hemispherical, or globular aggregates	one perfect and one good cleavage	alpha = 1.520–1.535 beta = 1.526–1.543 gamma = 1.545–1.561	ortho-rhombic
xenotime	small pris-matic crystals; coarse radial aggregates; rosettes	uneven to splintery fracture	epsilon = 1.816–1.827 omega = 1.721–1.720	tetragonal

SULFATE MINERALS

These minerals are naturally occurring salts of sulfuric acid. About 200 distinct kinds of sulfates are recorded in mineralogical literature, but most of them are of rare and local occurrence. Abundant deposits of sulfate minerals, such as barite and celestite, are exploited for the preparation of metal salts. Many beds of sulfate minerals are mined for fertilizer and salt preparations, and beds of pure gypsum are mined for the preparation of plaster of paris.

All sulfates possess an atomic structure based on discrete insular sulfate (SO_4^{2-}) tetrahedra, i.e., ions in which four oxygen atoms are symmetrically distributed at the corners of a tetrahedron with the sulfur atom in the centre. These tetrahedral groups do not polymerize, and the sulfate group behaves as a single negatively charged molecule, or complex. Thus, sulfates are distinct from the silicates and borates, which link together into chains, rings, sheets, or frameworks.

Sulfate minerals can be found in at least four kinds: as late oxidation products of preexisting sulfide ores, as evaporite deposits, in circulatory solutions, and in deposits formed by hot water or volcanic gases. Many sulfate minerals occur as basic hydrates of iron, cobalt, nickel, zinc, and copper at or near the source of preexisting primary sulfides. The sulfide minerals, through exposure to weathering and circulating water, have undergone oxidation in which the sulfide ion is converted to sulfate and the metal ion also is changed to some higher valence state. Noteworthy beds of such oxidation products occur in desert regions, such as Chuquicamata, Chile, where brightly coloured basic copper and ferric iron sulfates have accumulated. The sulfate anions generated by oxidation processes may also react with calcium carbonate rocks to form gypsum, $CaSO_4 \cdot 2H_2O$. Sulfates formed by the oxidation of primary sulfides include antlerite [$Cu_3(SO_4)(OH)_4$], brochantite [$Cu_4(SO_4)(OH)_6$], chalcanthite [$Cu^{2+}(SO_4) \cdot 5H_2O$], anglesite ($PbSO_4$), and plumbojarosite [$PbFe^{3+}_6(SO_4)_4(OH)_{12}$].

Soluble alkali and alkaline-earth sulfates crystallize upon evaporation of sulfate-rich brines and trapped oceanic salt solutions. Such brines can form economically important deposits of sulfate, halide, and borate minerals in thick parallel beds, as the potash deposits at Stassfurt, Ger., and the southwestern United States. Many of the sulfate minerals are salts of more than one metal, such as polyhalite, which is a combination of potassium, calcium, and magnesium sulfates.

Sulfate minerals common in evaporite deposits include anhydrite, gypsum, thenardite (Na_2SO_4), epsomite ($MgSO_4\cdot 7H_2O$), glauberite [$Na_2Ca(SO_4)_2$], kainite ($MgSO_4\cdot KCl\cdot 3H_2O$), kieserite ($MgSO_4\cdot H_2O$), mirabilite ($Na_2SO_4\cdot 10H_2O$), and polyhalite [$K_2Ca_2Mg(SO_4)_4\cdot 2H_2O$].

Groundwater carrying sulfate anions reacts with calcium ions in muds, clays, and limestones to form beds of gypsum. The massive material is called alabaster or plaster of paris (originally found in the clays and muds of the Paris basin). If such beds become deeply buried or metamorphosed (altered by heat and pressure), anhydrite may form by dehydration of the gypsum.

Numerous sulfates, usually simple, are formed directly from hot aqueous solutions associated with fumarolic (volcanic gas) vents and late-stage fissure systems in ore deposits. Noteworthy examples include anhydrite, barite, and celestine.

SULFATE MINERALS				
NAME	COLOUR	LUSTRE	MOHS HARD-NESS	SPECIFIC GRAVITY
alum	colourless; white	vitreous	2–2½	1.8
alunite	white; grayish, yellowish, reddish, reddish brown	vitreous	3½–4	2.6–2.9

NAME	COLOUR	LUSTRE	MOHS HARD-NESS	SPECIFIC GRAVITY
alunogen	white; yellowish or reddish	vitreous to silky	1½–2	1.8
anglesite	colourless to white; often tinted gray, yellow, green, or blue	adamantine to resinous or vitreous	2½–3	6.4
anhydrite	colourless to bluish or violet	vitreous to pearly	3½	3.0
antlerite	emerald to blackish green; light green	vitreous	3½	3.9
barite	colourless to white; also variable	vitreous to resinous	3–3½	4.5
botryogen	light to dark orange red	vitreous	2–2½	2.1
brochan-tite	emerald to blackish green; light green	vitreous	3½–4	4.0
caledonite	deep verdigris green or bluish green	resinous	2½–3	5.8
celestite	pale blue; white, reddish, greenish, brownish	vitreous	3–3½	4.0
chal-canthite	various shades of blue	vitreous	2½	2.3
coquim-bite	pale violet to deep purple	vitreous	2½	2.1

NAME	COLOUR	LUSTRE	Mohs HARD-NESS	SPECIFIC GRAVITY
epsomite	colourless; aggregates are white	vitreous; silky to earthy (fibrous)	2–2½	1.7
glauberite	gray; yellowish	vitreous to slightly waxy	2½–3	2.75–2.85
gypsum	colourless; white, gray, brownish, yellowish (massive)	subvitreous	2 (a hardness standard)	2.3
halotrich-ite	colourless to white	vitreous	1.5	1.7 (pick) to 1.9 (halo)
jarosite	ochre yellow to dark brown	suba-damantine to vitreous; resinous on fracture	2½–3½	2.9–3.3
kainite	colourless; gray, blue, violet, yellowish, reddish	vitreous	2½–3	2.2
kieserite	colourless; grayish white, yellowish	vitreous	3.5	2.6
linarite	deep azure blue	vitreous to subadaman-tine	2.5	5.3
mirabilite	colourless to white	vitreous	1½–2	1.5
plumbo-jarosite	golden brown to dark brown	dull to glistening or silky	soft	3.7

NAME	COLOUR	LUSTRE	MOHS HARD-NESS	SPECIFIC GRAVITY
polyhalite	colourless; white or gray; often salmon pink from included iron oxide	vitreous to resinous	3.5	2.8
thenardite	colourless; red-dish, grayish, yellowish, or yellow brown	vitreous to resinous	2½–3	2.7

SULFATE MINERALS				
NAME	HABIT	FRAC-TURE OR CLEAVAGE	REFRAC-TIVE INDICES	CRYSTAL SYSTEM
alum	columnar or granular massive	conchoidal fracture	$n = 1.453–1.466$	isometric
alunite	granular to dense massive	conchoidal fracture	omega = 1.572 epsilon = 1.592	hexagonal
alunogen	fibrous masses and crusts	one perfect cleavage	alpha = 1.459–1.475 beta = 1.461–1.478 gamma = 1.884–1.931	triclinic
anglesite	granular to com-pact massive; tabular or pris-matic crystals	one good, one distinct cleavage	alpha = 1.868–1.913 beta = 1.873–1.918 gamma = 1.884–1.931	ortho-rhombic

NAME	HABIT	FRAC-TURE OR CLEAVAGE	REFRAC-TIVE INDICES	CRYSTAL SYSTEM
anhydrite	granular or fibrous massive; concretionary (tripestone)	two perfect, one good cleavage	alpha = 1.567–1.580 beta = 1.572–1.586 gamma = 1.610–1.625	ortho-rhombic
antlerite	thick tabular crystals	one perfect cleavage	alpha = 1.726 beta = 1.738 gamma = 1.789	ortho-rhombic
barite	usually in tabular crystals; rosettes (desert roses); massive	one perfect, one good cleavage	alpha = 1.633–1.648 beta = 1.634–1.649 gamma = 1.645–1.661	ortho-rhombic
botryo-gen	reniform, botryoidal, or globular aggregates	one perfect, one good cleavage	alpha = 1.523 beta = 1.530 gamma = 1.582	mono-clinic
brochan-tite	prismatic to hairlike crys-tal and crystal aggregates; granular mas-sive; crusts	one perfect cleavage	alpha = 1.728 beta = 1.771 gamma = 1.800	mono-clinic
cale-donite	coating of small elongated crystals	one perfect cleavage	alpha = 1.815–1.821 beta = 1.863–1.869 gamma = 1.906–1.912	ortho-rhombic

NAME	HABIT	FRAC- TURE OR CLEAVAGE	REFRAC- TIVE INDICES	CRYSTAL SYSTEM
celestite	tabular crystals; fibrous massive	one perfect, one good cleavage	alpha = 1.618–1.632 beta = 1.620–1.634 gamma = 1.627–1.642	ortho- rhombic
chal- canthite	short pris- matic crystals; granular masses; stalactites and reniform masses	conchoidal fracture	alpha = 1.514 beta = 1.537 gamma = 1.543	triclinic
coquim- bite	prismatic and pyramidal crys- tals; granular massive		omega = 1.536 epsilon = 1.572	hexagonal
epsomite	fibrous or hairlike crusts; woolly efflorescences	one perfect cleavage	alpha = 1.430–1.440 beta = 1.452–1.462 gamma = 1.457–1.469	ortho- rhombic
glauberite	tabular, dipy- ramidal, or prismatic crystals	one perfect cleavage	alpha = 1.515 beta = 1.535 gamma = 1.536	mono- clinic
gypsum	elongated tabular crystals (some 5 ft long; others twisted or bent); granu- lar or fibrous masses; rosettes	one perfect cleavage	alpha = 1.515–1.523 beta = 1.516–1.526 gamma = 1.524–1.532	mono- clinic

NAME	HABIT	FRAC-TURE OR CLEAVAGE	REFRAC-TIVE INDICES	CRYSTAL SYSTEM
halo-trichite	aggregates of hairlike crystals	conchoidal fracture	alpha = 1.475–1.480 beta = 1.480–1.486 gamma = 1.483–1.490	mono-clinic
jarosite	minute crystals; crusts; granu-lar or fibrous massive	one distinct cleavage	omega = 1.82 epsilon = 1.715	hexagonal
kainite	granular mas-sive; crystalline coatings	one perfect cleavage	alpha = 1.494 beta = 1.505 gamma = 1.516	mono-clinic
kieserite	granular mas-sive, intergrown with other salts	two perfect cleavages	alpha = 1.520 beta = 1.533 gamma = 1.584	mono-clinic
linarite	elongated tabular crystals, either singly or in groups	one perfect cleavage; conchoidal fracture	alpha = 1.809 beta = 1.839 gamma = 1.859	mono-clinic
mirabilite	short prisms; lathlike or tabular crystals; crusts or fibrous masses; granular massive	one perfect cleavage	alpha = 1.391–1.397 beta = 1.393–1.410 gamma = 1.395–1.411	mono-clinic
plumbo-jarosite	crusts, lumps, compact masses of microscopic hexagonal plates	one fair cleavage	omega = 1.875 epsilon = 1.786	hexagonal

NAME	HABIT	FRAC-TURE OR CLEAVAGE	REFRAC-TIVE INDICES	CRYSTAL SYSTEM
polyhalite	fibrous to foli-ated massive	one perfect cleavage	alpha = 1.547 beta = 1.560 gamma = 1.567	triclinic
thenard-ite	rather large crystals; crusts, efflorescences	one perfect, one fair cleavage	alpha = 1.464–1.471 beta = 1.473–1.477 gamma = 1.481–1.485	ortho-rhombic

VANADATE MINERALS

Vanadate minerals are made up of naturally occurring compounds of vanadium (V), oxygen (O), and various metals. Most of these minerals are rare, having crystallized under very restricted conditions. Although vanadinite occasionally is mined as a vanadium ore and carnotite as a uranium ore, most vanadates have no economic importance; they are prized by mineral collectors, however, for their brilliant colours.

The structures of the vanadate minerals are complex. Some vanadate minerals contain vanadate tetrahedra (VO_4), in which four oxygen atoms occupy the corners of a tetrahedron surrounding a central vanadium atom. Each vanadate tetrahedron has a net charge of -3, which is neutralized by large, positively charged metal ions (e.g., calcium, manganese, or ferrous iron) outside the tetrahedron. Unlike the similar silicate tetrahedra, which link to form chains, sheets, rings, or frameworks, vanadate tetrahedra are insular. The vanadates containing these tetrahedra are structurally and chemically similar to the phosphate and arsenate minerals; indeed, some vanadium in many of these vanadates often is replaced by phosphorus or arsenic, forming solid-solution series with both the phosphates and the arsenates. Like the phosphate and sulfate minerals, many vanadates are complexes of transition metals, particularly of ferrous iron, manganese, and copper.

Other vanadates, particularly those that contain uranium, contain $V_2O_8{}^{6-}$ ions, in which two atoms of vanadium are surrounded by eight atoms of oxygen arranged in two square pyramids that share one edge. Very complex clusters also exist but are usually classed with the complex oxide minerals rather than with the vanadate minerals.

NAME	COLOUR	LUSTRE	MOHS HARD-NESS	SPECIFIC GRAVITY
carnotite	bright yellow to lemon or greenish yellow	dull or earthy	soft	4–5
descloizite	brownish red to blackish brown; various shades from orange-red to black and green	greasy	3–3½	5.9–6.2
tyuyamu-nite	canary yellow; lemon to greenish yellow	waxy; also pearly	about 2	variable with water content
vanadinite	various shades of yellow, orange, red, and brown	subresinous to subada-mantine	about 3	6.5–7.1

NAME	HABIT OR FORM	FRAC-TURE OR CLEAVAGE	REFRAC-TIVE INDICES	CRYSTAL SYSTEM
carnotite	powder of micro-scopic platy or lathlike crystals	one perfect cleavage	alpha = 1.750 beta = 1.925 gamma = 1.950	monoclinic

NAME	HABIT OR FORM	FRAC- TURE OR CLEAVAGE	REFRAC- TIVE INDICES	CRYSTAL SYSTEM
des- cloizite	crusts of inter- grown crystals; rounded fibrous masses	no cleav- age; uneven fracture	desc mott alpha = 2.18–2.21 beta = 2.25–2.31 gamma = 2.34–2.33	ortho- rhombic
tyuy- amunite	compact to crypto- crystalline massive; scales and lathlike crystals; radiating crystal aggregates	one perfect, micalike cleavage		ortho- rhombic
vanadi- nite	hairlike or barrel- shaped (frequently hollow) prismatic crystals	uneven to conchoidal fracture	omega = 2.628–2.370 epsilon = 2.505–2.313	hexagonal

SULFIDE MINERALS

Sulfide minerals make up a group of compounds that join sulfur with one or more metals. Most of the sulfides are simple structurally, exhibit high symmetry in their crystal forms, and have many of the properties of metals, including metallic lustre and electrical conductivity. They often are strikingly coloured and have a low hardness and a high specific gravity.

The composition of the sulfide minerals can be expressed with the general chemical formula $AmSn$, in which A is a metal, S is sulfur, and m and n are integers, giving A_2S, AS, A_3S_4 and AS_2 stoichiometries. The metals that occur most commonly in sulfides are iron, copper, nickel, lead, cobalt, silver, and zinc, though about fifteen others enter sulfide structures.

Almost all sulfide minerals have structural arrangements that belong to six basic types, four of which are important. These arrangements are close-packing combinations of metal and sulfur, governed by ionic size and charge.

The simplest and most symmetrical of the four important structural types is the sodium chloride structure, in which each ion occupies a position within an octahedron consisting of six oppositely charged neighbours. The most common sulfide crystalling in this manner is galena (PbS), the ore mineral of lead. A type of packing that involves two sulfide ions in each of the octahedral positions in the sodium chloride structure is the pyrite structure. This is a high-symmetry structure characteristic of the iron sulfide, pyrite (FeS_2O). The second distinct structural type is that of sphalerite (ZnS), in which each metal ion is surrounded by six oppositely charged ions arranged tetrahedrally. The third significant structural type is that of fluorite, in which the metal cation is surrounded by eight anions; each anion, in turn, is surrounded by four metal cations. The reverse of this structure—the metal cation surrounded by four anions and each anion surrounded by eight metal cations—is called the antifluorite structure. It is the arrangement of some of the more valuable precious metal tellurides and selenides among which is hessite (Ag_2Te), the ore mineral of silver.

In virtually all of the sulfides, bonding is covalent, but some have metallic properties. The covalent property of sulfur allows sulfur-sulfur bonds and the incorporation of S_2 pairs in some sulfides such as pyrite. Several sulfides, including molybdenite (MoS_2) and covellite (CuS), have layer structures. Several rare sulfide varieties have the spinel (*q.v.*) structure.

Phase relations of sulfides are particularly complex, and many solid state reactions occur at relatively low temperatures (100–$300°$ C [212–$572°$ F]), producing complex intergrowths. Particular emphasis has been placed on the experimental investigation of the iron-nickel-copper sulfides because they are by far the most common. They also are important geologic indicators for locating possible ore bodies and provide low-temperature reactions for geothermometry.

Sulfides occur in all rock types. Except for dissemination in certain sedimentary rocks, these minerals tend to occur in isolated concentrations which make up mineral bodies such as veins and fracture fillings or which comprise replacements of preexisting rocks in the shape of blankets. Sulfide mineral deposits originate in two principal processes, both of which have reducing conditions: (1) separation of an immiscible sulfide melt during the early stages of crystallization of basic magmas; and (2) deposition from aqueous brine solutions at temperatures in the 300–600 °C (572–$1,112$ °F) range and at relatively high pressure, such as at the seafloor or several kilometres beneath Earth's surface. The sulfide deposits formed as a result of the first process include mainly pyrrhotites, pyrites, pentlandites, and chalcopyrites. Most others occur because of the latter process. Weathering may act to concentrate dispersed sulfides.

Pyrite (FeS_2) and pyrrhotite ($Fe_{1-x}S$) are the most common sulfide minerals. Brassy yellow pyrite, often called "fool's gold," occurs variously as an accessory mineral in many rocks, in veins, and even as a chief component of some fossils. Pyrrhotite, which typically has a bronze-like appearance and is slightly magnetic, is a common accessory mineral in mafic igneous rocks. Both of these minerals, which are associated with each other in some deposits, have yielded large quantities of sulfur recovered for uses such as the production of sulfuric acid.

Sulfide minerals are the source of various precious metals, most notably gold, silver, and platinum. They also are the ore minerals of most metals used by industry, as for example antimony, bismuth, copper, lead, nickel, and zinc. Other industrially important metals such as cadmium and selenium occur in trace amounts in numerous common sulfides and are recovered in refining processes.

SULFIDE MINERALS				
NAME	COLOUR	LUSTRE	MOHS HARD-NESS	SPE-CIFIC GRAVITY
argentite	blackish lead-gray	metallic	2–2 1/2	7.2–7.4
arsenopy-rite	silver-white to steel-gray	metallic	5 1/2–6	6.1
bornite	copper-red to pinchbeck-brown, tarnishing quickly to iridescent purple	metallic	3	5.1
chalcocite	blackish lead-gray	metallic	2 1/2–3	5.5–5.8
chalcopy-rite	brass-yellow, often tarnished and iridescent	metallic	3 1/2–4	4.1–4.3
cinnabar	cochineal-red to brownish or lead-gray	adamantine to metallic	2–2 1/2	8.1
cobaltite	silver-white to red; steel-gray or grayish black	metallic	5 1/2	6.3
covellite	indigo-blue; highly iridescent; brass-yellow or deep red	submetallic to resinous (crystals); subresin-ous to dull (massive)	1 1/2–2	4.6–4.8
cubanite	brass- to bronze-yellow	metallic	3 1/2	4.0–4.2

NAME	COLOUR	LUSTRE	MOHS HARD-NESS	SPE-CIFIC GRAVITY
domey-kite	tin-white to steel-gray; tarnishes yellowish brown, becoming iridescent	metallic	3–3 1/2	7.2–7.9
galena	lead-gray	metallic	2 1/2–3	7.6
gree-nockite	various shades of yellow and orange	adamantine to resinous	3–3 1/2	4.9
krenne-rite	silver-white to light brass-yellow	metallic	2–3	8.6
linnaeite	light gray to steel- or violet-gray, tarnishing to copper-red or violet-gray	brilliant metal-lic (when fresh)	4 1/2–5 1/2	4.5–4.8
loellingite	silver-white to steel-gray	metallic	5–5 1/2	7.4–7.5
marcasite	tin-white, deepening with exposure to bronze-yellow	metallic	6–6 1/2	4.9
mauch-erite	reddish platinum-gray, tarnishing copper-red	metallic	5	8.0
metacin-nabar	grayish black	metallic	3	7.65
millerite	pale brass-yellow, tarnishing iridescent gray	metallic	3–3 1/2	5.3–5.7
molybde-nite	lead-gray	metallic	1–1 1/2	4.6–4.7
niccolite	pale copper-red, tarnishing gray to blackish	metallic	5–5 1/2	7.8

NAME	COLOUR	LUSTRE	MOHS HARD-NESS	SPE-CIFIC GRAVITY
orpiment	lemon-yellow, golden-yellow, brownish yellow	resinous; pearly on cleavages	1 1/2–2	3.5
pentland-ite	light bronze-yellow	metallic	3 1/2–4	4.6–5.0
pyrite	pale brass-yellow	splendent to glistening metallic	6–6 1/2	5.0
pyrrhotite	bronze-yellow to pinchbeck-brown, tarnishing quickly	metallic	3 1/2–4 1/2	4.6–4.7 4.8 (troilite)
realgar	aurora-red to orange-yellow	resinous to greasy	1 1/2–2	3.5–3.6
rickardite	purple-red	metallic	3 1/2	7.5
sphalerite	brown, black, yellow; also variable	resinous to adamantine	3 1/2–4	3.9–4.1
stannite	steel-gray to iron-black	metallic	4	4.3–4.5
stibnite	lead- to steel-gray, tarnishing blackish	metallic	2	4.6
stromey-erite	dark steel-gray, tar-nishing blue	metallic	2 1/2–3	6.2–6.3
sylvanite	steel-gray to silver-white	brilliant metallic	1 1/2–2	8.1–8.2
tetrady-mite	pale steel-gray, tarnishing dull or iridescent	metallic	1 1/2–2	7.1–7.5
umangite	dark cherry-red, tarnishing quickly to violet-blue	metallic	3	5.6
wurtzite	brownish black	resinous	3 1/2–4	4.0–4.1

NAME	HABIT OR FORM	FRAC-TURE OR CLEAVAGE	REFRACTIVE INDICES OR POLISHED SECTION DATA	CRYS-TAL SYSTEM
argen-tite	cubic or octa-hedral crystals, often in groups; arborescent or hairlike massive	subcon-choidal fracture	faintly anisotropic	isomet-ric
arseno-pyrite	cubic or dodeca-hedral crystals having rough or curved faces; granular or com-pact massive	one distinct cleavage	strongly anisotropic	mono-clinic
bornite	prismatic crys-tals; columnar, granular, or com-pact massive	uneven fracture	isotropic in part; pinkish brown	isomet-ric
chal-cocite	short prismatic or thick tabular crystals; massive	conchoidal fracture	weakly anisotropic	ortho-rhombic
chalco-pyrite	compact mas-sive; tetragonal crystals	uneven fracture	weakly anisotro-pic; often shows lamellar and polysynthetic twinning	tetrago-nal
cinnabar	rhombohedral, tabular, or pris-matic crystals; massive; earthy coatings	one perfect cleavage	omega = 2.756–2.905 epsilon = 3.065–3.256	hexago-nal

NAME	HABIT OR FORM	FRAC-TURE OR CLEAVAGE	REFRACTIVE INDICES OR POLISHED SECTION DATA	CRYS-TAL SYSTEM
cobaltite	cubic or pyrito-hedral crystals with striated faces	one perfect cleavage		isomet-ric
covellite	massive; rarely in hexagonal plates	one highly perfect cleavage	strongly anisotropic	hexago-nal
cubanite	thick tabular crystals; massive	conchoidal fracture	anisotropic	ortho-rhombic
domey-kite	reniform or bot-ryoidal masses	uneven fracture	isotropic	isomet-ric
galena	cubic crystals; cleavable masses	one perfect cleavage	isotropic	isomet-ric
gree-nockite	earthy coating	conchoidal fracture	omega = 2.431–2.506 epsilon = 2.456–2.529	hexago-nal
krenne-rite	short prismatic crystals	one perfect cleavage	strongly aniso-tropic; creamy white	ortho-rhombic
lin-naeite	octahedral crys-tals granular to compact masses	uneven to subcon-choidal fracture	isotropic	isomet-ric
loellin-gite	prismatic or pyramidal crys-tals; massive	uneven fracture	very strongly anisotropic	ortho-rhombic

NAME	HABIT OR FORM	FRAC- TURE OR CLEAVAGE	REFRACTIVE INDICES OR POLISHED SECTION DATA	CRYS- TAL SYSTEM
marca- site	tabular or pyra- midal crystals; spear-shaped or cockscomb-like crystal groups	one distinct cleavage	strongly aniso- tropic and pleochroic; creamy white, light yellowish white, and rosy white	ortho- rhombic
mauch- erite	tabular crystals	uneven fracture	weakly anisotro- pic; pinkish gray	tetrago- nal
meta- cinnabar	tetrahedral crys- tals; massive	subcon- choidal to uneven fracture	isotropic; grayish white; shows lamellar twinning	isomet- ric
millerite	very slender to capillary crystals in radiating groups, sometimes interwoven	two perfect cleavages	strongly anisotropic	hexago- nal
molyb- denite	hexagonal tablets; foliated massive, in scales	one perfect cleavage	very strongly anisotropic and pleochroic; white	hexago- nal
nicco- lite	reniform massive; also branching	no cleavage	strongly anisotropic	hexago- nal
orpi- ment	foliated, fibrous, or columnar mas- sive; reniform or botryoidal masses; granular	one perfect cleavage	alpha = 2.4 beta = 2.81 gamma = 3.02	mono- clinic

NAME	HABIT OR FORM	FRACTURE OR CLEAVAGE	REFRACTIVE INDICES OR POLISHED SECTION DATA	CRYSTAL SYSTEM
pentlandite	granular aggregates	conchoidal fracture	isotropic	isometric
pyrite	cubic, pyritohedral, or octahedral crystals with striated faces; massive	conchoidal to uneven fracture	isotropic; creamy white	isometric
pyrrhotite	granular massive; sometimes platy or tabular crystals	uneven to subconchoidal fracture	strongly anisotropic	hexagonal
realgar	short, striated prismatic crystals; granular or compact massive; incrustations	one good cleavage, three less so	alpha = 2.486–2.538 beta = 2.602–2.684 gamma = 2.620–2.704	monoclinic
rickardite	massive	irregular fracture	strongly anisotropic and pleochroic	orthorhombic
sphalerite	tetrahedral or dodecahedral crystals, often with curved faces; cleavable masses	one perfect cleavage	n = 2.320–2.517	isometric
stannite	granular massive	uneven fracture	anisotropic	tetragonal

NAME	HABIT OR FORM	FRAC- TURE OR CLEAVAGE	REFRACTIVE INDICES OR POLISHED SECTION DATA	CRYS- TAL SYSTEM
stibnite	aggregates of needle-like crystals; crystals are easily bent or twisted	one perfect cleavage	alpha = 3.184–3.204 beta = 4.036–4.056 gamma = 4.293–4.313 white; strongly anisotropic	ortho- rhombic
stro- meyer- ite	pseudohex- agonal prisms; compact massive	subcon- choidal to conchoidal fracture	strongly anisotropic	ortho- rhombic
sylva- nite	short prismatic, thick tabular, or bladed crystals	one perfect cleavage	strongly aniso- tropic and pleochroic; creamy white; shows polysyn- thetic twinning	mono- clinic
tetrady- mite	foliated to granular massive; bladed crystals	one perfect cleavage	weakly aniso- tropic; white; sometimes shows a graph- like intergrowth	hexago- nal
umang- ite	small grains; fine-grained aggregates	uneven fracture	strongly aniso- tropic; dark red-violet; apparently uniaxial	tetrago- nal

NAME	HABIT OR FORM	FRAC- TURE OR CLEAVAGE	REFRACTIVE INDICES OR POLISHED SECTION DATA	CRYS- TAL SYSTEM
wurtzite	pyramidal crystals; fibrous or columnar massive; concentrically banded crusts	one easy cleavage	omega = 2.330–2.356 epsilon = 2.350–2.378	hexagonal

SULFOSALTS

Sulfosalts constitute an extensive group of minerals, mostly rare species, marked by some of the most complicated atomic and crystal structures known to inorganic chemistry. They conform to the general composition $AmBnXp$, in which $m, n,$ and p are integers; A may be lead, silver, thallium, or copper; B may be antimony, arsenic, bismuth, tin, or germanium; and X may be sulfur or selenium. Formerly it was believed that the sulfosalts were salts of complex hypothetical thioantimonic or thioarsenic acids (e.g., $HSbS_2$, $H_{18}As_4S_{15}$, H_3AsS_3), but X-ray diffraction analyses indicate that the atomic structures of many sulfosalts are based on structural fragments of simpler compounds such as galena (lead sulfide; PbS) blocks and stibnite (antimony trisulfide; Sb_2S_3) sheets. No encompassing theory has been evolved to rationalize many of these curious compounds. The complexity of many of the structures evidently results from their having crystallized at low temperatures and the consequent high degree of ordering of the metal atoms. Syntheses of such compositions at higher temperature usually result in structures simpler than the complicated low-temperature forms.

Although sulfosalts are much rarer than the sulfide minerals with which they are often associated, some

MOLYBDATE AND
TUNGSTATE MINERALS

These naturally occurring inorganic compounds are salts of molybdic acid, H_2MoO_4, and tungstic acid, H_2WO_4. Minerals in these groups often are valuable ores.

The structural unit of these minerals is a tetrahedral group formed by four oxygen atoms at the corners of a tetrahedron surrounding a molybdenum or tungsten atom. Each MoO_4 or WO_4 tetrahedron has a net charge of -2, which is neutralized by metal ions outside the tetrahedron. Unlike the silicate or borate minerals, which form chains, rings, sheets, or framework structures by sharing oxygen atoms between adjacent tetrahedra, the molybdate and tungstate minerals share none; they are similar in this respect to the phosphate, vanadate, arsenate, and chromate minerals. Because the molybdenum ion and the tungsten ion have similar radii, they may substitute for one another within the structure of any naturally occurring example; thus, they tend to form solid solution series.

Among the molybdate and tungstate minerals, only the powellite-scheelite series (calcium-bearing molybdate/tungstates) and wulfenite (lead molybdate) are noteworthy. Scheelite is a valuable tungsten ore; wulfenite is a minor ore of lead.

One other series of tungstates is important. Wolframite, another name for the hübnerite-ferberite series of manganese/iron tungstates, is perhaps the most important ore of tungsten. These minerals have a structure, unlike that of the other tungstates, based on WO_6 octahedra—i.e., each tungsten atom is surrounded by six oxygen atoms arranged at the corners of an octahedron. These minerals are classed with the complex oxides and are related to the niobates and tantalates.

localities are truly remarkable for the variety of species encountered. At the Lengenbach Mine in Switzerland, for example, more than 30 distinct species have been recognized, 15 of which are not found elsewhere. Most sulfosalts have formed at low temperature in open cavities, usually in association with copper–zinc–arsenic sulfide ores. Very often they occur in cavities of calcite and dolomite, as at the Lengenbach Mine. Most are lead gray in colour with a metallic lustre, brittle (rarely malleable), crystalline, and difficult to tell apart without recourse to X-ray diffraction and electron microprobe analyses. The thallium-bearing sulfosalts often are deep red and transparent, as sometimes are the sulfosalts of silver.

Although under exceptional circumstances some sulfosalts may constitute silver ores (i.e., proustite, pyrargyrite, and stephanite), and other species have constituted ores of silver (in minor amounts), mercury, arsenic, and antimony (i.e., boulangerite, livingstonite, enargite, and tennantite-tetrahedrite), their economic importance is trivial. Aside from mineralogical curiosities, the sulfosalts are of interest because their electronic properties are related to those of semiconductors.

SULFOSALTS				
NAME	COLOUR	LUSTRE	MOHS HARDNESS	SPECIFIC GRAVITY
argyrodite	bluish to purplish black; steel gray when fresh	metallic	2½	6.1–6.3
bournonite	steel gray to iron black	metallic	2½–3	5.8–5.9
enargite	gray black to iron black	metallic	3	4.4–4.5
polybasite	iron black	metallic	2–3	6.0–6.2
proustite	scarlet vermillion	adamantine	2–2½	5.6
pyrargyrite	deep red	adamantine	2½	5.8
stephanite	iron black	metallic	2–2½	6.2–6.3
tetrahedrite	flint gray to iron or dull black	metallic	3–4½	4.6–5.1

SULFOSALTS				
NAME	HABIT	FRAC-TURE OR CLEAVAGE	REFRACTIVE INDICES OR POLISHED SECTION DATA	CRYSTAL SYSTEM
argy-rodite	crystals and crystal aggre-gates; crusts; compact masses	conchoidal to uneven fracture	violet gray white; isotro-pic (canfieldite) or weakly pleo-chroic (argyrodite)	isometric
bour-nonite	prismatic to tabular crystals; crystal aggre-gates; granular to compact masses	subcon-choidal to uneven fracture	white; weakly anisotropic and very weakly pleochroic	ortho-rhombic
enar-gite	tabular crys-tals; granular masses	one perfect cleavage	gray to light rose brown; strongly aniso-tropic; weakly pleochroic	ortho-rhombic
poly-basite	tabular crys-tals; massive	uneven fracture	gray white; moderately anisotro-pic; weakly pleochroic	monoclinic
proust-ite	prismatic crys-tals; compact masses	one distinct cleavage	omega = 2.979–3.088 epsilon = 2.711–2.792	hexagonal
pyrar-gyrite	prismatic crys-tals; compact masses	one distinct cleavage	omega = 3.084 epsilon = 2.881	hexagonal

NAME	HABIT	FRAC-TURE OR CLEAVAGE	REFRACTIVE INDICES OR POLISHED SECTION DATA	CRYSTAL SYSTEM
stepha-nite	prismatic to tabular crystals; dis-seminated grains; com-pact masses	subcon-choidal to uneven fracture	strongly anisotropic	ortho-rhombic
tetra-hedrite	tetrahedral crystals; granular to compact masses	subcon-choidal to uneven fracture	gray to olive brown; isotropic	isometric

CONCLUSION

Quite literally, minerals provide the foundation upon which humans and other forms of life stand. By definition, they are naturally occurring homogenous solids composed of a single chemical compound. As such, they serve as the building blocks of rocks, and thus they are the primary components of mountains, valleys, ocean and lake basins, beaches, and other landforms.

Earth's minerals also serve as the ultimate source of many of the materials humans use. Humans derive such products as metallic goods, glass, ceramics, graphite (pencil lead), fertilizers, pigments, abrasives, and industrial tools and chemicals from minerals. A number of minerals also serve as prized gemstones. In addition, the weathering of landforms by water, wind, and other forces contributes minerals to the soil. Such minerals provide bulk to the soil and nutrients that aid in agriculture.

GLOSSARY

alluvial Relating to, composed of, or found in alluvium.

anion The ion in an electrolyzed solution that migrates to the anode; broadly a negatively charged ion.

axes A straight line with respect to which a body or figure is symmetrical—called also axis of symmetry.

carbonate A salt or ester of carbonic acid.

compound Something formed by a union of elements or parts; especially a distinct substance formed by chemical union of two or more ingredients in definite proportion by weight.

covalent bond A chemical bond formed between atoms by the sharing of electrons.

ferrous Of, relating to, or containing iron.

fluorescence Luminescence that is caused by the absorption of radiation at one wavelength followed by nearly immediate re-radiation usually at a different wavelength and that ceases almost at once when the incident radiation stops.

geochemical The related chemical and geological properties of a substance.

halide A binary compound of a halogen with a more electropositive element or radical.

hydrogen bond An electrostatic attraction between a hydrogen atom in one polar molecule (as of water) and a small electronegative atom (as of oxygen, nitrogen, or fluorine) in usually another molecule of the same or a different polar substance.

hydrothermal Of or relating to hot water—used especially of the formation of minerals by hot solutions rising from a cooling magma.

ionic bond A chemical bond formed between oppositely charged species because of their mutual electrostatic attraction.

lustre A glow of reflected light sheen; specifically the appearance of the surface of a mineral dependent upon its reflecting qualities.

magma Molten rock material within the earth from which igneous rock results by cooling.

mineral Any of various naturally occurring, homogeneous substances (as stone, coal, salt, sulfur, sand, petroleum, water, or natural gas) obtained usually from the ground.

morphology The external structure of rocks in relation to the development of erosional forms or topographic features.

nomenclature The act or process or an instance of naming.

ore A naturally occurring mineral containing a valuable constituent (as metal) for which it is mined and worked.

oxide A binary compound of oxygen with a more electropositive element or group.

petrology A science that deals with the origin, history, occurrence, structure, chemical composition, and classification of rocks.

polymorphism The property of crystallizing in two or more forms with distinct structure.

radioactivity The property possessed by some elements (as uranium) or isotopes (as carbon 14) of spontaneously emitting energetic particles (as electrons or alpha particles) by the disintegration of their atomic nucleus.

silicate A salt or ester derived from a silicic acid; especially any of numerous insoluble often complex metal salts that contain silicon and oxygen in the anion, constitute the largest class of minerals, and are used in building materials (as cement, bricks, and glass).

solubility The amount of a substance that will dissolve in a given amount of another substance.

specific gravity The ratio of the density of a substance to the density of some substance (as pure water) taken as a standard when both densities are obtained by weighing in air.

striated Marked with striations, or minute grooves, scratches, or channels, especially when one of a parallel series.

sulfide Any of various organic compounds characterized by a sulfur atom attached to two carbon atoms.

symmetrical Capable of division by a longitudinal plane into similar halves.

tetrahedron A polyhedron or a solid formed by plane faces that has four faces.

triclinic Of, relating to, or constituting a system of crystallization characterized by three unequal axes intersecting at oblique angles—used especially of a crystal.

twinning To grow as a twin crystal.

BIBLIOGRAPHY

Standard mineralogical reference works include Dexter Perkins, *Mineralogy*, 2nd ed. (2001); *Manual of Mineralogy (after James D. Dana)*, 23rd ed. by Cornelis Klein and Barbara Dutrow (2007); William D. Neese and Daniel J. Schultze, *Introduction to Mineralogy and An Atlas of Minerals in Thin Section* (2004); Chris Pellant, *Smithsonian Handbooks: Rocks & Minerals* (2002); and Michael Fleischer, *Glossary of Mineral Species, 1995*, 7th ed. (1995). Useful texts and monographs include Robert M. Garrels and Charles L. Christ, *Solutions, Minerals, and Equilibria*, 2nd ed. (1990); Paul C. Hess, *Origins of Igneous Rocks* (1989); Cornelis Klein, *Minerals and Rocks: Exercises in Crystal and Mineral Chemistry, Crystallography, X-ray Powder Diffraction, Mineral and Rock Identification, and Ore Mineralogy*, 3rd ed. (2007); Anthony R. Philpotts, *Principles of Igneous and Metamorphic Petrology* (1990); and Tibor Zoltai and James H. Stout, *Mineralogy: Concepts and Principles* (1984).

MINERAL DEPOSITS

Two texts for nonspecialists on the subject that also address questions of how the use of mineral resources affects the use of other resources and the environment are James R. Craig, David J. Vaughan, and Brian J. Skinner, *Earth Resources and the Environment*, 4th ed. (2010); U. Aswathanarayana, *Mineral Resources Management and the Environment* (2003); and James R. Craig, David J. Vaughan, and Brian J. Skinner, *Resources of the Earth: Origin, Use, and Environmental Impact*, 3rd ed. (2001). Three excellent references dealing with the broad topic of the genesis of mineral deposits, but written at a level requiring at least a beginning familiarity with geologic terminology, are Laurence Robb, *An Introduction to Ore-Forming Processes* (2005); Richard Edwards and Keith Atkinson, *Ore Deposit Geology and Its Influence on Mineral Exploration* (1986); and John M. Guilbert and Charles F. Park, Jr., *The Geology of Ore Deposits* (2007). More specialized texts deal with specific classes of mineral deposits or with specific processes that form mineral deposits. In all instances, such texts presume a working knowledge of the technical terms used in geology. Among the best specialized texts are Hubert Lloyd Barnes (ed.), *Geochemistry of Hydrothermal Ore Deposits*, 3rd ed. (1997); J. Barry Maynard, *Geochemistry of Sedimentary Ore Deposits* (1983); Anthony J. Naldrett, *Magmatic Sulfide Deposits* (1989); F.J. Sawkins, *Metal Deposits in Relation to Plate Tectonics*, 2nd rev. ed. (1990); B.R. Berger and P.M. Bethke (eds.), *Geology and Geochemistry of Epithermal Systems* (1985); J.A. Whitney and Anthony J. Naldrett (eds.), *Ore Deposition Associated with Magmas* (1989); and E.R. Force, J.J. Eidel, and J. Barry Maynard (eds.), *Sedimentary and Diagenetic Mineral Deposits: A Basin Analysis Approach to Exploration* (1991).

SILICA MINERALS

Silica minerals are considered in W.A. Deer, R.A. Howie, and J. Zussman, *An Introduction to the Rock-forming Minerals*, 2nd ed. (1996); Frederick H. Pough, *Field Guide to Rocks and Minerals*, 5th ed. (1998); and Dougal Dixon, *Practical Geologist: The Introductory Guide to the Basics of Geology and to Collecting and Identifying Rocks* (1992).

AMPHIBOLES

Amphiboles are considered in B.E. Leake (compiler), "Nomenclature of Amphiboles," *American Mineralogist*, 82:1019–37 (1997); David R. Veblen (ed.), *Amphiboles and Other Hydrous Pyriboles: Mineralogy* (1981); David R. Veblen and Paul H. Ribbe (eds.), *Amphiboles: Petrology and Experimental Phase Relations* (1982).

FELDSPARS AND FELDSPATHOIDS

General descriptions of feldspars and feldspathoids are provided in William L. Brown (ed.), *Feldspars and Feldspathoids: Structures, Properties, and Occurrences* (1984) and Joseph V. Smith and William L. Brown, *Feldspar Minerals*, 2nd rev. and extended ed. (1988).

OLIVINES

Olivines are described in William D. Neese, *Introduction to Optical Mineralogy*, 3rd ed. (2003).

PYROXENES

The topic of pyroxenes is covered in Robert J. Lauf, *Collector's Guide to the Pyroxene Group* (2010) and N. Morimoto et al., "Nomenclature of Pyroxenes," *American Mineralogist*, 73(9–10):1123–33 (1988).

CALCITE

Solid treatments of carbonate rocks are provided in C.J.R. Braithwaite, *Carbonate Sediments And Rocks: A Manual for Geologists And Engineers* (2005); and Maurice E. Tucker and V. Paul Wright, *Carbonate Sedimentology* (1991).

Terence P. Scoffin, *An Introduction to Carbonate Sediments and Rocks* (1987), is a well-illustrated, easy-to-read book about limestones and dolostones. Both Albert V. Carozzi, *Carbonate Rock Depositional Models: A Microfacies Approach* (1989), an extensively illustrated treatise of the author's ideas about the geneses of carbonate-rich sedimentary rocks; and Richard J. Reeder (ed.), *Carbonates: Mineralogy and Chemistry* (1983), a collection of summaries that deal with the carbonates, including calcite, are written at the professional level.

DOLOMITE

A general description of dolomites is provided in B.H. Purser, M.E. Tucker, and D.H. Zengerand (eds.), *Dolomites* (1994). Terence P. Scoffin, *An Introduction to Carbonate Sediments and Rocks* (1987), is a well-illustrated, easy-to-read book about limestones and dolostones. A review article by Laurence A. Hardie, "Dolomitization: A Critical View of Some Current Views," in *Journal of Sedimentary Petrology*, 57(1):166–183 (1987), emphasizes the problems involved with accepting the most commonly embraced models of dolomitization and concludes that direct precipitation models (among other things) should receive more attention and study. Vijai Shukla and Paul A. Baker, *Sedimentology and Geochemistry of Dolostones* (1988), a collection of symposium papers, covers organogenic dolomites and the geochemistry of dolomite textures. John K. Warren, *Evaporite Sedimentology: Importance in Hydrocarbon Accumulation* (1989), includes a chapter on dolomites and dolomitization, a good recent summary of the pertinent data and hypotheses; the bibliography includes most of the noteworthy articles published in English. Bruce Purser, Maurice Tucker, and Donald Zenger, *Dolomites: A Volume in Honor of Dolomieu* (1994), provides a review of recent scientific progress and remaining scientific and economic problems concerning the mineral dolemite.

CLAY MINERALS

Treatments of various aspects of clay mineralogy are provided in Duane M. Moore and Robert C. Reynolds, Jr., *X-ray Diffraction and Identification and Analysis of Clay Minerals*, 2nd ed. (1997); Ernő Nemecz, *Clay Minerals* (1981); Toshio Sudō et al., *Electron Micrographs of Clay Minerals* (1981); Simonne Caillère, Stéphane Hénin, and Michel Rautureau, *Minéralogie des Argiles*, 2nd ed. rev., 2 vol. (1982); Friedrich Liebau, *Structural Chemistry of Silicates: Structure, Bonding, and Classification* (1985); Robert H.S. Robertson, *Fuller's Earth: A History of Calcium Montmorillonite* (1986); A.C.D. Newman (ed.), *Chemistry of Clays and Clay Minerals* (1987); S.W. Bailey (ed.), *Hydrous Phyllosilicates (Exclusive of Micas)* (1988); J.B. Dixon and S.B. Weed (eds.), *Minerals in Soil Environments*, 2nd ed. (1989); Charles E. Weaver, *Clays, Muds, and Shales* (1989); Bruno Velde, *Introduction to Clay Minerals: Chemistry, Origins, Uses, and Environmental Significance* (1992); B. Velde, *Origin and Mineralogy of Clays* (1995); and A. Parker and J.E. Rae (eds.), *Environmental Interactions of Clays* (1998). Technical works that consider the topic of clay minerals include Bruce Velde, *Origin of Clay Minerals in Soils and Weathered Rocks* (2009) and M.H. Repacholi (ed.), *Clay Mineralogy* (1994).

INDEX

A

accessory minerals, 6, 151, 256, 263, 264, 280, 309

agate, 24, 235, 239, 241

Agricola, Georgius, 91, 234

Algoma-type deposits, 100, 103

allophane, 196, 213–214, 215, 217, 219, 221

alluvial (stream) placers, 107, 108–109

amphiboles, 1, 6, 68, 111, 125–126, 158, 167, 172, 175, 179, 183, 237, 239
  chemical composition of, 126–128
  crystal structure of, 128–131
  origin and occurrence of, 133–135
  physical properties of, 131–133

anhydrite, 63, 265–266, 298

aragonite, 3, 33, 60, 61, 134, 184, 201, 247, 248–249, 250, 255, 256, 257

arsenate minerals, 64, 268, 273, 305, 319

assemblages, explanation of, 71–72

atomic substitution, explanation of, 79, 82

B

banded iron formations (BIFs), 100–102, 104, 106, 110

bauxites, 57, 104

beach placers, 108, 109

Biot, Jean-Baptiste, 188

biotite, 6, 71, 72, 131, 134, 146, 187, 188, 190, 191, 192, 193, 206

borates, 36, 62–63, 268, 271, 278, 297, 298, 319

Bragg, W. Lawrence, 36

C

calcite, 32, 33, 60, 61, 84, 93, 134, 184, 201, 247, 248, 249–250, 258, 259, 260, 263, 265, 319
  chemical composition of, 250–251
  crystal structure of, 251–253
  origin and occurrence of, 255–256
  physical properties of, 253–254
  uses of, 256–257

caliche/caliche deposits, 99, 277–278

carbonates, 16, 30, 33, 36, 59–61, 80, 82, 84, 93, 97, 99, 134, 148, 149, 242, 247–249, 265, 268, 272, 278, 297
  aragonite, 3, 33, 60, 61, 134, 184, 201, 247, 248–249, 250, 255, 256, 257
  calcite, 32, 33, 60, 61, 84, 93, 134, 184, 201, 247, 248, 249–257, 258, 259, 260, 263, 265, 319